IRA ATEN:
Last of the Old Texas Rangers

by
Harold Preece

2024
Copano Bay Press

Originally published in 1960 under the title
Lone Star Man—Ira Aten: Last of the Old Texas Rangers

CONTENTS

ACKNOWLEDGMENTS

Writing is an exacting chore, tempered by all those who help an author, in one way or another, while he is gestating his book. And so I make grateful acknowledgment to the following persons who aided me, through inspiration and practical help, with this work:

To the Atens, of Texas and California, for all the hard, patient digging they did into family records and personal memories.

To Leo Margulies, who published my very first magazine article on Ira Aten.

To Judith Rosen, fellow Texan, and her husband, Jack, at whose New York City home I prepared the initial synopsis.

For research and related assistance, I am indebted to Dorman H. Winfrey, Texas state archivist; to my sister, Lenore Preece; and to Mrs. Helen Swanson, historical reference librarian of the Austin, Texas, Public Library.

Thanks for varied favors are due Carolyn Marshall, Francis Bartlett, Thelma and Jay Johnson, and Katherine and Sam Luparello. Also to Henry Biederman, Carlos Ashley, W. A. Askew, John Farwell, and M. H. Dowd.

It would be hard to find adequate words of appreciation for my editor, Don Ward, of Hastings House, an authority on the Old West in his own right. A tribute has to be rendered in memory of my wife, Ruth Kruskal Preece; she read my magazine articles about Ira Aten during her lifetime, and kept urging me to interpret him in a book.

H. P.

INTRODUCTION

On a quiet day in 1953, there died an aged man whose life had been accented by the hard thud of buck shot and the strident clip of hoofs.

Ira Aten was ninety years old when he closed eyes that had witnessed so much. He had lived almost half a century in his adopted state of California, which knew him as a public spirited citizen with a shrewd intelligence, matched by his unqualified honesty. For three decades before, he had lived in Texas, to whose heroic history he had added his own supplement of enduring courage.

Farmer he was. Rancher. Bank director. Pioneer. Involuntary political leader. Cottonpicker once, during a vexing hiatus told in this book.

But, first and last, he was an enforcer of law: a man who, over the greater part of seventy years, wore one or another badge conferred upon him by one or another authority. Even when the emblem was honorary, he gave it meaning by going after lawbreakers with straightforward determination and bull dog tenacity.

Many frontiers and two Western states felt the impact of Ira Aten, with that sheer courage of his, which was never vulgarized by the gaudy exhibitionism that characterized many early-day lawmen. Born to the badge he may have been—but it was one of his few boasts that he had never bullied a man with it.

If he made a mistake or committed an injustice while serving in his official capacity, he was the first to acknowledge it and the first to correct it.

As a sheriff, Aten can be compared justly with Pat Garrett, Jim East, Bill Tilghman, and other fearless officers who challenged so effectively the bristling outlaw combines which, more than all the calamities of nature, blocked the advance of civilization in the West. As a range detective he was, without doubt, the peer of John Poe, who upset Billy the Kid. As a division manager of the world's largest ranch, the XIT, he proved himself not only to be an outstanding administrator but a leader and organizer of cattlemen harassed by the rustler rings in the Panhandle.

It was primarily through his services as a Texas Ranger, however, that Ira Aten earned the immortality that is so indelibly his. The Ranger image was his constant one of himself as I have said in a chapter of this book. It is—these seven decades since—Texas's constant image of him.

His name would be on any list of the score or so greatest officers who have ridden and battled in that outstanding corps of lawmen during the many memorable generations of its functioning. He had the bravery and the seasoned initiative of the Texas Ranger in the finest definitions of those terms. Forever, too, there centered around him that peculiar, very justifiable, romanticism with which America invests the Ranger symbol as such. Horse and spur—riata and .45—outlaw trails and gun scourged cowtowns—these are the physical trappings of the mythos.

They all fitted Ira Aten.

The reader may wonder why his saga remained untold so long. Incomplete bits of it did appear in this and that publication during his lifetime. A substantial and durable bit, in the form of disconnected personal memoirs, was issued by the distinguished Southwestern historical journal, *Frontier Times*. The man was too great to become obscure. But he had the hesitant modesty of so many outstanding frontiersmen about trumpeting his own horn.

"I have always thought a person's memoirs should be released to the public only after his death," he wrote in a preface for *Frontier Times*. Then there would be no controversy with him over what had been written. But upon the insistence of admiring friends, he consented to relate some of his experiences as law enforcer and frontiersman—yet not enough nor in sufficient detail.

Many capable writers approached Ira Aten with the intent of portraying him in proper dimension. Gently and courteously, he turned them away. Through a fortunate combination of circumstances, this author finally became his close friend and chosen biographer.

In 1950, I was doing a series of articles on notable Texas Rangers for a national magazine. Till that time, I had had no personal contact with Mr. Aten. But through research I developed an account of his dramatic experiences on the Mexican border entitled *Knight of the Mesas*.

To my surprise I received, a few weeks after publication of this article, a long, handwritten personal letter from Ira Aten himself. He thanked me for the manner in which I had interpreted him, then added: "You must be from Texas, too."

And, of course, I am. Proudly so, though I emphatically disassociate myself from a certain type of professional Texan who makes our homeland ridiculous by the florid chauvinism he exhibits when he strays outside the bounds of the Lone Star State. A cordial correspondence then developed between a former Texas Ranger, living in California, and a nostalgic Texas writer whose work made New York a necessary permanent camp.

Through the few years that remained before his death, the ties of friendship between Ira Aten and myself kept broadening because of our many common associations "back home." We had come from adjoining Texas counties, and from the same general area of Round Rock, which Mr. Aten claimed as home town, where his father had offered spiritual consolation to the dying outlaw, Sam Bass. Three older members of my family had been Texas Rangers. One of them, Richard Lincoln Preece, my grandfather, had helped prepare the way for homesteaders in the Jim Ned country where my honored correspondent later destroyed the fence-cutting gang.

So Ira Aten started sending me more material about himself. Through research and my widespread personal contacts in my native state, I began collecting additional data. While he was still alive, I published many articles dealing with his pursuits and ordeals as an officer in a number of nationally circulated magazines.

Not once did I have any dispute with him over my factual statements or the manner in which I characterized a protagonist who was not only still living but keenly critical. So truthful himself, he hated the type of biography that he described as "being tinged with a degree of fiction which generally borders on the impossible."

Actually, my only difficulty in our whole collaboration was his reluctance to state names of men whom he had arrested. Believing in no doctrine of inherited blood guilt, he didn't want to embarrass living children and other descendants of outlaws. So it is that here and there, to provide a character with identity for the reader, I have given some minor criminal another name from that which he bore in life. Here, also, I have been influenced by the example of Ira Aten because I, too, have known respectable men whose wayward kin got hanged for horse stealing. Almost every Texan has.

Otherwise the book has a complete and scrupulous authenticity. It is based upon his correspondence, his memoirs, the recollections of old-timers still living who knew him, and careful addenda recently provided by his oldest son, Marion Hughes Aten, of El Centro, California, as well as his niece, Mrs. Viola C. Webb, of Round Rock, Texas. Legend has been sifted from legend in the inevitable Aten saga. Apocryphal material has been included only where it could be substantiated by traditional and personal recollections that are reputable.

Some "Aten stories" were rejected because they proved, upon investigation, to have centered around other Rangers. This sort of thing always happens within the folk tradition itself. Dialogue has been constructed from his correspondence, his memoirs, and from the recollections of people who heard him speak.

Ira Aten was a giant figure in the whole epic of the West. This is his long overdue, but deeply appreciative, tribute in print. Of all the letters I have from pioneers in my files, I value his most. Of all the Rangers I have written about, I rate him highest. May his spirit continue in an age when so many of us are too comfortable—and too easily cowed.

HAROLD PREECE.

New York City,
September, 1960.

"If there was mercy for a thief who died on the cross, there might be some for a thief found dying in a cow pasture."

BOOTS DOWN FOR SAM BASS

Summer was an annual torpor enveloping the little trading center that was bisected by sluggish Brushy Creek into Old Round Rock and New Round Rock. It was a season when all creatures lapsed into a self-preserving slackness under the scalding Texas sun. Cattle and horses browsed less in the pastures, lazed more under the oak groves. Lizards clung in a trance to fern stalks and algerita bushes.

Women took more time with their house chores and kids dawdled longer over their marble games. Men gabbed sparingly though Texans loved the spark of a good tongue. Even the gobble of the turkeys in the back yards was muffled and desultory.

Drowsy calm reigned during the hot months. Except on Saturdays. Then the entire community, called just Round Rock, echoed to a different pitch as country folk streamed in for gossip and commerce. Confectioners were busy serving cool strawberry milk shakes and draughts of iced sarsaparilla to lines of customers. Farmers rubbed shoulders with ranchers in shifting, bantering groups along Main Street. The town lay on the great geographical dividing line of the Lone Star State so that it drew business from both the cotton-decked prairies to the east and the rugged cattle ranges of the hill country to the west.

From morning till dusk, every Saturday, housewives from both areas brought eggs and butter to exchange for snuff and calico. Peddlers of watermelons and cantaloupes parked their wagons at convenient intersections to haggle over prices with passers-by. Professional horse traders from Waco and San Antonio camped with their merchandise on the hoof near the creek and roamed the streets soliciting swaps or sales. Cronies whose eyes still held the glint of battle gathered at corners to reminisce about the Civil War, thirteen years finished. Families sat themselves down to free dinners served at general stores whose owners were anxious to attract and keep steady customers.

Round Rock stirred on its big day even when the temperature topped a hundred in the shade. But on that certain Saturday of July 20, 1878, the weekend tempo was commotion rather than the usual pleasant excitement. Mid-afternoon though it was, the confectioneries were all but deserted. Voices were loud, keyed with tension. Merchants were standing outside their stores gazing at incoming crowds of strangers instead of feeding familiar William son County citizens with plates of chicken and dumplings. A few of the visitors—tall, grim-looking men—were wearing guns, openly displayed in their holsters. Fidgety watchers pushed and jostled. For the first time since its founding, the little rural village had a big-town traffic problem.

A farm wagon, freshly painted in green, rolled down the street, headed toward the post office in the center of the five-block business section. Halfway to its destination, the vehicle was halted by a crush of buggies and surreys filled with eager, voluble passengers. The driver of the wagoh was a frowning, puzzled, gray-haired man dressed in neat black serge. He jerked at the reins, then spoke to two gangling teenage boys sharing the wide seat with him.

"Frank—Ira—keep a watch to see that we don't get rammed from behind."

Then he called to a man trying to maneuver a buggy through the blockade, "Mr. Davis, what's all this uproar? What's happening?"

Davis flicked a whip across the back of his buggy horse.

"Didn't you hear, Preacher? Sam Bass got shot. Shot to pieces right here in Round Rock. Everybody's come to watch him cash his chips."

The boy named Ira jumped to his feet, the older man put ting a hand on a shoulder to prevent his leaping from the wagon.

"You mean Sam Bass the train robber from Dallas?" the boy shrilled. "The one that the Rangers have been chasing? Did they run him clear to Round Rock?"

Davis laughed as the wheels of the buggy edged past a carriage full of strangers. "Yep. Same Mr. Bass, sonny. He was fixin' to rob our bank when the Rangers filled his craw with lead."

Looking silent and concerned, the man in serge got his wagon under way again. By temperament, the Reverend Austin C. Aten disliked anything florid and spectacular. He had no more use for these impromptu carnivals of sensationalism than he had for the brazen, paid-admission tent shows that occasion ally played one-night stands in this part of central Texas. Ten yards from the post office he announced a decision to his sons.

"Boys, we'll take care of the business we came for. Picking up the mail. Buying groceries and horse feed from Kopperel's store. Right afterwards, we'll go home and prepare for the Lord's Day tomorrow."

Both youngsters looked disappointed. Ira made a plea for both of them.

"Aw, Dad, can't we go see Sam Bass? Everybody else is."

Preacher Aten shook his head. "Guess not, Ira. Bass is probably dying. He's a bad man. But any man—even a bad one—has the right to die in peace."

Ira was the only one of the seven Aten children who ever dared argue with his father. "But, Dad, Sam Bass just isn't any man. Everybody's been talking about him since he started robbing those trains up in North Texas last fall."

The minister was firm. "That may be, son. But decent Christians don't make a circus out of death."

Finally the wagon reached the post office. The preacher stepped out, followed by his boys. A chorus of voices greeted him from a group clustered around the building.

Howdy, Brother Aten. Reckon you heard about Sam Bass....

Shot yesterday in front of Highsmith's livery stable after he'd done in Deputy Grimes and plugged Deputy Morris Moore from Travis County right through the lungs...

Got his dose of lead from the Rangers...

Sebe Barnes killed with him—but Frank Jackson got away...

Been hidin' out in a cemetery—and they'll be a-buryin' Sam Bass where he slept...

Preacher Aten tried to make some reply and ask some questions, but his own quiet words were submerged in the babble rising higher as more tongues joined to swell it. He looked around to see, approaching them, a group of citizens whom he knew to be church people.

Detaching himself from the noisy crowd and beckoning to his sons, he walked forward to meet what turned out to be a delegation.

"Brother Aten," their spokesman said, "Sam Bass has brought bloodshed and a crowd of rubbernecks to our community. But we don't think it would be right to let him die without trying to save him from hell."

Preacher Aten nodded solemnly. "I agree, since Bass has already suffered his earthly punishment. How bad off is he?"

"Very bad. He was bleeding like a stuck pig when the Rangers found him under a tree at the edge of a pasture last night. Dr. Cochran says he can't last more than forty-eight hours."

Preacher Aten looked thoughtfully toward the blue Texas skies as if hoping to find some inch of its spaciousness where a hellion could squeeze through. "All right, brethren," he replied. "I'll go with you. If there was mercy for a thief who died on the Cross, there may be some for a thief found dying in a cow pasture."

Ira found a pair of hitching posts for the wagon team. He noticed one of the armed men stepping into the post office as he made the reins tight around the short poles. His shining face paid silent homage. This must be one of the Texas Rangers, one of the men who'd run Sam Bass from Salt Creek, on the North Texas prairies, to Brushy Creek right here in Round Rock.

Ira and his brother Frank brought up the rear of the churchly procession marching toward the vacant house that Round Rock had provided as a dying place for a visiting outlaw. Other morbidly curious people were massed in the yard when the party got there. Still others were arriving. A Ranger stood on the steps by the front door.

"Only one visitor at a time, ladies and gentlemen," he was saying. "No children admitted, no conversation with the prisoner, and nobody to stay but a minute. Orders of Major Jones."

The leader of the delegation spoke to the guard. "Ranger, we've brought the Methodist circuit rider, Brother Aten, to bring Sam Bass to repentance. These"—indicating the boys—"are his two sons."

The Ranger addressed Frank. "How old are you, boy?"

"Seventeen," the preacher's eldest son answered.

"Old enough. You can go in." Then, to Ira: "What's your age?"

"Fifteen," Ira replied, adding hastily, as he saw the expression on the officer's face, "going on sixteen."

"Too young," the Ranger declared.

"*Too young*," Ira repeated in a daze. He took a defiant step toward the door till he was stopped by ingrained obedience to adults. His father had taught him to respect the authority of grown people, and this man carried authority. The authority of law represented by the Texas Rangers. Yet disappointment must be countered with some assertion of self.

"Do you know," Ira said in a voice half-cocky, half-tremulous, "I'm going to join the Rangers when I get a little older?"

The guard chuckled. "I'll be looking for you, son."

Frank Aten smiled at his brash younger brother before entering the house. Ira waited till the Ranger was occupied with other rubberneckers before slipping around the side of the frame building to peer through a window. So many people were inside the room where Sam Bass lay that Ira saw little, not even the face of the dying bandit. But by straining his ears and tuning them to the familiar voice of his father, he managed to make out the conversation that went on inside.

"Howdy, Mr. Bass," he heard his father say. "I'm Brother Aten, a preacher. The folks in this town wanted me to come and beseech the Lord for you."

Then the response of Sam Bass, feeble and cynical: "I've lived a dog's life, Parson. And I'll die a dog's death."

"Well, sir, if I can't do you any good, I'll go," Austin Aten rejoined.

"No, wait—Preacher. Come here a minute. If you don't mind, you can kneel and say a prayer for me."

Reverend Austin Aten prayed. Then, charitable duty performed, he took his boys home to the farm, seven miles outside Round Rock.

Sam Bass died the next day, the twenty-seventh anniversary of his birthday. One thing in common, and by accident, he had shared with the Atens, whom he'd never heard of till he lay dying on a mattress in a strange town.

Like them, he had come from the Midwest after the Civil War. As a mawkish ballad testifies, Sam Bass called Indiana his "native home." In Texas, he had progressed from cotton-picker to cowhand to race-track gambler, and finally to leadership of mounted rowdies whose reward was much more notoriety than it ever was tangible loot. His forebears were of those semi-derelict wanderers who lived by luck and scrapings on the thin margins of every frontier society during America's periods of pioneer expansion.

Ira Aten's father was a descendant of early Dutch colonists who had settled in New York during the early part of the seventeenth century. The original family name, Van Aten, was shortened to Aten after several generations in America. One part of the connection remained in the East; another moved westward. From this branch, Austin Van Aten was born in Ohio, some years after the War of 1812.

Like his kinsmen, he was religious, frugal, an admirer of learning. Deeply influenced by the Great Revival that continued in America for half a century, he became a Methodist minister, marrying a young woman of his denomination and holding various pulpits in Illinois. There his two eldest children were born—Frank in Peoria on August 26, 1860; Ira in Cairo on September 3, 1862.

During the Reconstruction period following the Civil War, Austin Aten came to Texas as a circuit rider for his church. His devoutness and his personal goodness offset any feelings that former Confederate Texans might have had against him as "a Yankee." Eventually he settled on the farm near Round Rock, eighteen miles north of the Texas capital city, called Austin after the Yankee-born colonizer who had established the first permanent English-speaking communities in the state.

Of the two elder Aten sons, Frank was the quiet, stay-at-home type, destined to live in and around Round Rock for the greater part of a long lifetime. Ira was the adventurous, imaginative one who would influence two younger brothers, Edwin and George.

Naturally, it was Ira who would become completely absorbed in the enormous and spectacular pageant of Texas. The Lone Star State had taken a beating with the rest of the Confederacy after having shot its way out of both the Mexican and the American republics. It had re-entered the Union after the Civil War, having no choice. But defeat was salved by its peculiar mystique, which stemmed from its own fling at independence before it joined the United States.

With his own eyes Ira Aten saw the treaties that Texas had signed as a sovereign nation with the monarchies of Europe. Carefully preserved, the documents were in the State Library at Austin. Old men who had served as officials and legislators of that backwoods commonwealth, wrested from Mexico, were still alive during his boyhood. Ira might be a native of

Illinois, which had given a president named Abraham Lincoln to America, but he was more conscious of Sam Houston, who had been president of Texas. Old-timers in Williamson County told him how they had known Houston personally, how they had lifted a glass with the "Texas Washington." Similarly, Ira learned about the Alamo before he did about Bunker Hill; he knew the story of Goliad before reading in a schoolbook something about a place called Lexington.

Ira Aten was never the rabid Texas "nationalist" that so many of his contemporaries were, but he absorbed the legend and gave it meaning in his own life by all the fervent, innate romanticism with which he endowed it.

A few weeks after the Sam Bass killing he chanced to be in Austin with some citizens of Round Rock. In a store he saw a man built like a mountain, hair flowing to wide shoulders, his huge feet encased in Indian moccasins. At first Ira thought the giant must be an attraction of one or the other of the circuses which periodically played the capital. But after the mammoth figure had left, a clerk said reverently:

"That was Big Foot Wallace, the famous old Texas Ranger. He's got a ranch down in Frio County, but he lives here in Austin with his kinfolks."

Ira ran to the door to get another glimpse of the illustrious one. He saw only a receding back and a pair of mighty legs. Then he stumbled back to the counter, blinded by the sight of greatness.

Big Foot Wallace, the Texas Samson, had torn panthers to pieces with his bare hands and smashed anvils with one blow of a powerful fist; he was the last of the demigods who had shaped this vast and wonderful country from rock and sand and gunpowder. Hitched to a wagon by the Mexicans and worked like an ox when he had been their prisoner, he had paid them back later, with a thousandfold interest, in that strange conflict called the Mexican War.

Above everything else, Big Foot Wallace personified the Texas Ranger who whipped his weight in wildcats or in wild men. The living forerunner of those who had strewn the corpses of the Sam Bass gang from the boundary of Indian Territory to the outskirts of the capital.

When Ira got home, he repeated the promise he had made to himself when Sam Bass was dying.

"I'm going to be a Texas Ranger when I grow up," he told his father.

Preacher Aten might not approve of a boy's ambitions, but he was no man to mock them. He did say that, with so much good land to be had for just about nothing, he had hoped his son would be a farmer and stock raiser.

Ira never heard the answer, being off in his dream again. But now all his idealizing about Texas had a focus that was direct and intimately personal. From all available printed matter and from the tales that the old-timers spun, he learned of those heroic men who had built the Ranger saga by their quick wit and their audacious courage:

Jack Hays, the first outstanding commander when the Rangers had comprised the Republic's standing army of fifty men, defending a country twice the size of Germany. Sam Walker, who had changed the history of Texas and the West by replacing the old-fashioned single-shot weapons with the modern repeating ones turned out by Samuel Colt of New Jersey. Lonnie Moore, who had been a Ranger at twelve, carrying with him on the Texas frontier a Kentucky long rifle that Lonnie's kinsman, Daniel Boone, had borne in the Cumberlands. Mustang Grey, who had jumped his pony into a hail of gunshot across Mexican barricades after General Zachary Taylor had called the Texas Rangers "the finest light-horse cavalry in the world."

In Ira's time, there were June Peak, who had set the trap for Sam Bass, and John Jones, who had driven the outlaw into its jaws. John Armstrong, slated to run down Texas' bloodiest gunman, Wes Hardin, in Florida, and bring Hardin in, something no other officer ever accomplished. L. H. McNelly, with his tiny band, rounding up or driving out an incredible five thousand outlaws who were robbing and killing along the Mexican border.

America, so Ira read in his schoolbooks, had once had her Minute Men. Texas, a land that cherished guts and gallantry, still had her Rangers. The boy from Round Rock was bent on being one of them.

To qualify himself for later enlistment, Ira began to practice riding and shooting. His father's horses were docile animals long broken to the plow and the wagon. So the boy offered to break more spirited saddle ponies for his neighbors. The ponies pitched and bucked; they sent him sailing to the ground many times. Each time he swung back in the stirrup till even the wildest mustang would acknowledge him as conqueror and master.

When he reached his late teens, he was rated as one of Williamson County's best marksmen. His father loved quiet while preparing his sermons, so Ira mounted empty tin cans on stumps in the secluded woods and perforated them with bullets from rifle and revolver. He stalked deer in the hills and pot-shotted rabbits, at increasingly longer ranges, on the prairie.

One day on Cypress Creek, just across the line in Travis County, he brought down a running deer at a hundred yards. "If I can shoot a running buck from that far away," he remarked to his hunting partner, "I could do the same with a running outlaw."

Ira Aten, now twenty, that night mailed an application to Texas Ranger headquarters at Austin, asking to join the force.

Two weeks later he received a reply signed by State Adjutant General William H. King. The letter asked him to come to Austin for an interview and to bring along written recommendations from Williamson County peace officers.

Ira was in the capital the next day. He was nervous and a bit shaky when he was admitted to see General King.

General King never won a reputation for having an angelic disposition, but he soon put the prospective recruit at his ease. Ira found that the way had been unexpectedly paved for him.

"Calm yourself, Aten," the general said. "I know a peace officer who speaks highly of you and your family—Sheriff Emmett White here in Austin."

Ira beamed. "Yes, sir, Sheriff White is a right close friend of ours." The general studied the young man carefully. "Do you owe any debts?"

"No, sir," Ira replied, "not a penny."

"That's good," the general commented. "We don't like to get letters from people saying that Rangers owe them money. You know what our pay is to start. No more than you'd earn as a cowpuncher—and for a whole lot rougher work—thirty dollars a month and your keep thrown in."

Ira made no protest about the wages and answered "yes" when General King asked him if he had his father's consent to enlist. He wanted to tell the general just how he felt about the glories of Rangering, but King didn't seem to be in the mood to listen.

The general finally told him he would do; he would have to report for formal enlistment two weeks hence.

Leaving that office, Young Ira Aten was walking on the warm Texas air.

"I was always expecting the impossible, such as attempting to rescue some pretty girl from the bandits infesting the border along the Rio Grande."

RANGER ROOKIE

On a breezy March day in 1883 Ira Aten stood waiting impatiently for the train that would carry him from his dusty little home town to Austin. There would be done what was necessary to make him an official member of the Texas Rangers. Ira felt a little like Galahad qualifying for the Round Table. His gray Stetson hat was freshly cleaned and blocked stiffer than Williamson County cedarwood. He was wearing a brand-new blue serge suit, bought with money earned by the despised drudgery of cotton picking. Well, he had learned from a reading of Tennyson at the Literary Society that the Round Table's Gareth had served as a kitchen pot wiper before sallying forth to roust bandits out of castles.

All the Atens, dressed in their best, had ridden in a surrey with him to the squat frame depot where trains stopped briefly to throw off mail sacks and pick up passengers. Family friends and other admiring citizens kept arriving by ones and twos to tell the preacher's starry-eyed son goodbye.

Ira accepted handshakes of congratulation from Robertsons, Gandys, Hills, and other townsfolk whom he'd known all his life. In a community whose daily life was generally pretty humdrum it was something for a local boy to become a Ranger! Like a local girl's finishing normal school and leaving home to teach.

A grocer said, with appropriate civic-mindedness, "Maybe, Ira, you signing up with the Rangers will help this town live down the bad name it got from the Sam Bass fight. Why, they're even comparing Round Rock to them gun-slinger nests like Tascosa and San Saba."

Ira made a silent vow to reform Tascosa, up in the Panhandle, as well as San Saba, closer home in the bullet-bit Texas hills. It would have been boasting before his neighbors had he said so out loud.

"I'll try to do Round Rock proud," he solemnly promised the merchant.

Anxiously, Ira pulled out his dollar Ingersoll watch, comparing hour and minute with the schedule for the train's arrival that was chalked on a blackboard near the ticket window. *On time* was the comment written in the station agent's very legible script.

But it was already five minutes late on its two-hundred mile run from Dallas, where Sam Bass had first started acting so ornery. Had one of the other brigand outfits now prowling Texas halted this train? Maybe at some curve of the track, along some desolate right of way, they had raided the very coach he'd be riding to Austin to swear his vows. What a comedown that would be on this, the supreme day of his life!

Ira was nervous with apprehension. He edged toward the ticket window, meaning to ask the agent if there were any news of the delayed train. Halfway there, he heard a whistle blow.

The train paused for a grudging five minutes at this small, next-to-last stop between Dallas and Austin. Ira hoisted his bag, hurriedly kissed his mother, and stepped into a car. The wheels had already started moving out of Round Rock when he waved a departing salute to the friends and kin who had come to see him off.

Half an hour later he was striding up Austin's main street— Congress Avenue—toward the state capitol. When he reached the capitol, he reported for duty to Adjutant

General King, commander of the generally-inactive Texas militia and the always active Texas Rangers.

King looked up from a stack of letters and documents as the rookie entered. "Howdy, Aten. Right here when I expected you. Good start for a Ranger."

Ira made some polite answer and stood waiting for instructions.

"You ever been on the Mexican border?" the head of Texas's military forces demanded.

Ira's face flushed with excitement. The Mexican border, where the bandits roved and the Rangers struck! Just the right patch of hell for a Ranger to make his name and win his spurs.

"No, sir," he answered; "but I'd hoped you'd send me to the border."

The general's laugh grated on Ira. "Don't look so happy, boy. A lot of the people down there don't even know they're in Texas, and wouldn't give a damn for its laws if they did. One Ranger after the other has been killed in that blasted brush—a lot more crippled for life." Then, irritably: "Follow the orders of your captain and forget all the fancy stories you've read about Rangers—unless you want the state of Texas to bury you."

He handed Ira an envelope. "Here's your train ticket to Uvalde, not far from the border. You'll report there to Captain L. P. Sieker of Company D. He's expecting you as a replacement for a man who had the good sense not to re-enlist. You're now an enrolled Texas Ranger—or will be as soon as you step down the hall to let Governor Ireland swear you in."

Only for a moment did Ira feel chastened as he left the adjutant general's office to seek out Governor John Ireland. Only for a few paces, as he trod the wide stone floor, did he feel the proverbial cold water dousing so much soaring ambition. He walked jauntily into the Executive Department, gallantly removed his Stetson, and presented himself to the elderly clerk handling callers in the reception room.

"I'm Texas Ranger Ira Aten. General King sent me here to take the oath from the governor."

The clerk seemed a little bored. Many a brash youngster had come tramping up to his desk, making this same kind of announcement in almost the same language. But Governor Ireland demanded that all visitors be received cordially. So the oldster shook hands and said gravely: "Welcome, Ranger Aten. Just take a seat where you see those other people, and I'll tell the governor you're here."

For more than an hour Ira fidgeted in his chair as the clerk led Texans, come for different errands, into the governor's private office. Farm women with tearful, swollen eyes, were there to plead for pardons for sons doing time in the state prison at Huntsville after getting liquored up and stabbing somebody at one or another Saturday night frolic. Politicians, wanting jobs or favors, lounged and smoked and chatted while waiting to bend John Ireland's ear. Sheep ranchers were on hand to complain about the depredations of cattle ranchers, and cowmen to protest the inroads of the hated flocks on their grass.

Finally the clerk approached Ira. "The governor will see you now, Ranger. Right this way."

Ira walked into the private sanctum, his heart beating faster than a blacksmith's hammer. Sitting at a long desk, under a Lone Star flag and a wall painting of Sam Houston, was a big man wearing expensive black broadcloth, speaking in a patrician manner modified by the easy democracy of a frontier state. Southern-born Governor Ireland came from the Guadalupe Valley town of Seguin which, till its saturation by abolitionist German immigrants, had clung to the decorous social traditions of Charleston and Baltimore.

"Glad to know you, Ranger," the governor said. "I hear you're from Round Rock. Why didn't you bring in Frank Jackson and let the state treasurer pay you a reward?"

Frank Jackson, Ira knew, was the only member of the Bass gang still at large. He failed to see the twinkle in John Ireland's sharp eyes. Anything to do with Rangering had to be taken seriously. "I'll go after Frank Jackson if you want me to, Governor," he promised solemnly. "I think I'd recognize him from his pictures I've seen on posters in the Georgetown courthouse."

Governor Ireland laughed. "That's up to Captain Sieker, Aten. Chances are he may want you to catch some other fellows first."

Then the governor bade the rookie raise his right hand and repeat the Ranger oath. Ira Aten always remembered that as the most dedicated moment of his life.

The Lone Star flag, the faces of Sam Houston, who had shaped Texas, and of John Ireland, who now ran it, were swimming blurs in the young recruit's eyes as he repeated the words that Ireland dictated. He promised to obey and enforce the constitution and laws of the state of Texas and of the United States without fear or favor, to obey implicitly the orders of his superiors in the field and of the governor as his commander in chief.

Ira took leave of Governor Ireland in a mumble of thanks, and almost forgot to say goodbye to the old clerk in the outer office. After leaving the capitol he flagged a horse-drawn hack.

"Take me to the depot," he ordered. "I'm a Texas Ranger and have to get to Uvalde—my post."

A day and a half it took him to journey two hundred and fifty miles in a state where railroads were still something new, with the majority of travelers still depending on saddle horses or stagecoaches. Language and skin hue changed with terrain as he entered southwestern Texas, legally and politically a part of the United States but, culturally and ethnically, a detached appendage of Mexico.

Southward the slow-moving coaches carried him, eighty miles from Austin to San Antonio, where he had to lie over for some hours while awaiting a second train that he would take west to Uvalde. He wandered the streets of this old city, founded before Baltimore, but cheerfully accepting antiquity as a matter of course rather than building shrines to ancestral mummies. Pimps in the Mexican quarter offered to "fix him up" with *muchachas bonitas*—pretty girls. Tamale peddlers vending their fiery tidbits, wrapped in corn shucks, shouted to him from the streets, "Nice fresh tamales, señor—ten cents a dozen." Store signs bore inscriptions in a language he couldn't read but knew to be Spanish. He stopped for a few minutes to rest on a bench in a park and listen to an orator, mounted on a cart and making a wildly applauded speech to a crowd of shabby brown men.

"*Muerte a Díaz! Muerte a Díaz!*" Ira made out those words because the speaker shouted them every other minute. But of their meaning he had no idea. He turned to another blond Anglo who had that moment sat down opposite him on the bench.

"Do you understand his talk?" Ira asked the stranger. "What's he hollering about?"

The Anglo laughed. "Listen to him—*muerte a Díaz*. That means death to Díaz—Porfirio Díaz, the president of Mexico."

Ira's face wrinkled in a puzzled frown. "Aren't these people citizens of the United States?"

"Yep." The stranger chuckled. "Most of 'em. Their families have been in Texas for hundreds of years—a damned sight longer than lots of our folks."

Ira was worriedly trying to get at something. "Chester A. Arthur is president of the United States. Why get so riled up about Porfirio Díaz, the president of Mexico?"

The stranger yawned. "Mister, you sure don't know Mexicans. Chet Arthur would be just another gringo if they ever heard of him. But Díaz—he's one of their own bad hombres and they'd cut him up for chili meat if they could lay hands on him. Know what the business of that fellow on the box is?"

Ira shook his head.

The Anglo bit deeply into a plug of Star Navy chewing tobacco. "Recruiting Texas Mexicans to cross the Rio Grande and fight in a revolution against Díaz. A lot of 'em will sign up, too."

Ira's face reddened with anger. He was of a mind to make his first arrest as a Ranger by pulling the anti-Díazista off the box and delivering him to the United States marshal for enlisting American citizens to fight in a foreign war. Then the caution of a man asserted itself over the impetuosity of a boy.

There would be lots of Mexicans in the country where he'd be serving. These revolutionists probably would be all over it trying to enlist men who'd be better off herding sheep or wrangling horses. But Captain Sieker probably had a policy about it—and he'd better ask the captain before making any moves.

When he got up to go the stranger had begun to counter the oratory with loud snores. Ira strolled along some more narrow, zigzagging streets, listening to the babble of strange talk around him, being eyed coldly by out-of-town vaqueros standing in front of cantinas that gringos seldom entered unless they were spoiling for trouble. Ira felt ill at ease: displaced from every reality he'd ever known.

It was a country boy's first contact with a puzzlingly different culture, and the rub was raw. Before this, Ira had known Mexicans only by the handfuls as seasonal cotton pickers in Williamson County or to see them bunching around the cheap stores along Austin's mart of the poor—Pecan Street. Here he felt overwhelmed by Mexicans, as outnumbered as those Anglo Texans who'd fought that immortally unsuccessful battle in the tumble-down Spanish mission called the Alamo.

It was the Alamo where he finally took refuge. He sought out the venerated stone structure in the center of town as do most Anglos, their primness offended too brazenly and too soon by the rampant exoticism of this casually wicked community.

Ira's eyes were reverently moist as he looked at wide splotches of brown imbedded in the masonry of the inner walls. Another visitor told him that the spots were the dried blood of the hundred and eighty defenders—though this

may have been one more furbish of legend added to the
Texas sequel of the American Revolution.

Silent and thoughtful, the Ranger recruit moved in and
out of different chambers whose identifying signs testified
to the bravery of men who had died defying twenty-to-
one odds. The broad front room where Travis and Bonham
had fallen beside their cannons. The crumbling remains of
the picket stockade held by gray-bearded Davy Crockett,
intending in Texas to buck his old Tennessee political opponent, Sam Houston, rather than to die and let Sam become
a president. The quarters where sick Jim Bowie had risen
from his pillow and slain thirty of his foes, sprawled in a
circle around his cot, before dying himself, bullet-riddled
and spitting blood.

An anteroom where a stack of gunpowder had been left
by a previous Mexican commandant before the Texans had
taken their stand in this fiery cradle of their four-day-old
republic. And, by a legend that Ira knew, the very last one
alive was supposed to blow up the powder and blast Santa
Anna's four thousand troopers to kingdom come.

He left the shrine and strolled to the neighboring plaza where the corpses of the Alamo had been stacked like
cordwood and burned to ashes. Texas patriotism—stirred
by all he had seen—restored Ira's mood of dedication; made
him feel, in an almost fanatical imagery, that he'd joined an
order of elect fighting men by enlisting in the Texas Rangers—had been accepted into a group of hard-riding cavaliers
stemming in some lineal descent from the heroes of the Alamo, if you reckoned descent by blood that was shed rather
than blood that was sired.

Exaltation continued after Ira had boarded a train for
Uvalde. Crockett and Bowie—the Alamo's demigods—had
slain their share of invaders from over the Rio Grande. Ira
Aten, idolizing them, meant to get his share of outlaws from
both sides of the big river.

Maybe he'd start with Frank Jackson, uncaught henchman
of Sam Bass. Ira wondered whether Governor Ireland had

been dropping some broad hint about running down Jackson, who had been reported variously as hiding in New Mexico, Indian Territory, and the Texas Cross Timbers where the Bass gang had vacationed between holdups. Any Ranger who brought in Jackson would not only collect a reward but, even more satisfyingly, write his own commission of rank. After Frank Jackson, there were still more bad men that Ira Aten meant to tame...and tough towns along with the tough men. Tascosa, whose dubious enforcer of law was Henry Brown, now municipal constable after having been a swaggering gun slinger for Billy the Kid. Hempstead, down near Houston, better known by its well-deserved nickname of Six-Shooter Junction. There a restaurant keeper had drawn a forty-five and scattered a man's brains for mildly criticizing the pie. Fort Worth, gateway to the Cattle Kingdom stretching from Texas to British Columbia, and also the center where hired killers were recruited for western range wars by certain detective agencies. Red Rock, close to Austin, where taxpayers saved board money on prisoners by hanging them all whenever the jail reached its maximum capacity of seven. Possibly even Austin, with its saloon touts trying to elect the West's worst killer, Ben Thompson, as city marshal. All the more now the Texas capital needed a stiff purgative of law since decent boys and girls from every county would be enrolling in the newly-founded state university.

The train swept across high, brushy country, jungles of cactus and cockleburs skirting the miles of tracks. Flocks of quail, panicked by the thunderous passage of the iron horse, soared from clumps of mimosa and huisache shrubs, to take refuge in temporary, circling ascent till the last thudding echoes had faded. Thorn-scratched cattle fled the right of way when the engine whistle keened its shrill, impatient warning. A buzzing legion of swarming bees battened for a moment at the closed windows of the coach where Ira sat. Herds of the sword-tusked, bristlingly undomesticated pigs called javelinas rutted and dueled in wallows inherited from the now annihilated buffalo.

Wild life—fecund, assertive, gregarious—was everywhere. Human life—existing differently, still maintaining only precarious supremacy—manifested itself less along this tenuous roadway of iron freshly spanning an ancient land. Man—blond or brown—became a rarer species as Ira kept observing the grimly forbidding topography of what some army engineers had called the Texas Bad Lands. Now and then he saw a vaquero sitting mounted, waiting to cross once the train moved on. Sometimes the man on horseback would wave to the people in the coaches, but often he would vouchsafe only an indifferent stare. Ira guessed that most of these riders had yet to set foot on a train.

Hamlets marking the route also became fewer and fewer. The nearer the Mexican border, the scarcer the towns. Tired from absorbing so many sensations in just two days, Ira slumped down into his seat. There was so much to be learned about this unwelcoming wilderness before he could interpret or master it. Or must a man first let himself be overwhelmed by it before attempting mastery?

The train stopped at a place where Ira could see a big clock leering from the steeple of a two-story building he judged must be a courthouse. Uvalde—end of the line and his destination. Eagerly he grabbed his bag from the overhead rack and walked in a long, quick stride out of the coach to the station platform. There he looked for one or another Ranger who should be able to recognize him by intuition and have a horse waiting for him to make that short, last lap of the journey.

He stood there waiting as he shunted off hawkers for a couple of hotels. Others who had been on the train were being met by spouses or relatives grabbing their baggage and showering them with embraces. But a Texas Ranger—a guardian of the state's peace—was being given the non-reception of a nobody by fellow Rangers.

Ira felt hurt and confused. It was a hell of a way for an outfit to treat a brother in arms. Across the tracks he saw some cowboys fooling around a loading corral used in the shipment of cattle. He walked to the pen and spoke to one of them.

"How far is it to Camp King, the Ranger headquarters?"

The cowboy put the last licks on a homemade cigarette before he answered. "'Bout ten miles. You come here to join up?"

"Already joined up," Ira replied. "Where's the nearest livery stable?"

His informant jabbed a thumb in the direction of the main street. "Down that way a little piece."

Feeling humiliated and embarrassed, Ira Aten, a Ranger without a horse, walked to the livery stable and rented one. After promising to send it back by the first member of the force who'd be riding into town, Ira started toward Camp King, named for Adjutant General King, and located on the little Leona River, not far from the larger, more important Nueces.

It was suppertime and the Rangers were in the cook shack eating when he finally got there. He entered the hut, sniffed hungrily when he saw the plates of beef and beans on the table, then caught the eye of a robust man some years older than himself.

The man stood and greeted the tired recruit. "Howdy. You must be Aten, the new private we've been expecting. Sit down and I'll make you acquainted with the boys while the cook is bringing you some grub."

He grasped Ira's hand. "I'm Frank Jones, the sergeant of this outfit."

"Maybe I'd picked the wrong time to be a Ranger..."

TEXAS ALSACE

For some weeks Ira nursed an unspoken umbrage that no fellow Ranger had shown up to glad-hand him at the Uvalde railroad station. That had been quite a letdown for an epic-fed youngster all ready to climb into saddle and start rounding up bands of freebooters.

Yet anticlimaxes are common techniques of molding men in military organizations and in semi-military groups such as the Texas Rangers. Else how contain the ebullient impulsiveness that recruits always display when they are eager volunteers rather than conscripts?

Soldiering and policing—Rangers did both—never afford continuous opportunities for heroism. Routines transcend valor in daily functioning, although a Ranger without valor would have been a contradiction of that legend which is Texas. Duty work is often necessarily dull work. And to Ira's keen dismay, a great deal of Ranger activity was just so much dull, dedicated duty.

It was serving writs and warrants on sorry wrongdoers, craven and submissive before men wearing badges no matter how much slapping around of ordinary citizens they might do. It was rough, tedious patrol work across steep, sullen mountains and broad, treacherous canyons where bobcats and chaparral cocks were more common than the humans who clustered for gregariousness and safety around the widely separated little towns. On levels that would have taxed the devotion of the Round Table's Gareth, it was doing that extra share of camp drudgery naturally expected from a rookie.

Loading pots and provisions on pack mules for the eight hundred-mile round-trip patrols from the Pecos River Bottoms, on the north, to Rio Grande City, at the very edge of the Mexican border on the south. Washing pans and skillets, with sand for detergent, on these long, wearying trips. Building campfires; sometimes coaxing flame from dead boughs and driftwood dampened by rain or the waters from overflown creeks. Fetching hay for the wooden feed troughs of horses and mules when the company was bivouacked at headquarters.

So ran the course of Ira Aten's apprenticeship as a lawman. So began that awkward, but imperative, change from romantic into Ranger.

His coming from Round Rock, the scene of the Sam Bass fight, attracted a flurry of interest during his first few days in camp. Ira's comrades wanted to hear his personal account of what had happened on that sizzling July day. Since the rookie had not been an eyewitness to the fight, he talked more about the bravado the outlaw had shown on his deathbed.

"Sam Bass figured prayers wouldn't help," chuckled Sergeant Jones. "Probably thought there'd be reward posters tacked on the Pearly Gates."

Jokes and opinions about Sam Bass inevitably brought up the question of which Ranger had pumped the fatal bullet into the outlaw. Some Company D men argued that the honor of potting Sam belonged to Dick Ware. Others upheld the contending claim of George Harrell.

Tactfully Ira avoided a commitment for either man, not wanting, as a new Ranger, to be caught in an intramural crossfire. Instead, he hesitantly mentioned that Frank Jackson was still running loose and ought to be caught.

"Oh, Frank Jackson." A Ranger yawned. "Knew him when he was a one-gallus plow-pusher in Denton County. Well, we'll pick him up if we see him in our territory."

"Yeh," drawled another. "If Jackson's still in Texas, he's laying low and letting the trains roll by. There's a lot more men Company D's having to keep an eye on just now."

Ira got the point without putting up any impudent back talk. Rangers of any corps were duty-bound to arrest any wanted man who drifted into their particular patrol area.

But no company could go larking all over Texas for one desperado just because he was notorious and uncaptured. Outlaws who had suspended operations were less of a threat than those still brandishing guns and swinging long ropes. Law-enforcement officers had to place practical emphasis on hellions active and contemporary.

Ira heard some of the Rangers in the company discuss Ben Thompson, then running for marshal of Austin. The lack of rancor displayed toward Thompson amazed him whenever the campfire gossip turned to the merits and demerits of different pistol geniuses. Dodge City Marshal Bat Masterson, who should have known, had publicly branded Ben and his brother Billy Thompson as the West's two deadliest gunmen. Yet the majority of the men in Ira's outfit admired the courage and trigger art of the two "Thompson boys" even as they deplored the uses of those considerable talents made by the two hell roarers from Austin.

"Ben stood by us Texas cowboys when he ran saloons in Kansas," Ira heard a comrade say once. "He backed us with shootin' irons and bail money whenever some high-and-mighty bunch of Jayhawkers tried to hurrah us."

"And it was a Ranger, Nap Jennings, who let Bill get across the Rio Grande when a posse of Laredo Mexicans took after him," a second Ranger recalled. "Sure, Ben did some cuttin' up in that town. But that gang of star-wearin' Pedros would have robbed him, cut his throat, and dumped him in the river if they'd caught him."

"Sure would," a third man commented. "I'd have damned well looked the other way, too, if I'd been in Nap Jennings's place."

Heads nodded in general agreement. Ira may have dissented, but he did so silently, knowing that pattern of Texas patriotism which even decked Ben and Bill Thompson in some mantle of regard for having challenged outlanders. Several members of Company D had formerly been hands driving cattle up the long trails to the towns of Kansas which loved Texas money while detesting Texas men. But any saloon managed by Ben Thompson had been a friendly outpost on enemy soil—and, unfailingly, Ben went along with his country men: right or wrong.

Mexicans, by the traditional Texas chauvinism, belonged in a category of aliens even more disliked than the Yankee-descended Kansans. These brown-skinned, mixed-blood descendants of Spanish grandees and Aztec Indian concubines spoke a strange tongue, adhered to a strange religion, and were "white" only legally. Rangers often regarded Mexican sheriffs and constables elected in the border counties as being but one degree above "bandits" and disliked even minimum dealings with them. The dark folk, in turn, thought of the different Ranger commands not as detachments of gallant caballeros but as foreign garrisons occupying land wrested from their fathers during the Mexican War less than forty years before.

However, festering cultural conflict did not prevent Ira from picking up the rudimentary knowledge of Spanish required by Rangers serving on the border. Without it, he would have been severely handicapped when sent on some assignment to a village where the only English-speaking resident might be a priest with but a limited grasp of the language imported by the Anglo conquerors.

Ira noticed, too, that ancient, mutual biases still allowed for some cautious personal relationships between Anglos and Mexicans. Hospitality was graciously offered him in the meanest jacal or at the most comfortable rancho. Richly clad grandee or barefooted sheepherder treated him with the exquisite courtesy of a people for whom manners were a way of life. Sometimes Ira was irked by their bland denials—"*No, señor—no veo*," ("No, sir—no see")—when he asked for information about some Mexican on his wanted list.

To his credit, Ranger Aten never clubbed any poor peon on the head with a pistol to force either information or a confession. As he went along, learning, he began sensing the nuances he must respect to help preserve some measure of tranquility in this brooding, forever-explosive Alsace Lorraine of Texas.

Discussions of religion were strictly taboo. Let the Mexicans have their altars with the never-extinguished candles and their *santos* paraded around the fields to invoke plentiful rains and good crops. Ira's Protestant backbone had stiffened when he'd first seen such odd goings-on in the name of Christianity. The echoes of a hundred anti-Roman sermons drummed in his ears. Then he remembered that dark-faced village priests never bothered to ask his creed—nor, for that matter, showed much interest in proselyting Anglos. The cue had a historic subtlety—but Ira Aten grasped it.

Next he learned never to mention, in private conversation, the boiling politics of Mexico across the river. There he'd been helped by the bluff pragmatism of his company commander, Captain Sieker.

"We can't stop Texas Mexicans from swimming the Rio Grande to fight for or against Porfirio Díaz. We can't take time off to round up recruiting agents for either side because that's the business of the federal army and secret service—even if they don't attend to it." So the captain had told Ira when the Rookie had dutifully reported the incident he'd witnessed in the San Antonio park. "We Rangers take a hand only when Díazistas and anti-Díazistas try pulling one of their damned blood sprees on *this* side of the river."

Mexicans, on broad levels, regarded Texans—even the courteously polished ones—as invaders and pirates grabbing land that generations of families had possessed under patents granted by kings of Spain. Texans equated the humblest, most inoffensive Mexican with Santa Anna's professional soldiers who had perpetrated those massacres of the Alamo and Goliad. Santa Anna, exiled by his own country, had been dead but a few years when Ira joined the Rangers. Elderly Anglos, who had helped Sam Houston rout the Mexican dictator at San Jacinto, were still alive to keep an old feud edged with recollections.

Prejudice smoldered in the pineboard settlements of the gringos and the adobe hamlets of the *peones*. Ira, though never a crusader for ethnic equality, found that he got along

best with the dark people by exercising authority tactfully rather than bluntly. A Mexican, wanted for rustling or
smuggling, was generally too surprised to reach for gun or
blade, although Ira had to deal more emphatically with resisting offenders of both races.

No man, embodying gringo power, could really be loved by
the Mexicans. But if they didn't love Ira Aten, these original
Texans at least learned to respect him.

For the first few months of his apprenticeship Ira "broke
in" with older Rangers. "Older" these men were in terms
of official seniority. By chronology most of them, like him,
were young men in their early twenties. But soon the recruit
was being trusted to handle individual assignments where
his only allies were wit and his badge.

Most of the prisoners he brought in were men whom
county sheriffs couldn't find or were afraid to hunt. Some
were captured through the cooperation of informers who
bore them personal grudges and "tipped" the Rangers on
their whereabouts. Others Ira recognized from circulars and
reward posters received through various official sources by
Captain Sieker at headquarters.

As the young officer learned increasingly to work on his
own, he outgrew his resentment that nobody had met him
at the railroad station on that disappointing afternoon. The
incident, he sensed now, had been a subtle test of his whole
potential as an enforcer of law.

Why should a Ranger have anticipated a red carpet and a
reception committee for doing anything as elementary as
reaching his post? How could a vain or a petulant man be
expected to quell some seething mob or resolve some grisly vendetta in a place where he might be the only officer
detailed for the job? A Ranger stood on his own. A Ranger stood by his comrades. Ira quickly absorbed these two
time-honored rules, so inseparable and so interlinked.

By listening to the experiences of older men, he understood
why the arrival of a single Ranger in a turbulent community
was often sufficient to start heads cooling and Winchesters

lowering. To the public, every individual Ranger symbolized the courage, the power, and the hard-headed judgment of the whole force. Otherwise such a numerically small body could not have carried so much weight, such feared authority in a state as big and tempestuous as Texas.

Every Ranger knew that he might, at any time, have to play a lone hand in a hostile setting. Yet that rugged, forced individualism accentuated the natural sociability and comradeship between those committed by duty to risk and loneliness. There was not a man in Ira's outfit who wouldn't have sacrificed his life for any other man. Company D members nursed each other through sickness and lent each other money between pay days. Little attention was paid, either, to the fussy protocols of rank. The outfit's three leaders—Captain Sieker, Sergeant Jones, and Corporal B. D. Lindsey—ate from the same tables or on the same patches of camp ground as the privates. There was no saluting nor any wordy etiquette involving the use of "sir." In the border saloons, officers and men drew cards from the same decks and drank whisky from the same bottles.

That had been the general pattern during the sixty years since the Rangers had started as volunteer local militia units, democratically electing their own commanders, while Texas was still a neglected, unpoliced province of the chaotic Mexican Republic.

As the months went by, Ira rode so many patrols that the very trees between Uvalde and Rio Grande City became as familiar as the faces of the people who had lived between Round Rock and Georgetown. He undertook solo missions and wondered what kind of reports Captain Sieker was mailing to General King about him. He never did ask because that would have made him seem anxious for favor. As he conscientiously reviewed his work, he realized that he'd performed some tasks well, some middling, and some badly.

As yet, Ira had come up against only the sorry human scrapings that his outfit flushed without much trouble from caves and lean-tos on their patrol course. When would he

find foes worthy of a Ranger's steel? Men who didn't cringe
and whimper when caught on the scout or beg and bawl
when arraigned before a judge.

No man he'd arrested had shot at him, though several had
threatened. No law hater had tried to bushwhack him. Not
once had he been sent in hot pursuit of smugglers sneaking
stolen merchandise over the Rio Grande or rustlers trans-
ferring cattle from the Texas side of the river to the Mexican
side. Never had he been called upon to fight Apaches; after
all, there were none left to battle—in fact, the only Indians
around were a few part Negro Seminoles serving as scouts
for the United States Army.

Where were the bandits riding in savage gangs to challenge Texas Rangers to swap lead? Where were the really
bad men supposedly infesting the border?

Sometimes he felt that life might have been more exciting
if he'd stayed home and got himself appointed deputy constable of Round Rock precinct, which included several mighty
boisterous communities. There would have been swaggering,
knife wielding drunks to disarm at the cedar-brake dances
and Saturday afternoon street brawls to break up. Posses, too,
in which he could have ridden after shoot-it-out rapists and
killers fleeing to the tangled slopes of the Austin hills. General King had been ribbing him because he was a greenhorn, Ira
decided. Or else he'd picked the wrong time to be a Ranger.

His twenty-first birthday came. He was now old enough to
vote and to run for office. He heard that the chief constable
of Round Rock precinct was retiring. An obvious temptation
had to be resisted. He could ask to be discharged from the
outfit, go home, and get elected—young as he was—because
he'd been a Ranger.

He thrashed the matter over for a few days then came to
a decision. It wouldn't be fair to the Rangers or the home
folks. He'd be running on a title he'd worn instead of a
reputation he'd won. He had signed up for three years; he
would stick for three years.

"By God—let's go get 'em."

DEATH ON A HILLTOP

Spring came, accentuating Ira's itch for action. Panthers mated on the mountain slopes; raccoons licked the fresh sap trickling down the trunks of trees. Huisache and gigantic bushes of laurel flowered along the trails that Rangers rode. Flocks of Mexican eagles soared over the pack mules, hopeful for dropped scraps of bacon and dried beef. Days were as benign as they could be in rough country.

Also, spring brought out the long riders. They were regrouping and rearming after McNelly's cleanup, which had turned so many of their roosts into graveyards.

From Laredo there came an urgent appeal for help. Horse thieves were prowling the large ranches of the Rio Grande Valley and driving off prize hoof stock across the international boundary. Appeals to Webb County Sheriff Dario Gonzales had brought suave promises but no posses. Old Dario, as the disgusted ranchers called him, was not only the kingpin of the corrupt Laredo political ring with its inner council, nicknamed The Forty Thieves; he was also believed to be receiving a handsome percentage of all money realized from the sale of stolen horse herds at Nuevo Laredo on the Mexican side.

The ranchers furnished descriptions of a gang led by one Mario Sanchez, who had missed McNelly's rope. Seven Rangers, headed by Corporal Lindsey, went to the big county and began a search. Five veterans were riding out front on that May morning of 1884, when the patrol detected the prints of many hoofs at San Ambrosio Creek, eighty miles above Laredo. Two rookies—Ira Aten and Ben Reilly—assigned to pack-mule detail were idly chatting and had dropped some distance behind in violation of strict Ranger rules about

close formation. After examining the prints, Lindsey concluded that the drivers of the ponies were bound for the Rio
Grande, a few hundred yards farther on. Then, suddenly, he
saw two men, each riding a horse and leading a horse, hurrying toward the river.

Already the pair had crossed Ambrosio Creek. But when
they caught sight of the Rangers they abandoned their lead
horses and rode furiously toward a high, rugged peak overlooking Old Mexico.

"At 'em, boys!" shouted Corporal Lindsey. "Head 'em off
before they hit the border."

The Rangers lashed their ponies and gave chase. Ira and
Ben Reilly headed across a cutoff away from the channel of
the creek. Their five comrades in front plunged headlong
into the stream. Three horses bogged down in a pocket of
deep mud, then fell, pitching their riders into the water.
Ranger C. W. Giffin's mount tumbled on its master, smash-
ing his collarbone and wrenching a shoulder painfully. Frank
Sieker, younger brother of Captain Sieker, managed to make
it across. In a few minutes he had joined Ira and Ben Reilly,
who were charging toward the hill.

Reilly's fast horse sprinted ahead. Halfway up the hill the
rookie overtook the bandits and rode straight toward them.
Ira was close behind as Reilly pulled up his pony. Frank
Sieker was a few yards farther in the rear.

"We're Texas Rangers!" Reilly shouted. "You're under arrest—" He got no further; the two desperadoes raised rifles and shot him from his saddle. As he fell, thigh bone
shattered, he drew his pistol and fired, but his shot did no
damage.

The bandits turned their guns on the other two Rangers.
Ira was firing his Winchester as rapidly as he could. Frank
Sieker was blasting with a Colt six-shooter. A bullet from
Ira's gun struck one outlaw in the shoulder and the man's
rifle slid to the ground. Lying across his horse, clutching its
mane to keep from falling, he goaded the pony into a run.
As he sped down the opposite side of the hill, Ira sent an-

other shot after him, but without effect. Then came a gasp of pain from Frank Sieker.

Ira wheeled his pony. Sieker was reeling backward in the saddle. His six-shooter was still gripped tightly in the young Ranger's hand when he fell to the ground, shot through the heart.

Ira boiled with anger when, as he said later, he saw "that game boy murdered by thieving hellions." He drew a fine bead on the remaining outlaw and squeezed the trigger. His shot hit the bandit in the right hand and shattered the stock of his opponent's rifle.

The gun fell from the outlaw's hand. Ira tried to get in another shot but his rifle jammed. The second desperado, sprawled across his horse like the first, disappeared at breakneck speed down the hill.

All during the fight Ira's horse had been carrying him farther up the hillside. When he reached the summit, he looked from his saddle to see Frank Sieker's horse below and Reilly's still farther down, where the shooting had started. Then he turned his gaze in the direction of the outlaws' flight.

He saw a group of adobe houses at the foot of the hill. People down there were dashing around in an excited manner. It must be a settlement of Texas Mexicans, Ira thought. He'd have to go down there and claim the pair of bandits as prisoners. He realized it would be no easy job. No doubt those two had friends and allies in the hamlet below. Nevertheless they had to be taken. Their bullets had killed one Texas Ranger and wounded another. Ira reloaded his Winchester. He was about to direct his pony downhill when he heard hoofbeats on the other slope.

He turned to see three men riding full speed up the side of the hill. When they drew nearer Ira recognized them as his comrades who had bogged down in the creek, except for Ranger Giffin, out of commission with the fractured collarbone.

Ira saw the Rangers dismount for a moment where Ben Reilly had been tumbled by the barrage of outlaw gunfire as they rendered Reilly some temporary aid before resuming the chase. They made another short stop where Frank Sieker lay dead. Hats were lifted from heads. A Ranger bent over the slain man and covered the boyish face with a red bandanna handkerchief.

Ira cupped his hands to his lips. "Hello!" he called. "This is Aten."

Corporal Lindsey yelled back. "Ira, are you hurt? Where are you?"

Ira shouted an answer. "No, not hurt. I'm here on top of the hill."

A few minutes later the three Rangers had ascended the summit. "Where are those son-of-a-bitching killers?" Lindsey thundered.

Ira pointed toward the hamlet. "Down there, Corporal."

Lindsey spoke to his men. "By God, come on—let's go get 'em."

The four Rangers rode recklessly down the steep irregular decline. When they reached bottom, Lindsey ordered a slowdown. Guns cocked and ready for action, the men rode cautiously into the settlement.

The whole population was milling around as the Rangers halted at a little plaza in the center of the village. Armed men had called their wives and children from the shacks to greet the Americanos with hot words and cold stares. A wrinkled old man, who must have been ninety, was sharpening a rusty bowie knife on a chipped whetstone grasped in his palm.

Ira said, "Looks like we're going to fight the second battle of San Jacinto."

"Not with all these women and kids around," Lindsey replied. "But we are going to take those damned gun slingers back to Laredo."

The corporal ordered his men to ignore the abuse and stay in their saddles. A strapping, portly man waddled from the crowd and approached the Rangers. He was a mestizo but demanded in snarling English, "This is the Loyas Ranch. Who are you, riding here with guns to threaten our people?"

Corporal Lindsey said coldly, "We're threatening nobody, mister. We're Texas Rangers come to arrest a couple of murdering horse thieves your people are harboring."

The big man scowled. "There are two vaqueros here who were attacked and shot by *Americanos* on San Ambrosio Creek. I am Prudencio Herrera, deputy sheriff of this district for Don Dario Gonzales, sheriff of Webb County. I have no reason to believe that these men are murderers or horse thieves."

Ira wanted to jump from his pony and collar this pompous charlatan. A deputy who protected gun slingers against Rangers! But he restrained himself as Corporal Lindsey went on talking.

"We do know these men to be what they are, Deputy Herrera—by their descriptions, by their killing one of my command and wounding another. We are not leaving here without them."

Herrera countered with mocking courtesy, "Have you warrants for the vaqueros, Mr. Ranger?"

Lindsey refused to be bluffed. "No warrants are needed when crimes are committed in the presence of officers." He jerked his head toward Ira. "Ranger Aten here witnessed what they did."

Ira nodded curtly to Herrera. The fat deputy reached a reluctant decision. "Very well, gentlemen, I will arrest them and help you escort them to the courthouse at Laredo."

Lindsey flushed. Plainly he didn't like this alternative. He and Herrera glared at each other in what Ira interpreted as the perfect standoff.

Herrera was bound as a county lawman to respect, however grudgingly, the authority of state police. Lindsey was forbidden by Ranger rules from superseding local officers in making arrests except under special and very carefully defined circumstances.

"Very well," the corporal said resignedly. "We agree. But we will hold you strictly responsible for the delivery of the prisoners at Laredo."

Herrera's words dripped venom: "And you Rangers will be held responsible for the lives of the prisoners. Else these people would never let me take them from this rancho."

Herrera turned and addressed the crowd in rapid Spanish. Sullenly the *Mejicanos* withdrew to their adobe shanties, all except the ancient villager, still whetting his bowie knife. The Rangers dismounted to work out practical procedures with Deputy Herrera. Ira learned afterward that he had fought in Santa Anna's army against Sam Houston's.

Corporal Lindsey finally accepted the arrangements proposed by the deputy. Endless quibbling might mean the death of badly wounded Ben Reilly back on the hill and more suffering for injured Ranger Giffin at the creek.

"After much parleying," Ira wrote later, "it was agreed that the so-called deputy sheriff of law and order, would take the two wounded prisoners in a buggy to Laredo. We were to follow as guards and turn them over to the sheriff of Webb County."

Herrera dispatched two men in a mule-drawn wagon to pick up the Ranger casualties after giving Corporal Lindsey his word that the rescuers would not harm the pair still living. Sieker's corpse and the two injured Rangers were transported to the Votaw ranch, fifteen miles away. Votaw then sent a cowboy on a fast horse to fetch the nearest doctor, who lived fifty miles away. Eventually, Giffin was carried for additional medical care to Eagle Pass, eighty miles up the river from the Loyas settlement and Frank Sieker's body was left with an undertaker there. Giffin recovered without too much difficulty, but for a long time Ben Reilly hovered between life and death at the Votaw ranch before he finally recovered.

Votaw's cowboys rounded up the strayed pack mules. The animals were then transferred, through the Western relay system, from one Anglo rancher to another till they wound up at Camp King, the Ranger headquarters.

On the morning after the battle of San Ambrosio a strange procession started down the Rio Grande toward Laredo. In the big rubber-tired buggy sat the deputy with the two prisoners, free of shackles because Herrera had forbidden his fellow lawmen to use them. Two on each side of the vehicle, the state officers rode, making only necessary talk with Herrera at the reins. Ordinarily a pair of Rangers would have been assigned to ride in front of the buggy, a couple more to serve as guards at its rear.

This time, mutual fear prompted mutual wariness. The Rangers felt that they would be risking shots in the back if they assumed their customary formation. Deputy Herrera probably suspected that the prisoners might be slaughtered for revenge unless he kept vigilant watch over them, for Rangers were supposed to be sheer hell on those who killed their comrades.

Late on the second day the odd cavalcade reached Laredo. It was the first time that any members of this patrol had ever seen the lusty border town where probably not more than one quarter of the population spoke any English. Ira felt an eerie uneasiness as they entered the city limits, strewn with junk and goat droppings—a something far transcending the sense of being "lost" that he'd experienced on that baffling day in San Antonio. He looked at the faces of the other Rangers to see the same dubious misgivings.

By all absolutes, the Spaniards never conquered the Mexicans. Sometimes Texans realize that they never did either.

Deputy Herrera escorted Rangers and prisoners to the office of Sheriff Dario Gonzales in the courthouse. The sheriff received his Anglo visitors with frigid handshakes and purposely scant English. But he greeted the prisoners as old friends and was deeply solicitous when he saw that their arms were in slings.

"Amador, Victorio," he said anxiously in Spanish, "what has happened? Who has harmed you, *mis compañeros?*"

The prisoner called Amador pointed an accusing finger at the Rangers. "*Los Americanos,* Don Dario. They shot Victorio and me when we were but riding the range for Señor Loyas."

Victorio took the cue and chimed in. "*Es verdad*—it's true—Don Dario. They chased us to our homes and would have killed us but for *el valiente deputado Herrera*—the brave deputy Herrera."

Herrera beamed in acknowledgment of the compliment. Corporal Lindsey, who understood Spanish but spoke it lamely, interrupted in English.

"Sheriff, these fellows are goddamned liars. They killed one of our men and badly wounded another when we spotted them heading toward the border to join the rest of Mario Sanchez's gang. Ranger Aten here is our witness."

Ira spoke. "Corporal Lindsey is correct, sir. I saw them kill Ranger Frank Sieker and wound Ranger Ben Reilly. We know, from their descriptions on wanted circulars, that they're members of the Sanchez horse-stealing ring. In fact, they were making off with two broncs when we caught them."

Don Dario banged on his desk and his English came easy. "Silence, gentlemen! I am conducting this investigation." He switched back to Spanish when he asked the prisoners: "Victorio—Amador—are you employed by the bandit, Mario Sanchez?"

Victorio coughed. "No, Señor Sheriff. You know that we are vaqueros for Señor Loyas. He ordered us to deliver those horses to a buyer in Mexico, and—"

Corporal Lindsey tried to be heard. "The horses were—"

Don Dario pounded again. "Señor Lindsey, I have heard enough about the horses." He resumed his questioning of the prisoners. "Now, hombres, tell me truthfully, did you slay the Ranger called Sieker and the one named Reilly as these men charge?"

Both vaqueros looked sad. "That, señor, we do not know," Amador answered quaveringly. "We shot to protect ourselves—then ran."

Don Dario rose abruptly from the desk. "Señores Rangers," he barked, "I find that these poor cowpunchers acted only in self-defense after you started a fight with them. By the authority vested in me as sheriff, I am releasing them from custody."

"Releasing them!" Lindsey echoed. "Why, damn it—!"

"Yes, releasing them," the sheriff replied coldly. "And let me warn your force not to come again to our county and shoot our citizens."

Corporal Lindsey raised his hand disgustedly as a signal to leave. The Rangers filed out into the courthouse lobby. They had gone some twenty paces when they were suddenly encircled by a cordon of Mexican deputies who had followed them from Don Dario's office.

"Gentlemen," rasped Deputy Herrera, "you are under arrest for assault with intent to murder Amador Rodriguez and Victorio Nuñez."

The Rangers stared in disbelief at the group, then tempers exploded.

"Under arrest!" Ira yelled. "We're officers of the state of Texas!"

Ranger O. D. Baker challenged Herrera. "I'm damn tired of being pushed by you, Potbelly. Let's have it out."

"Let's all have it out," insisted Ranger Grant, the fourth member of the outfit. "Let's shoot it out."

Corporal Lindsey vetoed any battling in a courthouse. "Keep your guns in your belts, boys," he ordered. "All right, Herrera, you say we are under arrest. Then release us on our personal parole till we can hear from state authorities in Austin."

Herrera refused. The Rangers were stripped of their weapons, as if they had been so many rustlers caught in the chaparral. Then they were marched to the Webb County jail and locked up on the bogus charges.

They stayed there for twenty-seven days. For the first time in history Rangers had been imprisoned by local officials for doing their duty. There was to be further humiliation before freedom. After the Rangers had made continued demands, Old Dario condescended to visit them in jail. Then, after much argument, he agreed to walk them around town to see if they could find somebody who would post the heavy bail his hand-picked judge demanded.

As the Rangers trudged along with him, they kept looking for a store with an English sign that might lead to somebody who would give them a needed hand. Block after block shops were labeled *bodega* or *cantina*, never a one that read "grocery store" or "saloon." Footsore and low in spirit, they finally noticed a sign: GRANT'S FEED STORE.

The Rangers entered the store with the sheriff, identified themselves, told their troubles, then asked this *Americano* businessman to post their bail. "Sure, I'll go your bond," he answered unhesitatingly.

The Rangers were so overcome that only Ira could speak: "Mr. Grant, finding your store was like locating a spring in a desert."

Merchant Grant, no relation to Ranger Grant, checked out Old Dario and invited the Rangers, famished from jail fare, to stay for a meal. "Turn these men loose now, Sheriff," he said. "I'll be over at your office in an hour to sign the bond."

The sheriff left, not wishing to quarrel with a leading tax-payer and voter. Ira always believed that the Rangers started things moving toward an eventual cleanup of the town by braving the old rogue.

A day after their release the Texas attorney general arrived in Laredo, having been sent by Governor Ireland. Dario's judge dismissed the charges against them when the state intervened. Before the Rangers left, Ranger O. D. Baker fired a parting shot in print at the border dictator.

Said Baker, later a state legislator, to a reporter for the San Antonio *Express*: "Old Dario Gonzales is the chief villain of the Forty Thieves who compose the county government of Webb."

His statement was widely reprinted in newspapers throughout South Texas, where enlightened citizens of both races were forming vigorous new political organiza-tions to oust the feudal county regimes of the border. Don Dario's popularity began waning as Texans such as Baker, kept warring on him in the press. Early in 1886 he was oust-ed as sheriff on charges of malfeasance brought before a Texas district judge. A few months later many of his "Forty Thieves" were slain in a bloody street battle which his faction provoked with the opposing party, led by City Marshal Stephen Boyard.

Old Dario finally died in disgrace. The two thieves Ira had shot escaped into Mexico shortly after their release by the sheriff, but one of them, Amador Rodriguez, died of blood poisoning from the bullet in his shoulder. Ira shed no tears when he learned about it.

He would have preferred to avenge Frank Sieker in a fair fight. But nature had inflicted the penalty for him; and one more outlaw was wiped off the "wanted" roster of the Texas Rangers.

"Many rustlers lost a whole winter's work and whined mightily."

PISTOL SIGHTS & MAVERICK BRANDS

Ira never regretted placing obligation above opportunity. His reward was completely unexpected. But it came because a smoldering old feud required a corps member to accept appointment as a local officer.

The year was 1884, when social convulsions throughout America were having their peculiar reverberations on the farms and pastures of Texas. Ranger intelligence sources in Austin received word that brooding grudges between rival German and Anglo-Saxon cowmen threatened a renewal of the savage Mason County cattle war. Rope and trigger had been the fierce weapons of both factions when racial and political tensions had erupted into bloodshed during the mid-seventies. The Germans had been led by the sheriff, who had finally been run out of the county. A main executioner for their opponents had been the notorious Johnny Ringo, who was later bushwhacked by Buckskin Frank Leslie in Tombstone.

Corpses had dangled from pecan trees. Men were called to their doors at night and gunned to death before their families. Ranchers and cowboys were butchered on rocky roads, then dumped like the carcasses of wild goats into mountain gulches and creek bottoms. These were the memories of Ranger veterans who had gone to Mason County and, risking the rifle barrels of both sides, had stopped the slaughter.

It would take a man with Ranger prestige to prevent a violent flare-up of the conflict that had been considered ended when the county courthouse was mysteriously burned and all indictments were destroyed with it. At the request of the current sheriff, Adjutant General King had released Ranger P. C. Baird to become Mason County chief deputy. Meantime, Company D had undergone a shift in its commanding personnel.

Captain Sieker had been promoted to quartermaster of the entire Ranger organization and had left the tents of the Frontier Battalion for a desk in Austin. Frank Jones, the sergeant, had succeeded Sieker as head of Company D, and Corporal Lindsey had assumed Jones' former post. For a brief time, Ranger Baird had taken Lindsey's place as the third officer of the corps. After Baird had left, Captain Jones called a mounted muster to announce his successor:

"Ranger Ira Aten—promoted from private to corporal."

Ira nearly tumbled from his saddle. Most of the men in the company had months or years of seniority over him. But now he had the answer to that nagging question he'd never asked: What was his rating at Austin?

With rank came fresh and more satisfying activities as an officer. The border had been relatively quiet for some years after an immortal Ranger commander, L. H. McNelly, had rounded up five thousand desperadoes and fugitives in an all-out campaign never surpassed by any other Western officer. But the Mason County war had been a blazing prelude to still other troubles of its kind. Violence had become the entrenched and accepted pattern of the range with the constant expansion of the cattle industry in Texas. Only Rangers could handle the deepening crisis in newly organized counties whose sheriffs were often simply cowhands wearing stars, with no background of law enforcement experience.

Soon after Ira's promotion a range feud threatened to erupt in a spot that happened to be the exact geographic center of the state. McCulloch County's fertile pastures stretched in a broad sweep from the slopes of the rugged Brady Mountains to deep, loamy valleys lying between the Colorado and San Saba rivers. Everybody in the county was busy with the roundup of cattle from the open range. Disputes were raging over the ownership of maverick calves and stock bearing brands unregistered at the county courthouse in Brady City. So far, no one had been killed, but tempers were growing hotter than the irons in the branding pens.

McCulloch County was right next door to Mason County—scarcely an omen of peace. From Austin came urgent instructions to Captain Jones. He was to rush his command to the trouble section and stay there till threatening hatchets were buried.

Captain Jones decided not to take the slow, overland horseback route across peaks and canyons to McCulloch County. Although it would mean a wide detour, the Rangers might avert bloodshed by boarding a fast train for the initial lap. McCulloch County lay almost due north of Ranger headquarters in Uvalde County. But from Uvalde town the outfit traveled east to San Antonio, then northwest, hundreds of miles, to Fort Worth and to Cisco, the nearest railroad point to Brady City. A railroad company provided a special unit of passenger cars and stock coaches. Ira, as company corporal, supervised the loading of ponies, pack mules, camp equipment, and an ample arsenal.

Railroads valued the good will of Texas Rangers for catching train robbers and always sped companies along. So the "Jones special," as Ira called it, was given the right of way above all other traffic on the long trip. At Cisco the lawmen mounted their horses for the second, less comfortable lap. Pack mules loaded with food and bedding, a supply wagon clattering in front, the outfit headed for McCulloch County, well over a hundred miles to the southwest in the fast-developing Central Texas rangeland.

A forced march brought the Rangers to the county's northern boundary, on the Colorado River, in the late afternoon of the second day. Captain Jones had meant to call a rest after the crossing, but the horses' hoofs had barely touched dry ground before another rider, probably a county deputy, came racing down a dirt road toward them.

"Hey, fellows!" he shouted. "There's a ruckus stirring at a big roundup two miles from here. If you want to get in on it, you'd better hurry."

"Lead us to it," Captain Jones responded.

The local man wheeled his mount. The tired Rangers spurred their weary horses to follow. Captain Jones rode at the head of the company. Close behind were his two subordinates—Sergeant Lindsey and Corporal Ira Aten. In twenty minutes or so the company reached the place that was serving as a central site for the roundup. Cattle of many brands and no brands were milling around a water hole, having been driven in from their grazing ranges by different groups of cowboys. Scared calves, snatched from their mothers, were bawling in branding pens and temporary corrals. Hobbled horses were cropping at grass. Two groups of about twenty men each were lined up on opposite sides, arguing vehemently and apparently on the point of shooting it out.

"Them's my calves you goddam rustlers put your maverick brand on," Ira heard a rancher in one contingent bark to somebody in the other.

"Shut your son-of-a-bitchin' mouth," came a snarling answer. "You range hogs claim every independent brand in this county is a maverick one!"

"None of your damn brands are registered in the courthouse," a second rancher yelled at the crowd called rustlers. "So that makes 'em maverick brands. You git 'em off this range or we'll blast you outta your saddles."

A tall man, who wore ragged chaps and sat a beat-up saddle, rode out from the circle of mavericks. "Just say that again, mister," he growled.

The rancher made no reply, but his eyes strayed toward the pistol butt protruding from his belt. The shabby man glanced back toward his supporters. The approaching Rangers halted, still unnoticed by the two bristling groups.

"One more move on either side," Ira said to Captain Jones, "and there'll be a massacre."

"The next move will be made by us," Captain Jones replied. He spurred forward quickly and came to a stop right in the middle of the angry factions.

"All right, gentlemen," he called out. "If there's any shooting to be done, we'll do it."

Both groups stared at him in wrathful surprise. "Who in hell are you?" demanded the character in the shabby chaps. "Some God-damn gun slinger from Mason County?"

The captain looked at him coolly. "I'm Frank Jones, commander of the Texas Rangers." He jerked a thumb toward his outfit. "And over there—my men of Company D."

Both groups turned in saddle to gaze in stony hostility toward the Rangers. "Who asked you all to butt in here?" a ranchman snapped. "We don't need no help to take care of these damned brand burners."

"Nobody asked us, sir," Captain Jones answered dryly. "But seeing that we're here, let's everybody cool off and stop the war talk."

Ira and the other Company D men dismounted after the two opposing groups got out of their saddles to confer with Captain Jones. Then the Rangers divided to mingle with both of the enemy camps as a precaution against any spontaneous gunplay's developing at some point in the parley.

Frank Jones watched faces while trying to mediate a truce. Ira kept his eyes lowered to watch gun hands. By warning gestures he kept itching fingers from straying toward triggers. If any hand edged an inch too far, he was ready to confiscate the pistol it was seeking.

After much palaver both sides accepted a peace proposal made by Jones. The roundup would continue under a no-shooting agreement. But all cattle with the unregistered marks called maverick brands and the altered ones known as burned brands were to be turned over to the Rangers for final disposal.

Ira had never been a working cowhand like so many men of the force, but now he found himself wrangling steers under a Ranger's commission. During the next four weeks he learned firsthand about the skulduggery, the thievery, the daily criminality that played such a prominent part in the development of the cattle industry in the West.

For convenience and to end the dispute-provoking roundup as quickly as possible, Captain Jones divided McCulloch

County into three districts and his company into three corresponding squads. By confirmation of the county sheriff,
each squad was to have almost unlimited authority in its
assigned section. It could arrest any man whose conduct
promised trouble and bring him into Brady City where he
would be put under bond to keep the peace. Rangers might
ride into any roundup center to inspect cattle, and their
judgment was to be final about any stock carrying disputed
brands. Should the citizen fail to respect Ranger authority,
Captain Jones would ask the governor to impose martial law
on the county.

Captain Jones took command of the squad covering the
largest and most explosive span of range. Sergeant Lindsey
headed a second detail whose assigned territory bordered
Mason County. Corporal Aten was in charge of a unit covering a zone that included the tough little cowtown and
county seat, Brady City.

The hard, thankless labor kept Ira busy, with scarcely
a break, from sunrise to sunset. Till he had to cope with
this disguised sort of rustling he'd had a Texan's common
knowledge of cattle brands. Now the duties of an officer
forced him to become an expert on the West's most controversial subject.

As he stopped wordy brawls in roundup camps, he had
to be able to tell infallibly whether a brand had really been
changed by somebody claiming cattle or whether the ac-
cuser was trying to increase his own herd by making the
charge. Let a Ranger make one mistake, and cries of partial-
ity would rock the county.

By examining contested markings, Ira learned how an
original brand could be changed by superimposing upon it
another brand that would resemble or encompass the first.
Those who specialized in this sort of trickery were contemptuously called "brand artists" by honest, law-abiding
cow folk.

As he kept patrolling his district, Ira also discovered another common trick of brand burners. Where a given brand

could not be changed easily, the thieves would turn it into an unreadable blotch by superseding it with a radically different marking—a practice called "brand blotting." Since possession was nine points of the law, the rightful owner of the animal would have an even harder time proving ownership than in a case of ordinary brand changing.

Ira generally tried to resolve such controversies by applying his general impression of the claimant and whatever knowledge he'd picked up about him. Very often, the conscientious corporal realized, "the man who hollered the loudest was the one who packed the running iron."

But there was a sure way of establishing ownership when Ira couldn't decide—although it meant driving the animal into a corral. "Slaughter it," he would say, pointing to the creature destined to be beef in any case. Almost always it was possible to make out the imprint of the original brand on the flesh side of the fresh hide.

Ira's own deeply ingrained honesty made him hate all brand burners—even though he knew that dubious practices had furnished the start of more than one highly respected cattle business. He would have enjoyed slapping every such McCulloch County offender in jail, but Captain Jones had ordered the Rangers to make no arrest except for breaches of the peace.

Ira felt even more disgust for the maverickers than he did for the out-and-out brand artists. Runners of maverick brands were not only odious hypocrites in his mind, but also clever tax dodgers unwilling to pay their just share of the expenses of keeping up roads and schoolhouses. To Ira, holding property without paying taxes was as reprehensible as siring children without marriage. His contempt for the maverickers soared when he saw who they were and how they accumulated their scanty herds.

They were men who had entered the cattle business with no capital except a bronc and a branding iron. Shirttail operators, they were, generally owning not one acre of land but grazing their stock on everybody's acreage under the custom of the open range. Driven out of one section, they moved into another, laying their irons across the hides of calves trailing cows bearing registered, tax-paying brands. Trouble spewed at roundups when "reps," or inspectors, from the established ranches noted this discrepancy and laid claim to the calves. Who got the young beeves depended on who put up the biggest bluff or carried the fastest guns.

Ira was soon familiar with all the prominent brands in McCulloch County. But being absolutely scrupulous, he went to the courthouse and asked the county clerk to give him a list of all the registered ones. These marks he and his detail memorized. Then the corporal came down hard on the maverickers.

He declared that an unregistered brand on any animal was prima-facie evidence of rustling. A mavericker could keep the stock only by going to the courthouse, recording the brand, and settling the taxes. Otherwise, Ira had his detail drive the longhorns to the bulging county pound in Brady City.

The same thing happened to cattle transferred under bills of sale which identified the stock by maverick brands. Ira laid a burden of proof on the purchaser, suspecting that these "sales" were often convenient transactions between maverickers to prevent the Rangers from seizing the stock. If the buyer couldn't prove that he was not a receiver of stolen property or didn't behave forthrightly, Ira would tell his detail:

"Look after the cattle, boys. If we're mistaken, this gentleman can take us into court and get 'em back."

Rangers were meeting a harsh situation in the rough-and-ready manner of the frontier. Only eight years had elapsed since McCulloch had been an unorganized county without elected officials, having been attached to an adjoining county for governmental purposes. The Texas cattle boom had increased its population from two hundred to two thousand in a little more than ten years. Maverickers and brand burners had swarmed to its wide, unfenced grazing lands along with the more responsible ranchers. By being arbitrary, the outside lawmen helped strengthen the forces of social control that were being subjected to strain by the strong pressures of lawlessness.

None of the crooked-brand crowd ever preferred a court charge against Ira or any other man of Company D. There were boozy mutterings and threats of dry gulchings as the expropriated rustlers gloomily downed their drinks in the Brady City saloons. But boasts never sprouted the guts of action. As Ira said afterward:

"It was safer to fight John Barleycorn than the Texas Rangers."

For four weeks—a busy, grueling month—the outfit scouted the roundup. By the end of that time the Rangers had driven six hundred head of cattle with suspicious brands to the corrals of the county pound. Then, as a final move, Captain Jones ordered the arrest of half a dozen better-known thieves. One of these was the arrogant fellow who wore the beat-up chaps.

The rustlers were indicted and turned loose on bond pending trial. Rightful owners of cattle came to the pound and were given back their stock by presenting acceptable proof. Maverickers blustered and threatened legal action when the Rangers refused to surrender stock. "But," Ira wryly commented in his memoirs, "our side of the argument generally prevailed particularly as it would be backed up by about twenty armed men."

All the remaining cattle were sold at auction by the county sheriff following advertisements, required by law, in the local newspaper. For several weeks after the roundup the Rangers remained, knowing that their testimony would be needed at the trials of the brand jugglers.

One day Ira decided to treat himself to the rare luxury of a barbershop shave. It happened that one burly citizen doubled as town barber and town blacksmith. Whiskers long, anticipating a session of hot towels and cooling lotions, Ira walked into the dirt-floored shop housing both chair and anvil.

The "barber" was beating a red-hot chunk of metal into shape on his forge. "Yes, sir, Ranger," he said, "just sit down and I'll give you the best shave a man ever had."

Fifteen minutes later Ira staggered from the barber chair feeling something like a plucked chicken. The barber-black Smith had borne down on his face with plenty of muscle and a minimum of lather. Whiskers had been scraped out by the roots. Ira had asked that the customary neck shave be omitted, not wanting to go down in history as the Texas Ranger who was beheaded by a blacksmith. After that, he shaved himself.

With the other Rangers, Ira waited impatiently for the trial of the accused rustlers. To their disgust, courts and juries let all the defendants go scot free. In those days, it was next to impossible to get convictions for cattle stealing. Local opinion generally preferred the six-shooter method of handling brand burners and wide-loopers. Sometimes it was the only effective way, since jurors often feared retaliation for bringing in verdicts of guilty.

Yet the work of the company had been outstandingly successful. Some of the boldest rustlers had fled the area to escape prosecution. Ira knew that Rangers would eventually be meeting them elsewhere. Most of them would, finally, get their just desserts, he was sure.

Best of all, the slim treasury of McCulloch County had been enriched by several thousand dollars realized from the sale of the confiscated cattle. "Through this action," Ira wrote proudly, "many rustlers lost a whole winter's work and whined mightily."

A day before the Rangers left, Ira passed the combined barber-blacksmith shop. His hand started trembling as he ran it reflectively across his face.

"What's the matter, Ira," inquired Sergeant Lindsey, who was walking with him, "you sick?"

"No," the corporal declared solemnly; "but see that place? I think only two kinds of men go to hell. One is a lawyer who tells cold lies. The other is a blacksmith who hammers cold iron."

Ira's fingers patted his jaw. "I think this blacksmith is in that class."

*"I'd just as soon dig gold out
of the mountains as try collecting it from those fellows."*

MAKING HELL PAY TAXES

A Ranger's dwelling was his tent at headquarters. His home was the house of his best girl.

Almost any bachelor wearing the badge rated as a top matrimonial catch. Leading Texas families encouraged Rangers to court their daughters and often gave big tracts of land as dowries. Wherever companies were based, local girls set caps for the men whose dependable courage personalized the romantic Ranger legend. Uvalde County's main appeal for the members of Company D was its marriageable young women showering them with attention and platters of fried chicken.

Many a Uvalde girl was wearing a Ranger ring. Captain Jones himself was one of those receiving mail with the Uvalde postmark during the McCulloch County stint. After the trials of the rustlers, the men had expected an immediate return to Camp King and their sweethearts. But the unpredictable luck of Rangers willed otherwise; a gang of stagecoach robbers crimped romance.

Company D was ordered to Pegleg Crossing of the San Saba River. There road agents had held up the stage nine times in nine months. Ira had no particular heart interest. But, wishing to relax after the range feud, he shared his comrades' disappointment.

He rode with the grumbling men to the barren Crossing and saw that it offered no natural protections against bad weather. Stunted bushes were its only natural growths. Nobody lived near the San Saba's chalky banks except a few ragged squatters having few words and less friendliness for lawmen.

The company pitched camp on a windy plain overlooking the Crossing. Ira, with two other Rangers, dug a latrine, then took the wagon and loaded it with river driftwood to build fires. A straggling cowtown called Menardville lay ten miles away. Once a week someone rode there to pick up the mail, which generally consisted of official communications from Austin and the usual batch of pink envelopes from Uvalde.

As a blistering summer faded into a chilling early fall, the impatient outfit kept searching for the highwaymen. Twice daily the stagecoach forded the Crossing. Ira took his turns crouching in the damp bushes to spot any strange riders who might show up to meet it. His hands and his boots were caked with mud after these vigils. Disgusted, he cussed at the gang for not appearing so that accounts could be squared.

At other times he would be ordered to head a detail looking for the robbers. Eyes alert, he would halt his squad whenever he saw fresh hoof tracks or batches of empty cartridge shells littering up trails.

But the hoofprints always led to some ranch house, where a hot meal would be offered the baffled Rangers. Cartridges often proved, after investigation, to have been exploded by some settler hunting antelope. Other clues, such as stray dungaree buttons or rusty, dropped coins, proved equally fruitless. There were times when Ira felt that even the packs of mangy coyotes were laughing at the frustrated Rangers.

"Captain Jones," he finally said to his commander, "we're just wasting our time hanging around here. Nobody's going to hist a coach right under the noses of Texas Rangers."

The captain nodded agreement. "I think you're right, Corporal. Either the bunch has got more careful after sticking it up nine straight times in the same place, or more likely they've been tipped off—maybe by one of the squatters— that we're waiting for them."

Captain Jones shifted camp, the Rangers moving their tent to another plain nearer Menardville. He hoped this would tempt the road agents to pull a tenth holdup at the Crossing. It would give the gang a temporary advantage of flight, but he could then trail them to their rendezvous, he figured.

The stage went on unhindered at the Crossing, however. Morning and afternoon the coach rolled into Menardville on time. Balked, the Rangers kept up their constant prowl, bringing in a few long-wanted minor outlaws but not the gang they had been assigned to get.

Then there came along a cycle of those sudden tempests of howling winds that Texans call "blue northers." Winter struck D Company completely unprepared, since only summer supplies had been carried on the trip from Uvalde to Brady City. Cakes of ice were embedded in the skillets when men awoke mornings after bleak, freezing nights. Overcoats and extra blankets were all in the commissary at Camp King two hundred miles away. Nor could Captain Jones buy needed cold-weather supplies in Menardville till Austin honored a requisition he had sent in—and that would mean more dismal weeks under the slow procedures of the quartermaster's division.

Heavy snows fell to smother campfires. Sleet stung the faces of the patrol groups that futilely combed every mile of this dreary land to find the road agents. Many of the men were sneezing and coughing with grippe. Captain Jones believed that the freebooters had long since left the section. He requested Austin to let him take his sick, discontented command back to its headquarters in the warm Texas border country.

Austin's answer was no. Perhaps, as the men believed, some Texas politician owned stock in the stage line. But another order from the adjutant general called for two Rangers to be detached for tax-collecting service in the newly created border county of Val Verde.

Every man in the outfit hoped to be one of the two. Tax collecting was risky work in certain remote counties where hordes of squatters felt no obligation to help pay salaries of despised sheriffs and judges. In Val Verde they grabbed shotguns and ran out every tax man venturing up from Del Rio, the county seat. "But," as Ranger Ben Reilly said gloomily, "I'd damned sure rather be shot to death than freeze to death."

Ira was surprised when he was chosen as one of the pair to help Val Verde County's harassed tax collector. He had no girl to visit in Uvalde before a return to the camp that the Rangers had named "Fort Iceberg." Possibly, as he thought later, that was why the captain had selected him. His mind would be on collections instead of courting.

The next day Ira set out with a fellow Ranger. Rations for thirty days had been stacked aboard a pack mule. The two men rode southwest a hundred miles to Beaver Lake, between two streams with sinister associations—Pecos River and Devil's River.

The tax collector was a nervous little man whose authority was respected by nobody outside of the county seat. His face was twitching, his hands shaking when he greeted the Rangers.

"Boys," he sighed, "I hope you brought along plenty of hardware. Them people where we're goin' are so fierce they use wildcats for house pets and owls for chickens."

Ira laughed. "How much do they owe the county in all?"

The tax man patted his saddlebag. "I got it all put down on some lists here. Around fifteen thousand dollars, it stands. The county treasurer'll be happy if I come back with a third of it."

Ira checked his guns and ordered the other Ranger to do the same. "I won't guarantee how much we'll bring back, but it'll be worth your trip. Let's go."

The collector climbed into a buckboard drawn by two mules; one Ranger rode in front of the wagon and another behind. The first stop was at an adobe shack standing in the middle of a sloping range where a herd of fat cattle grazed. There wasn't a human in sight. The tax collector put his hands to his mouth and called:

"Hello! Hello! Bart Shelby, I got business with you."

A door opened grudgingly and by fractions of inches. A Winchester barrel edged through the door, accompanied by a yell: "Who is it? What's your business?"

The tax collector started to tremble. "Shelby'll blast my brains out when he knows what I'm here for. Maybe one of you boys oughtta tell him my business."

Ira drew his forty-five and pointed it toward the door. His comrade followed suit. "Mr. Shelby," Ira shouted, "drop that gun and come out. We're Texas Rangers."

The rifle started bobbing up and down in the doorway. "Texas Rangers!" its owner exclaimed. "I ain't killed nobody and I ain't runnin' no hot iron."

Ira rode closer to the door. "Mr. Shelby," he called again, "we've got no warrants for you. But if you don't drop that Winchester and come on out, I'm driving off all your steers."

The gun eased downward to the floor. A tall man with a big paunch stepped to the porch, stared at the Ranger, and caught sight of the tax collector seated in the buckboard.

"So it's you, you sawed-off son of a bitch!" he roared. "Not man enough to face me by yourself so you up and bring the Rangers!"

Ira jumped from his saddle and strode to the porch. "The tax collector is not required to face you, Shelby. But you are required to pay your just obligations to the state and Val Verde County. Since you won't come to the courthouse and pay them like a gentleman, we're here to collect."

Shelby began haranguing and protesting. Suspecting that this might be a calculated stall, Ira glanced around and saw another gun barrel protruding from the loft of a barn.

He raised his revolver and fired. An answering shot sailed over his head and landed in a live oak tree. A second bullet from the Ranger's weapon caused the rifle to drop to the barnyard. Shelby jerked a small pistol from a hip pocket but the second Ranger reached out to wrest it from his hand with a deft flip. From inside the barn came the terrified, high-pitched voice of an adolescent boy: "Pa! I lost my shootin' iron! Them gun slingers'll kill us all."

Ira took the pistol from his partner's hand, unloaded it, pocketed its cartridges, then handed the weapon back to the furious squatter.

"We're not gun slingers, Shelby," he said. "If your boy is ever hurt, it will be your fault for making a bushwhacker out of him. Now, how about your taxes? Or do we have to take your cattle in payment?"

Shelby grudgingly pulled out a bulging leather pocketbook. Ira beckoned to the tax collector. The official climbed out of the buckboard and came forward.

"How much does Mr. Shelby owe?" Ira asked.

The tax man took out his list. "Ninety-nine dollars and thirty-three cents, including penalty for not paying on time."

Shelby opened the pocketbook. It was filled with the heavy gold coins commonly used during that era. The squatter handed five ten-dollar pieces to the collector.

"Here's fifty," he growled. "I'll pay you the rest next time I'm in Del Rio."

The Rangers were prepared to back the collector if he had demanded the full amount. Ira was chagrined when he gratefully accepted an installment.

"Thank you, Mr. Shelby," the official said. "Sorry we had to ask for it this way."

Shelby looked at the tax man with a contempt Ira couldn't help but share. But the dignity of the state had to be maintained even if this elected official wouldn't uphold it. He spoke to the squatter.

"Better lose no time going to Del Rio and paying the rest, Mr. Shelby. 'Specially since you probably don't even have homestead title to this land that you're making a good living off of."

The squatter looked uneasy. Ira had been told by the tax collector that all these people were occupying school land, reserved by the state to support public education, or railroad land allotted to the Southern Pacific as a consideration for having recently extended its lines from San Antonio to the Pecos country.

The party collected four hundred dollars in taxes that first day of the "invasion." Six more involuntary contributors to government Ira bluffed or disarmed. All payments were made in gold, greenbacks being tabooed by the squatters since so many bogus bills were being slipped across the Rio Grande by Mexican counterfeit rings. Burlap bags carried in the wagon kept filling with the yellow money as days went by. None of these delinquents ever paid in full, and nobody agreed to pay at all until Ira threatened to come back with a company of Rangers and attach his stock.

It was hard country they rode through. Rattlesnakes and copperheads slithered across wisps of roads nurturing clumps of murderous Spanish dagger and prickly pear that the wagon mules breasted gingerly lest their bellies be ripped. Patches of cat's-claw and crown-of-thorns were as ominously fierce as their name. Bears and mountain lions were more common than the harmless armadillo.

Val Verde County's place names were on a par with all the rest. The county's main stream was called Devil's River for the hell that sizzled along its banks. Devil's Lake, superstition declared, was filled with swarms of poison fish. Vinegarone was a brawling, lead-paved border village named for the vinegar smelling, whip-tailed scorpion whose sting could nearly kill a man.

Danger and deadliness were everywhere. Gaping skulls of men were sometimes to be seen scattered among rotting skulls of sheep and cattle. Solitary wood bees—a species having no liking for its kind—buzzed in and out of tree-trunk holes clearly gouged by bullets.

And to this section, Ira realized, had migrated the humans with little love for their kind. These squatters were of a different breed than Menard County's outcasts, still clinging to the fringes of society for whatever chewed-over manna it might offer. These Val Verde men ruthlessly wrested what they wanted from a land ill-disposed to give.

A week after the journey began the party approached the ruins of Old Fort Hudson, a federal army outpost abandoned after the ending of Comanche warfare. Fat sheep, tended by a Mexican herder, grazed on what had once been the parade ground. Ira noticed another immense flock on the nearby range. The tax collector drove the wagon through a break in the crumbling stockade.

"Quite a sheep spread here," Ira remarked. "And the rancher didn't even have to put up any buildings. Uncle Sam furnished them."

A rusty lizard made an investigative scramble around a wagon wheel as the party halted. "Yep," sighed the collector. "This feller Juan Ochoa ain't even a citizen, and this is still United States government property. But he's runnin' four thousand head of woollies here—and ain't never paid a nickel on 'em."

Ira saw more signs of prosperity: thoroughbred Percheron draft horses in rows of strong new corrals; a row of brightly painted Studebaker wagons, evidently used for transporting wool to the El Paso markets.

"Mr. Ochoa is going to pay this time," he said grimly. He called to the herder: "*Donde esta su jefe?*—where is your boss?"

The shepherd pointed toward a building that had once been army command headquarters. "*Alli*—there."

Ira directed that the boss be fetched. When the herdsman knocked on a door, five men came out. One was a burly mustached figure of about forty-five, wearing a livid, many-colored serape draped over an exquisitely tailored pink silk shirt. This was Don Juan Ochoa, the wool baron. Four were lean, high cheeked young Aztecs with two pistols each strapped around denim pants: Don Juan's guards, hired to do any shooting he might require.

The quartet spread out to flank their employer as they brushed sheep out of their way to stride toward the visitors. Perfect fighting formation, Ira thought. He signaled with his eye to the second Ranger. Both law men kept their hands on their gun butts.

Ten yards from the party the Mexicans halted. Don Juan removed his wide-brimmed straw sombrero, bowed, and said in English that echoed only a middling trace of Spanish: "Good morning, gentlemen. Will all of you get down and have some refreshment? Mutton and tequila."

Ira shook his head. "Thank you, señor, and excuse me for talking to you from a saddle. But we're Texas Rangers—not here for hospitality but to collect your taxes."

Don Juan frowned. Ira sensed the anger bubbling under the elegant courtesy. "Texas Rangers?" The guardsmen moved closer to their master, almost encircling him. "But I am a peaceful ranchero, not a border bandido."

The glint in Ira's eyes matched the edge on his tongue. "Señor Ochoa, we are not accusing you. But—your taxes, please."

Ochoa gracefully put his hat back on his head. "Taxes." He glanced toward the buckboard, where the silent collector sat, then past the man to the heap of burlap bags in the wagon bed.

A gleam of yellow showed through a sack that was frayed. "Taxes," Don Juan murmured. "Ah, yes, I recognize my friend, the tax man, and I believe that there is an unsettled matter between us." The ranchero moved closer. His guardsmen were staring boldly at the sacks as they kept pace with their master. The second Ranger reined his pony toward Ira's.

"No farther, Don Juan," Ira said tersely. "Now—your taxes. Twenty-one hundred dollars, by the records of the collector."

"But suppose I wish to protest these taxes, señor?" Ochoa's eyes flicked toward the four guards.

Ira knew what he meant and dropped the veneer. "Protest peacefully by suing peacefully in El Paso district court for their recovery or—" and he roared—"protest with your filthy gunmen and, by God, Texas Rangers will blow all your damned heads off."

He jerked on the pony's bridle. It reared high on its haunches. He plunged the horse toward the nearest guard and leaned from his saddle to jerk a sombrero from the man's head. All four of the gunmen scattered, their plan for gathering, deliberate battle spoiled by the Ranger's sudden move. Ira pulled the horse up short and threw the hat at the feet of Don Juan, who had stood his ground, his face writhing with hate.

"Don't hurrah the Rangers, señor," Ira said curtly. "And you'd better stop hurrahing the United States Government if you don't want the soldiers to come and chase you out. This is federal property—and you are an alien who's turned it into your private hacienda."

Ira jumped down from the saddle and held out his hand. "Now, for the last time, those taxes. Or do I have to send more Rangers with the soldiers to attach your blasted sheep?"

Don Juan Ochoa made another stately bow. "You have misunderstood me, Señor Ranger. I shall pay the taxes."

He clapped his hands loudly. A mousy little man, whom Ira judged to be a steward, appeared from somewhere. Don Juan Ochoa gave the flunky an order in Spanish. Ira dismounted and stood waiting.

A few minutes later the man came back, lugging a great pouch of gold coins. As Ira watched carefully, Don Juan counted out twenty-one hundred dollars. The tax collector wrote a receipt. Ira had some last words for the sheep lord: "Don't run your woollies on Texas soil without paying taxes unless you want them swimming back across the Rio Grande. Don't ever again threaten Texas Rangers with a slow draw and—" his eyes blazing—"don't commit suicide by following this wagonload of gold, or the empty sacks I've got will be all your damned shrouds."

Payments came more easily after the showdown at Fort Hudson. Messages flashed over the grapevine that this year the collector was accompanied by two Rangers who didn't have any more sense than to shoot it out. For the rest of the trip Ira and his fellow officer took turns guarding the wagon at night, fearing that Don Juan and his semi-bandidos might not be able to resist temptation.

But there was only one other incident of near gunplay during the campaign against the tax dodgers. At one ranch a man went into his house, following the usual arguments, and stayed there. After an hour the Rangers walked through the door with drawn revolvers to see what was detaining him. They found the rancher sitting in a rocking chair, a rifle across his knees, "ready and willing to give battle." But, as Ira described it, "with the help of his woman we finally persuaded him to give up his gold instead of his life."

The two Rangers spent almost a month extracting tax gold from those mountaineers on the Pecos and Devil's rivers. Between four and five thousand dollars had been accumulated for the treasury of Val Verde County by that time. The lawmen then escorted the collector to Pontoon Crossing on the Pecos. There he was met by a special Val Verde County posse, which conducted him safely to Del Rio.

Of all the delinquents, only Don Juan Ochoa had paid in full. But Ira hoped that Val Verde County's tax problem would be his no more as he returned with his partner to the frigid camp in Menard County.

The two were cold and shivering when they got there. To their grateful surprise the camp was being struck. Even Austin had tired of the farce that had victimized conscientious state troopers and decided that the stagecoach robbers had disbanded. Now the men were going back to Uvalde County, back to a warmer climate, back to their girls.

"You had it easy, Ira," a Ranger said as the hoof march began. "It'll take us weeks of sun to heal all our frostbites."

Ira laughed uncertainly. "Maybe so, boy. But I'd just as soon dig gold out of the mountains as try collecting it from those fellows."

"I began to think, maybe, I was too zealous in hunting down criminals."

"THE MEANEST THING I EVER DID"

Ira's dossier at Austin began filling with citations for difficult services performed. His outgoing personality and his instinctive sense of justice had made him one of the most popular men in the entire Frontier Battalion. His handling of the Devil's River tax situation had been an object lesson for other assessment dodgers up and down the border. In one county a harassed tax collector threatened to "send for Ira Aten" unless delinquents paid up. They paid.

Everywhere, on every mission, Ira demonstrated a capacity for cool judgment underscored by hard courage. His name was becoming a familiar one throughout the state. Now he was looking forward to being sent on one of the important roving assignments that were the hallmark of outstanding Rangers.

John Armstrong had gone to Florida and fetched back Wes Hardin, who ever since had been trying to win a pardon by teaching in the Texas prison school at Huntsville. Other Rangers were being sent on direct instructions from Governor Ireland to hunt down the most vicious desperadoes or do discreet jobs of detection.

High praise had come to Ira for his conduct at the fight on San Ambrosio Creek. As yet, however, his major tasks were still those involving teamwork. He made no complaint because by now obedience to orders was one of the constants governing his life. While he continued sharing the risks and responsibilities of concerted actions, he kept hoping for a chance to prove himself "on his lonesome."

One morning Captain Jones summoned Ira and ordered him to take three men for what was called "warrant patrol." Before setting out, the young corporal studied the sheaf of warrants that had been handed him.

All would have to be served in one of the state's worst outlaw belts—the interlocking chain of rugged canyons extending from a corresponding network of streams—the Sabinal, Frio, Nueces, Pecos, and Devil's rivers. This territory, remote from county seats and organized authority, was a convenient refuge for criminals from the eastern states as well as from east Texas. Many men were wanted on papers sent by state officers and Texas county sheriffs. One warrant interested Ira in particular, however.

It was for a man named James Epps, who had killed somebody in Tennessee thirty years before. Along with the warrant, sent from Nashville, came a description of the fugitive as he had appeared then and information that he was supposedly living near the Texas-Mexican border. Ira guessed that some traveling Tennessean had recognized Epps in one or another cowtown, then informed on him by letter to the officials of that state.

Ira had developed an abiding hate for killers since seeing Ranger Frank Sieker die at San Ambrosio Creek. More than any other type of bad man, he liked to bring in murderers and start them down the road of retribution. "We're going to find Brother Epps," he told his command as the patrol set out from Uvalde County. "Then we're giving him a trip he'll never come back from."

Four mounted men and one pack mule constituted the expedition. For three days the patrol journeyed over marked roads toward the outer reaches of Nueces Canyon, eighty miles west of Uvalde. Travel on these arteries presented problems with civilian sojourners, since horses drawing wagons stamped into the brush when they saw the pack mule with his outlandish burden of supplies topped by the inevitable Dutch oven. The mule, too, made scaring horses a perverse sort of sport. When he saw a team and a wagon, he would prick up his ears and pass on a dead run with the kitchen utensils he was carrying, "making a noise like the old-time charivari, only looking a great deal worse."

Ira was relieved when the party reached Nueces Canyon. From here on, passage would be largely by narrow mountain trails. Risky they were, but the sure hoofs of horses and mule could manage them without mishap. As the Rangers rode, Ira wondered where they would find James Epps. Thirty years was a long time for a killer to be at large. This man's debt to society was a big one, Ira thought—one Tennessee wanted to collect with accumulated interest that might be paid off only on a gallows.

For four or five days the Rangers scoured Nueces Canyon. They uncovered half-a-dozen fugitives named on the warrants and turned them over to a ranchman who'd had the unwelcome job of constable wished on him. The rancher swore in his cowboys as special deputies so that he would have a posse to take the prisoners to the county jail some fifty miles away.

While preparing for the trip, the local officer made some remark about being from Tennessee. Ira was immediately interested, but cautious, as he often was with part-time, non-professional law men.

"Tennessee?" He laughed. "Half of Texas came from there. Any more of you around here?"

The rancher-constable cinched the strings of a saddle and motioned a prisoner to get aboard. "Nope. Nobody but a feller named Jim Epps."

Ira kept a straight face. "Thought I knew all the settlers around here, but I don't remember meeting Mr. Epps."

The rancher shrugged his shoulders. "You'll never meet everybody in this spliced-up country, Ranger. Epps lives just about eight miles from here, but I don't see him more than once a month or so."

"Guess we ought to meet him," Ira replied. "Tell us how to find his place."

Suspecting nothing, the constable gave directions to the Epps ranch. The Ranger command took leave of him and the cowhand posse then rode down the first of a series of indicated trails.

"That Epps must be a nervy son of a bitch," a Ranger remarked when they were out of earshot. "Living here in Texas all this time and not even changing his name."

Ira agreed that he must be pretty bold. Most bad men who hit the state started wearing different handles right away.

He gave the patrol an order. "Check your Winchesters and Colts. See that there's plenty of ammunition in the magazines and in your belts." A killer who had been free for thirty years was likely to put up a husky scrap when the law came to take him in.

Within an hour and a half the Rangers rode down a dip in the canyon to spot a ranch that must be the one run by Jim Epps. Cattle and sheep were grazing all around an unfenced house built in the long, rambling style of Texas. The prankish pack mule saw the dwelling, ran snorting around it a couple of times as the pots and pans banged and clattered, then settled down to browse on the ample grass.

Ira heard the stirring of people inside the house. "Hello!" he hailed. The Rangers stiffened in their saddles, alert for trouble.

The door opened. A man stepped to the porch that ran the length of the structure. Ira had expected to see a shaggy, furtive recluse. But the ranch owner was a friendly, well-kept, middle aged man with a face that beamed a welcome.

"Howdy, gents," he saluted them. "Light down and have some vittles."

The Rangers eyed the man narrowly. He must believe them to be wandering punchers, but an invitation to hospitality might turn into a bid for battle when he learned their real identity.

"Thanks," Ira answered curtly; "but we didn't come for a meal. Are you James Epps?"

"Yes," the rancher admitted. "I'm Epps. Then, in a puzzled manner: "What do you want?"

Ira took out the warrant that bore the seal of Tennessee. "Looks like we want you, Mr. Epps." He read the warrant aloud, Epps listening intently to every word. When Ira finished, the rancher stood in silence. He looked dazed; his lips moved but he could say nothing.

Ira signaled his command to be at ease. The men relaxed in their saddles. "Mr. Epps," Ira said, "we're Texas Rangers. I'm Corporal Aten, in charge of this squad. You're under arrest—you'll have to come with us."

Epps stared at the outfit like a man in a trance. "After all these years," he mumbled brokenly.

The door swung open again. Out walked a woman with the seams of age and hard work on her face. Following her were a boy of fourteen and five younger children.

Ira felt a spasm of conscience. Desperadoes generally didn't have families and comfortable-looking houses. The Rangers had assumed automatically that Jim Epps must be another no-account trigger man batching in a hovel.

The woman looked sharply at the four mounted strangers and guessed that something was happening to her husband. "What is it, Jim?" she asked anxiously. "What are these men here for?"

Jim Epps put his face on his wife's shoulder and started to weep. Seeing their father break down, the children started wailing.

"I—I never told you about it," the rancher said. "I killed a man, back in Tennessee. These fellers are Rangers come to send me back for trial."

Mrs. Epps clasped her husband in her arms. "I—oh, God, they'll hang you in Tennessee." She clutched Jim more closely and began crying hysterically. The children, also clinging to him, sobbed, "Papa, don't go. Don't go, Papa."

Ira felt tears running down his own cheeks. Then he looked around at his own men. Not a dry eye could he see. But he had to cut short the farewell of Jim Epps to his family. At Ira's direction, the rancher saddled a pony, then bade good-by to his family. "I may never return," he told them sadly as they stood on the porch, still grieving.

The prisoner slumped dejectedly in his saddle as he rode away with the lawmen. Individual Rangers tried to console

him by little acts of kindness such as offering to roll ciga-
rettes. Each sympathetic gesture Jim Epps declined with a
worried shake of the head.

Five miles from the Epps place, the party passed another
ranch. "Who lives here?" Ira asked the prisoner.

"My neighbor, Ben Brown," Epps replied dully. Ira issued
a command to his force. "You boys ride on, and I'll catch up
with you. I want to talk to Mr. Brown."

Rancher Brown proved to be a large, swarthy man with
obvious part Indian features. He was mending a break in his
corral when Ira got down from the saddle and started talking.

"I'm Corporal Aten of the Rangers. Your friend, Mr. Epps,
is in a little trouble. My patrol's taking him into Uvalde."
Brown's jaw dropped and his face clouded over.

"Why, you crazy, damned coyote! I ought to cut your goddamned heart out. There ain't a better man in Uvalde County than Jim Epps."

Ordinarily, Ira, no more than any other Ranger, would
have submitted to such insulting language. But this time a
Ranger took it without challenge—and a little humbly.

Ira's reply was mild. "I'm sorry for Mr. Epps. But he'll be
back soon." The corporal's tongue halted as he realized the
sudden commitment he'd made—promising that Jim Epps
would be coming home when the authorities of Tennessee
might have a different notion.

Ben Brown went on wrathfully protesting the arrest of
a respected neighbor. Jim Epps had raised his young-uns
right. His branding iron never slipped. He'd ride twenty
miles to do a man a favor. Why the hell were the Rangers
wasting the taxpayers' money hounding him?

Ira felt as sheepish as he ever had when his preacher father had bawled him out for fishing on Sunday. "We didn't
hound your friend, Mr. Brown. He surrendered peacefully on
a warrant from Tennessee. I just stopped to ask if you'd look
after his family while he's gone."

Brown opened his lips and spat out a rivulet of tobacco
juice. "Hell, yes, I will. And Tennessee be damned. That's

where they ran out my grandfolks—for bein' Cherokee!" He strode to his back door. "Betty! Betty! Come here this minute."

Betty came running. Her face, too, was etched with age and work. Her husband told her brusquely to get right over to Miz Epps—this damn fool of a Ranger had done took off her husband.

Betty Brown got on a horse and rode off toward the Epps home. Her husband paid his last respects to Ira Aten; Jim Epps, he said, was just too good-natured to scatter Ira's guts in the middle of Nueces Canyon, like he would have done. He didn't want to see Ira hereabouts again unless he was bringing Jim Epps back with him. "Now git!" he ended.

Ira got.

The trip from Jim Epps' ranch to Uvalde town took three days. When Ira had arrested Epps, he'd decided to make the rough jaunt rather than humiliate the man further by turning him over to a fellow former Tennessean, the constable. Gradually, with the Rangers showing him so much consideration, Epps pulled himself together. He became more cheerful and spoke frankly with his unchosen companions about the crime that had risen up finally to haunt him.

He had, indeed, slain another Tennessean during his youth. But the crime had been a heated one of passion rather than a calculated one for gain. A girl in his native community had jilted him for a rival. And the victor, in the love tussle, had died by Jim Epps's gun. The pattern was a common one in the mountain South. "I oughtn't a done it," he told the Rangers soberly. "I found a better woman after I run off to Texas—one who stuck with me. But I was a fool kid and didn't have no more sense than to kill."

Ira had several long talks with the prisoner as the two of them rode in advance of the outfit. A basically honest man, Epps had never thought of changing his name as did so many migrants who came to Texas to live down old crimes. He had taken the precaution of living in thinly settled country and had finally landed in Nueces Canyon, where he had built up his little ranch with the help of his wife. But he swore that he'd never been in the slightest brush with the law during these thirty years in Texas.

Ira felt sure that Jim Epps was telling the truth. The rancher's conduct as a prisoner bore out his account of himself.

Because of his good behavior, Ira let him ride with his hands free during the daylight hours. Nights, Epps submitted cheerfully to sleeping with one of his hands cuffed to a Ranger. This was a customary procedure to relieve patrolmen of standing guard. The Rangers had leg irons in their equipment and had expected that they would have to use them on Jim Epps when they first set out to find him. But not once did the prisoner show any inclination to resist or escape.

Ira described him as "one of the most obedient and agreeable men I ever had to bring in." Uvalde County officers told the Rangers that Epps bore the reputation of being a peaceful man when they locked him up pending the completion of the necessary extradition procedure. The rancher made no effort to balk Tennessee, but went quietly back with a sheriff coming from that state.

The Rangers went back to the canyons. They dragged a good many sorry specimens of humanity from that criss-cross of malevolent pits and started dozens of them toward the gibbet or the rock pile. They confiscated enough guns to equip a small army but turned the weapons over to local sheriffs as possible items of evidence. But, as the number of caught men soared, Ira kept remembering one man—Jim Epps, who might be facing a scaffold in Tennessee.

For weeks, Ira tried to appease a gnawing conscience with the letter of legality. Epps *had* killed a man. He *had* run off to escape punishment. Rangers were *not* judges passing final decisions on facts. They had no leeway. Or did they? There were nights when Ira tossed in his blankets remembering the anguish of Jim Epps's family as they watched him being led away. A happy, well-ordered family it had been until the Rangers had appeared from nowhere to shatter the quiet, contained little world they had built.

Ira thought of sending a few dollars from his Ranger pay to Mrs. Epps. But he knew Texas women well enough to realize that she would tear the bills to bits and scatter the shreds to the wind. Charity from the man who had wrecked their life would be adding dire insult to injury.

"He'll be back soon." That pledge he had made to the aroused Ben Brown in the canyon, that had slipped out and surprised him so. The recollection of Mrs. Brown rushing off on the horse to help Jim Epps's wife now almost a widow. Women were few in that "sliced-up land" of the canyons. But, as everywhere, they maintained some intact sisterhood, from the swapping of recipes to helping deliver each others' babies.

Betty Brown and her husband would do whatever they could for neighbors crushed by the impersonal forces of the law. Yet they probably had children of their own to worry about, too. Jim Epps's fourteen-year-old son would now have to be the man of the house. Boys that age knew how to rope and brand and ride—but what protection would a youngster be against thieves who might now strike at the little ranch? And what about the five younger children, the ones who'd grabbed at their father's legs to keep him from going? All those six who Ben Brown declared had been "raised right."

"I didn't have to pick up that man," he kept telling his fellow Rangers. "I could have put him on his word to have stayed there till I could see what else might be done about that warrant. And we'd have found him right there the next trip we made."

Whenever Ira discussed that arrest with his comrades, they talked uneasily. It was as if the whole patrol shared a burden some collective shame. None wanted to criticize Ira because all felt culpable. But on a night when there were no prisoners to be tended, a young private said mildly:

"You know, maybe we oughta have asked that constable more about Mr. Epps before rampaging off and yanking him in."

"Yeh," another Ranger drawled reflectively, "we'd bust the

state treasury building jails if we locked up every man who'd
been in trouble before he hit Texas."

Ira's face was redder than the campfire. Why *hadn't* he
asked the constable more about Epps before snatching him
away from his world? Instead, he'd gone tearing off to serve
that warrant and grab a killer wanted for thirty years.

As Ira stretched out on his blankets he felt as foolish as
he'd been while a Ranger rookie ready to rescue ladies from
cliffs and wipe out all the bad men single-handed.

That night, on his bed under a dim, condemning moon, Ira
thought of all the men who'd come to Texas because they'd
been in trouble. A lot of them, like these devils rounded up
in the canyons, had blown in to make more trouble. But
more—far more than he'd ever allowed himself to believe—
had arrived to make the same industrious new starts that
Jim Epps had made.

They had stayed out of trouble by putting it wisely and
safely behind. And still in Texas you didn't ask a man, however respectable, much about his past if he'd come from
elsewhere. If he was a native son, you didn't quiz him too
much about his ancestry: every Texan knew that the state
had prospering, well ordered communities where scarcely a
citizen bore the original name of his father or his grandfather, back in some state where transgression had dictated
migration.

"G. T. T."—gone to Texas—was the phrase coined to de-
fine so much migration during the days when so many people got into so much trouble on so many frontiers. Such
had been the case in Tennessee, where statutes had not restrained a shotgun in the hands of a foolish frontier boy
named Jim Epps.

As an officer, Ira was obligated to uphold the written law
and punishment was one of its functions. But another of
its functions that he sometimes forgot was leniency, where
leniency was merited. Even—maybe particularly for those
who'd "gone to Texas" and had helped build it because it
had been a refuge, rather than a respite, from trouble.

Ira finally dropped off to sleep recalling one of the favorite texts of his father in brush-arbor revival meetings:

The letter killeth, but the spirit giveth life.

He awoke the next morning to the smell of bacon frying and coffee boiling. They were sweet scents combining with the pungent odors of the big canyon flowers. Ira brushed away a wild bee buzzing too close to his cheek. He swung out his arms to relax a kink or two and washed his hands in the overflow from a spring at the camp site. As he sat down to breakfast, he felt that he had grown the space of those thirty years that Jim Epps had been in Texas. Felt actually full grown, at a man's age of twenty-one.

"Boys," he said as he poured his third cup of coffee, "arresting Jim Epps was the meanest thing I ever did. Now, I'm going to try to do the best thing I ever did."

The patrol returned to Uvalde. There Ira gave himself that first individual assignment—upholding leniency as a function of law.

How he performed it is told best, without any fillips of literature, in his own memoirs:

> *I wrote a letter to the state officials [of Tennessee] telling all the circumstances about the family without protection in the far-away mountains, and the loved ones in his home. He stayed in jail about six months. As the State could not get the witnesses against him to make a case, some of them having died and others being out of Tennessee, he was released and immediately returned to his family in the mountains.*

And he added the moral of that experience: *I began to think, maybe, I was too zealous in hunting down criminals after this sad experience.*

Jim Epps looked up his deliverer, who had been his captor.

"Rube might have made a wonderful Ranger."

THE WORST OUTLAW SINCE SAM BASS

He rode into Camp King and found Ira thumbing another sheaf of "catch-'em papers."

"Thank you, Mr. Aten," Jim Epps said feelingly. "That letter you wrote sure helped me when the prosecutor read it."

Ira felt a surge of something even more gratifying than a Ranger citation. "I'm glad to hear that, Mr. Epps," he answered modestly.

Jim Epps's hand strayed gratefully around his throat. "Reckon they could have swung me just on my confession. I'm back home 'cause a lawman that lawyer never saw had a heart."

Ira didn't know what to say; he was struggling for words when Epps added:

"You know I ain't throwin' off on the law, Mr. Aten. But not many officers woulda put theirselves out for somebody in my fix. They'da been more interested in makin' a record than in savin' a man's neck."

The two shook hands. Jim Epps mounted a waiting horse. Then the settler rode back into happy obscurity and out of a Ranger's life.

Yet not quite out of his life. Their first encounter had left Ira tortured by a recurrent vision of Jim Epps dangling from a rope while a woman and six youngsters grieved. Now their second meeting became still another goad to a law enforcer's conscience. As poignantly as he recalled that sorrowful family in the canyon, Ira kept remembering an obvious truth voiced by its head—far too many officers would have been far more concerned with a record than a life.

Once again Ira found himself wondering what kind of record he wanted to make.

Courage was a recognized part of the reputation he had already built. Alertness and natural ability, too. All of them combined had earned him promotion from private to corporal within a very short time. The foolish part of his early romanticism had long since been outgrown. Its better part had remained to give his work the inspiration and imagination that made him an outstanding, completely trusted member of the force.

But the postscript to Jim Epps was a new element welded into ambition—the simple element of mercy.

Mercy, which Ira's good common sense would never let be diluted into sentimental drivel over "a man who ought to be hung."

As a Ranger and a frontiersman, Ira believed that ropes were often necessary and highly effective instruments of justice. Yet in a larger focus he wanted his record to be more than a footnote to a sheaf of death warrants.

His broader understandings met their first test a few months later. The test involved a man who was the complete opposite of Jim Epps—a wild man who had flirted many times with hemp but had managed to dodge its kiss.

Rube Boyce was a town rowdy who had launched himself on a lurid career of posse racing by shooting his own brother-in-law in a family fracas. Ira described him as being "one of the real bad men of western Texas in the early days."

The acquaintance was incidental rather than one dating from a sprint between lawman and outlaw. Boyce was enjoying a stretch of freedom in Llano, a hill country county seat, when Ira went there with a Ranger detail to guard a court whose sanctity was threatened by a scorching Texas feud.

Two families—the Carters and the Cogginses—had been improving already notable reputations for marksmanship by pot-shooting each other in the convenient Packsaddle Mountains of Llano County. At a former hearing, stemming from the feud, the warring clans had started aiming at each other in the district courtroom. They had finished the battle on the streets of Llano town, leaving men lying in the dust.

When the second trial opened, armed Rangers were present to help Sheriff George W. Shaw preserve order. Ira was assigned to guard duty in the courtroom. His chore was to keep an eye on the spectators and be sure that nobody testifying was "bullet knocked" out of the witness chair. He kept Carter partisans sitting on one side of the courtroom and Coggins warriors on the other. The presence of the Rangers made the truculent clans mind their decorum. What puzzled Ira, as the trial went along peacefully, was the odd behavior of Sheriff Shaw.

A tall, whiskered man with a face that was both hard and sad, Shaw kept himself posted below the judge's rostrum when he wasn't escorting witnesses to the chair. Ordinarily, a Texas sheriff maintained a hawk's watch on a trial as tense as this one. But Ira sensed that he sometimes wasn't even listening to the testimony of men living in his own jurisdiction. Often he barely heard instructions given him by the judge. Ira noticed that he was forever gazing into the middle of the crowd except when a bang of the gavel made him jump to duty.

"What's bothering the sheriff?" Ira whispered to a deputy on the third day of the trial.

The deputy jerked a thumb. "The fellow over there." Ira looked toward a section of benches that had been set aside for Llanoites who were neutrals. He saw a robust man who kept watching the proceedings with eyes that laughed at all the embellished follies of jurisprudence. Occasionally his chest would vibrate in some suppressed belly rumble when the judge was pompous or some witness fatuous. Now and then someone would glance around to see how this spectator was taking the trial before turning a head to hide an unbidden grin.

There was a certain negative magnetism about the man. A defying, elusive something that Ira just couldn't put a finger on. And obviously nobody felt whatever it was more uncomfortably than the stiff, lonely figure who was the sheriff of Llano County.

Ira saw Shaw's eyes stray again toward the fellow. There was a subtly teasing response on the face of the man as their glances met—like the subtle challenge of a confident wolf knowing that it can conquer a hound wanting to spring but not quite daring.

All afternoon Ira was fascinated with the byplay between the upset man of law and the man who might be anybody. The sheriff was fidgeting visibly as the session drew to a close. But his tormentor still showed that provoking self-assurance.

When the day's tourney of law ended, Ira followed the man into the corridor. There he stood, watching with twinkling eyes as Rangers supervised the downstairs exit first of Carters, then of Cogginses, making sure that none carried forty-fives.

Ira turned to the fellow as the last feudist began treading steps.

"Don't believe I've met you," he said. "My name's Aten —I'm here with the Ranger detail."

The man nodded and put out a hand. "So I know. Guess we should have met before. I'm Boyce—Rube Boyce."

Ira's hand froze in the clasp. Rube Boyce, smartest of all the tribe of stagecoach robbers. The man some Texas officers declared to be "the worst Outlaw since Sam Bass."

By God! Ira thought; *George Shaw ought to have jugged him long ago for his damned impudence.*

The Ranger saw that same satirical gleam that had been disturbing to Sheriff Shaw. "Hear you Rangers are camped outside town. Maybe I'll drop over to chin with you some night."

The cheek of this damned highwayman! Ira withdrew his hand.

"You do that, Boyce," he said curtly, then walked away. Around the campfire after supper Ira and the outfit recounted the sizable legend of Rube Boyce, who took what he wanted and twiddled his long gunman's fingers at the law. In Kimble County, a further extension of these hills, he had slain his brother-in-law. Kimble was such an undeveloped patch of rock and brush that, for several years, its "courthouse" had been two tall trees serving as twin gallows for felons condemned under their branches. A posse of cowpunchers had taken out after Rube, following the killing, but he had outrun them.

Then he had turned up as the nimble brain of a gang preying on the stagecoach lines of western Texas. Finally Rube and his followers had been bagged after robbing the Austin stage. His henchmen took their medicine of sentences served in the state penitentiary. But, as a Ranger remarked with a long sigh, "keeping their head man locked up was like trying to stuff a wolf in a tow sack."

Rube Boyce had also been condemned. Convicted, Ira guessed, while jousting in his peculiar game with the judge who had tried him. His wife had visited him often in the Austin calaboose, bringing him victuals to supplement "the jail grub which would just about keep a man alive." The jailer, feeling sorry for the pitiful girl, always admitted her for a tryst in Rube's cell after first making the customary check of her basket for hidden firearms.

Never a weapon or a getaway tool turned up in the straw container. One day Mrs. Boyce came while her husband's lawyers on the outside were engaged in some legal maneuvers for a stay of sentence. Perfunctorily, the jailer examined the basket to find nothing but fried chicken and trimmings. Graciously he then let the girl into the steel boudoir.

Two hours passed. Time to bring the baton down on the love symphony. The jailer went to Rube's cell—to find a forty-five pointing through the bars at his head. As Ira heard the story by the Llano campfire, the jailer walked into the cell; Rube Boyce and his wife walked out. They made their way to the unguarded hitching rack outside the building. There Rube boarded a good horse that was waiting and stayed ahead in a two-hundred-and-fifty-mile race to Mexico.

The jailer was released by a sheriff whose tongue blasted louder than Rube Boyce's six-guns ever had. A dropped basket on the cell floor spelled out the answer. When the angry sheriff ripped it apart, he found something never detected by his underling—a false bottom had concealed a cozy cache for a gun.

Nobody thought of prosecuting Mrs. Boyce. In fact, no Texas jury would have convicted a woman for standing by her man. Texans who detested outlawry chuckled over the break engineered by a slip of a girl. Public sympathy, as Ira remembered, began churning for the poor young wife left without the support of her husband. The romantics who kept shifting their Robin Hood projections from one knight of the swag to another now started making a popular hero out of a highwayman.

Jesse James—Sam Bass—now Rube Boyce. They had all "stolen from the rich and given to the poor," in one of the most enduring motifs of popular mythology. A climate of sympathy began generating in Texas for Rube, now enduring the less genial climate of Mexico.

He sweated out several years in the torrid southern republic, liking the country as little as had the batches of Texan filibusterers rounded up and thrown in presidios for violating a nation's sovereignty. Pesos from Mexican gaming tables came as easily to him as dollars had from American stage lines. As Ira had heard it said, "You could always count on Rube Boyce having a pocketful of money and a headful of sense."

But Mexican heat can evaporate even the cockiness of a Texan. Rube started writing letters to friends back home swearing that "he'd rather live in hell than in Mexico." It was another way of saying that he was just plain lonesome for Texas.

His wife found him a pair of smarter lawyers who got his case transferred on some technicality to the Federal Court in Austin. Rube returned to do a second jail stint while awaiting re-trial. This sojourn behind bars passed off tranquilly, Mrs. Boyce's visiting privileges being restricted. Rube made his due appearance before the court whose authority came from the Yankee capital in Washington. To the chagrin of Austin's sheriff, he was acquitted and walked away from custody, happily holding his helpmate's hand.

And now, as Ira had seen, he was a thorn getting sharper in the flesh of Llano's sheriff.

More days Ira watched the unfolding farce in the Llano courthouse. Even the way in which Rube Boyce toyed with a button on his shirt irritated Sheriff Shaw. His flick of an eye toward some demobilized feudist made the sheriff bristle. If he bent over to adjust his boot laces, Shaw's gaze would travel downward, too. Then when Boyce would look up again, Shaw would try to counter a barely sarcastic twinkle with stern visage, his whiskers vibrating, in a slow fitfulness, like grass ruffled by some puckish slow wind.

The other Rangers also began noticing that daily tussle between two men sharing nothing but strong wills and instinctive mutual dislike. At first Ira sympathized with the sheriff as a brother lawman and remained coolly aloof toward the slyly insolent highwayman. Sympathy, though, soured into gradual disgust as Shaw kept proving such a ready victim of every obvious trap.

"Rube Boyce surely gets the sheriff's goat," Ira remarked on another night in the Ranger camp. "And George Shaw stakes the goat right out for Rube to get."

"Yeh." A comrade laughed. "But I can't feel very sorry for Shaw standing up there every day and letting himself be hurrahed by a card-shark bandit."

Ira's own feeling for the sheriff began cooling. True, the presence of such a notorious bad man in the county was a standing reproach to George Shaw's dignity as its law enforcer. His humiliation was compounded by the fact that Rube Boyce was now technically as clean as the teeth of the hounds that the sheriff used to bay horse thieves out of the Packsaddle Mountains. How would any rural sheriff feel about a stellar, if inactive, outlaw taking up residence in his county and not even being able to order him out?

Rube Boyce had been a challenge to George Shaw on the day he was born, Ira decided; some men were just natural-born enemies. But an officer was also expected to show natural self control when dealing with an opponent whom some freakish process of justice had placed beyond his reach.

Then, much to his own surprise, Ira found himself getting friendlier with the outlaw. It began with a comment about the weather or, perhaps, some observation about quail hunting. Then it progressed to other and longer talk during recesses. For a while Ira wondered if Rube Boyce was trying to make a psychological ally of him in that silent feud with Sheriff Shaw. Finally he concluded that Boyce just wanted to be friendly in that normal camaraderie of Texans, always relaxed and sustained unless tempers flared suddenly.

One Friday night the gunman strolled casually into the Ranger camp. "Howdy, boys," he said in greeting. "Told Ira over there I'd been meaning to stop by some night."

Ira winced, feeling uncomfortable because the outlaw had for the first time referred to him by his given name. But that mention placed an obligation of sociability upon him. So he poured Rube Boyce a cup of coffee from the campfire pot and found him a box to sit on.

Boyce sipped and gossiped. Crime was a subject of mutual interest between lawmen and outlaw, if from different viewpoints. So there was much reminiscing about the gun slinging and banditry that gave the Lone Star State its continuing accent of notoriety. Ira noticed, however, that the guest was careful not to implicate himself in any flow of recollection, nor any other long rider about whom a fact mentioned was not general knowledge.

Rube was the smoothest bad man he had ever met, Ira thought. A man who made Sam Bass look like the crowing country boy Sam was.

After a while talk became concentrated on stage and train robberies. Rube Boyce helped himself to a second cup of coffee, then said in a voice whose matter-of-factness was edged with something else:

"Reckon the handiest bunch of stage histers was the one that robbed the coach at Pegleg Crossing nine times without being caught."

Ira almost jumped from the log where he was sitting. Memories swirled around him in an angry, churning fog. Recollections of those cold weeks and that mocking vigil when a Ranger patrol had kept searching, in stirrups caked with ice, for the Pegleg robbers. Other remembrances, too. The wheezing coughs of his comrades as they lay in their blankets on the frosty ground, sleeping in boots that didn't keep feet from freezing. The lonesomeness of the men for their girls in warm Uvalde. His own relief when he'd been given a rest from the howling "blue northers" to collect taxes on Devil's River.

And here, sitting carelessly before him, was the probable leader of the band that had given the Rangers such a futile, merry chase. Had Rube Boyce, from some safe hideout, many times spied on his weary pursuers and had more enjoyment out of it than he was now getting from taunting Sheriff Shaw? Was this an extra little gloating game that he'd started with the Rangers?

With difficulty, Ira managed to restrain himself. "Yep, Rube," he said with forced unconcern. "Those fellows who kept sticking up that stage certainly knew their oats." Ira had hoped to maneuver the outlaw into some slight boast, however indirect, that would lead eventually to an admission of the Pegleg robberies.

Instead, Rube stood up, stretched his muscles, and yawned lazily.

"Well, good night, gents. I'm moseying on back to the little woman."

After the visitor had gone, a Ranger said laughingly, "Ira, he sprung your trap before you ever got it set."

Ira couldn't help but laugh, too. "Guess so, Charlie. And I can't figure what bait to put out next."

Next morning Ira went to court expecting that Rube Boyce would try the same sort of artful psychological mayhem on him that he was performing on Sheriff Shaw. The gunman had taken him down the night before in a rather pointed way. And foxing a Texas Ranger before a crowd of people would be a much greater coup than the wordless bulldozing of a small-town sheriff. Ira was wondering how he would thwart such a ribbing. But he was determined not to let himself be flustered as George Shaw had been.

To his astonishment, Rube saluted him with an admiring grin and a jovial wave of a hand. The baiting of the sheriff continued. That was now as much a routine of the trial as the pen scratchings of the court clerk and the wrangling of the lawyers. But whenever Rube's eyes rested on Ira or any other Ranger, his expression was one of friendliness and respect.

"Seems like old Rube's kind of cottoning to us," a Ranger commented during the noon recess. "But what a picnic he's having out of Sheriff Shaw."

"Yes," Ira answered quietly. "He hates the sheriff. And the sheriff's deathly afraid of him."

A night or two later a local citizen ran breathlessly into the Ranger camp and almost fell into the fire. Ira gave him a steadying hand. "What's the matter, friend?" he inquired.

"Rube Boyce is drunk and getting ready to shoot up a saloon!" the townsman panted. "For God's sake, stop him!"

The commander of the detail said, "That's Sheriff Shaw's job. We're here only on court duty."

The citizen gasped. "George Shaw would no more get through the door than Rube Boyce would drop him dead. And we don't want no decent folks killed by that goddamn gunslinger."

Four Rangers, including Ira, were assigned to quell Rube Boyce. The townsman led them to the saloon where Rube was making his ruckus, then bolted. Shots were echoing from inside the place. There came the sound of crashing glass as whisky bottles, used for targets, dropped in shattered pieces to the floor.

"Whoopee!" the Rangers heard Boyce yell. "This is a hell of a fine night! Hooray for hell, gentlemen!"

More shots—more bottles crashing—shouts of alarm from Rube's captive audience.

Ira addressed his fellow Rangers. "He's finally busted loose—he's hitting at this place to do in the sheriff. Two of us had better go in the back, two in front." And one of them, he said to himself, might be expected to die.

A pair of Rangers walked into the saloon from the back door. Ira and the fourth man strode through the front entrance. At that moment Rube Boyce thrust out a leg to kick over a gambling table. Poker chips and stacks of silver coins scattered across the floor. Gamesters took whatever cover they could find or sprawled quiveringly on the floor.

"Rube!" Ira called. Then again, sharply: "Rube!"

The gunman wheeled around drunkenly. His forty-five was bobbing in his right hand, but his grip firmed when he saw two Rangers standing there.

"H-mph!" he grunted. "Come for a fight? All right, by God, I'll drill both of you!"

Ira answered coolly, "You might drill one of us, Rube, but not two of us. The man left would fill you full of holes before you got in your second shot."

Rube stared at the wobbling gun in his right hand, then at the raised revolvers of the Rangers. Ira saw that he wanted to aim, but that whisky had fogged his vision. The terrified customers were taking advantage of his confusion by tearing through the doors.

Swiftly Ira reached out and grabbed the desperado's pistol. "You're under arrest, Rube. And if you'll look behind you, you'll see that you'd have had four men to kill."

Boyce jerked his head around to see the pair of Rangers who had entered from the rear. "Four men to kill," he repeated heavily, then slumped into the one chair his boot hadn't upset. "I was just having a little fun cleaning out this saloon. Take me home to my wife."

Ira leaned over the chair to search Boyce for more weapons, and found none. "We're not taking you home, Rube, but I'll let your wife know where you'll be. Come on."

Another Ranger helped the gunman to his feet. Ira placed Boyce's pistol in his own pocket. Escorted by two officers walking beside him and two behind, the bandit started toward the Llano jail. The party had gone no more than a block when they ran into Sheriff Shaw and the sheriff's chief deputy. Boyce's hand reached quickly for the weapon that wasn't there. Then he brought his palm upward, his fingers twitching in the reflex action of a gun fighter who has been thwarted.

He looked hard at the county lawmen, then at the Rangers. "Six men to kill," he said in a hoarse whisper. "You devils framed this—"

Boyce didn't finish the sentence because Sheriff Shaw had reached out to grab him by the collar. "Damn you!" he shouted. "I'm going to tear you apart with my bare hands! I'm—"

Ira interrupted. "You're not going to do a damn thing to a man who's drunk and disarmed, Sheriff. Take your paws off of him."

He turned to the outlaw. "Rube, we four didn't bunch with these two as you think, but you're going to stand trial for what you did tonight." To the county officers he said curtly, "You fellows go on ahead to the jail. We'll bring Rube there."

At the jail, Ira sent a Ranger to inform Mrs. Boyce that her husband was being locked up. Then he laid down his own kind of law to Shaw, the lawman.

"This prisoner is under the protection of the Texas Rangers, Sheriff. Remember that after we leave him with you."

Next morning Sheriff Shaw triumphantly escorted Rube Boyce in handcuffs to the Llano justice of the peace. Suffering from hang-over and humiliation, Rube paid a large fine, then went home with his wife.

After that hectic night, Rube Boyce's game with the sheriff became a different one, with Llano's bedeviled law man gaining the upper hand. Rube stopped making his daily appearances in the district courtroom. From Sheriff Shaw's regular tormentor, he turned into the sheriff's regular guest. And by oddly contrasting circumstances, a Texas Ranger found himself being an instrument of mercy for Rube Boyce, the uproarious road agent, as he had been for Jim Epps, the penitent onetime offender.

An unwilling instrument, it was true, as Rube kept visiting Llano saloons to wreck them. When it came to the fundamental principles of law and order, Ira was unequivocally on the side of Sheriff Shaw and told the gunman so. But time after time Ira found himself intervening with Shaw for Rube's personal safety after delivering him into custody for hell raising.

"Aten," the sheriff snapped on one such occasion, "I don't like your interference. You Rangers are here today and gone tomorrow. But I have to put up with this rattler three hundred and sixty-five days a year—and he's a standing menace to the community."

Ira felt the sting of the rebuke and wondered what he would do if he were in George Shaw's place. But he had little time to grope with the question as he guarded the courtroom by day and curbed Rube's rampages by night. Every other evening Rube Boyce blew up somewhere. The Rangers would find him standing in the middle of wreckage and liquor puddles yelling at the shaking customers: "Help yourself, boys! Everything in this place is free!"

He gave the Rangers no resistance, except argument, whenever they came after him. But the saloonkeepers were protesting bitterly to Sheriff Shaw because evening trade was dwindling as patrons stayed safely at home. On alternate nights, when Rube was out of jail after paying his fine, he was always at the Ranger camp. There anybody whom his wife sent looking for him could always locate him.

"Rube," Ira commented one night, "I see your play now. You're trying to push Sheriff Shaw into a showdown."

Rube Boyce puffed on a corncob pipe and answered nothing. "You've taken him down enough," Ira persisted. "If I
was the sheriff here, you'd get that showdown."

Boyce knocked the ashes from his pipe. "Ira, that would be
a fight between two real men," he answered gravely. "Sheriffs are hardly worth killing. They're just cowpunchers and
plow pushers who've talked enough jaspers into voting for
them."

After Boyce had left, Ira understood now why the desperado held George Shaw in contempt. Shaw rated as a pretty
capable sheriff. But to Rube Boyce all local officers were so
many glorified nincompoops. Outride them across a county
line, and an outlaw could turn back to spit at them. Dependent they were on vote hustling, every two years, for their
jobs. Else return to cowpunching at twenty dollars a month
or plow pushing for even less.

Rangers were something else again. They represented that
society of larger stature against which Rube Boyce, a desperado of stature, had declared war. They were men fit to
be his opponents. Fit, too, for the occasional truces accorded
between equals.

Under different circumstances, as Ira would say later,
Rube Boyce "might have made a wonderful Ranger." He
was "shrewd and cunning—and fearless." But other circumstances had molded him into something else—something
no upholder of law could accept just because Boyce had an
interesting tongue and an engaging jib.

Underneath it all the outlaw's friendliness with Rangers
was only a truce. A foe he still was by definition—and in
fact. But who and what was a modest Texan named Jim
Epps?

A contrast between two men started Ira on comparisons
of two counties. Llano County, where George Shaw tried to
enforce the law and Uvalde County, where Jim Epps tried to
obey it. Two ordinary, average counties they were, varying a
little here and there because they were in opposite sections
of the state. More than two hundred other such counties,

with their individual peculiarities, made up Texas. County by county, since the days of the Lone Star Republic, regular or volunteer companies of Rangers had gradually brought law and order to the sprawling commonwealth.

They had done it, most often, with the help of average officers like George Shaw, who wangled ballots. With the help, too, of average citizens such as Jim Epps, sometimes giving their votes to raise a man from plow pushing, sometimes withholding the decisive slips of paper to send him back.

Rube Boyce had no more respect for a ballot box than he had for another man's purse. By calculated taunts, he flouted George Shaw's authority in the sheriff's own courthouse. By calculated terror, he would grab Jim Epps's purse on a train or a stagecoach.

Epps had impulsively killed a love rival in Tennessee. Boyce had committed a more reprehensible crime when he killed his own brother-in-law in Kimble County. Yet that average man had finally returned and offered himself for trial. The smarter man had simply thumbed his nose at warrants to commit more planned infractions of the law.

"Jim Epps would have surrendered as peacefully to Sheriff Shaw as he did to us Rangers," Ira reflected. "But if sheriffs or Rangers go out to take Rube Boyce—*bang!*"

Appreciation of Jim Epps suddenly made Ira feel more respect for Sheriff Shaw.

"The sheriff's trouble with Rube Boyce is a lot more dangerous than the one between the Carters and Cogginses," Ira said worriedly to fellow Rangers. "They're finally submitting to law and settling their troubles in court. After we leave, Rube Boyce will stop paying those fines to the J. P. He'll kill Shaw, then lope away to take in more towns."

The Carter-Coggins trial was nearing its close. A wise district judge had done much poulticing of old sores as the proceedings had gone along peacefully under the watchful eyes of the Rangers. Both families, Ira knew, would go back to their ranches under agreements of peace that ordinary people generally kept.

But there was still the other feud. The one now involving only two men—yet that could have serious repercussions throughout Texas.

Ira feared there would be "a showdown shooting as sure as shooting" after the Rangers departed. Sheriff Shaw might be able to stand up to Rube Boyce because of the increased self confidence gained from having had the outlaw in the lockup so many times. But the overwhelming probability was that Boyce, the professional trigger man, would rub out the country sheriff.

Only outlawry would gain if that happened. Gain everywhere in Texas. Once more Ira, as in the Epps case, gave himself a personal and private assignment. It was to stop the two-man feud before leaving Llano County.

The evening came when Ira knew that the Rangers would be making their last arrest of Rube Boyce. The usual call came from some townsman for what the rest of the detail was beginning to call "the Boyce squad." With the same three men who had gone with him the first time, Ira went to a saloon to pull out the roisterer.

Two behind, two ahead as usual, the Rangers began marching Boyce along the street. Again they met the sheriff and his deputy. The outlaw, reekingly drunk, began spitting oaths at Shaw. This time the county lawman lost all self-control. He jerked out his pistol and struck Boyce's skull with the barrel. The full force of the blow was warded off by one of the Rangers raising his arm quickly, but blood flowed from a gash in Boyce's scalp to pour down the outlaw's face.

"Damn it!" Boyce bellowed. "You're the first man who ever buffaloed me and you'll be the last." All four Rangers tussled with him as he tried to get at Shaw. The sheriff swung the pistol again. Two Rangers pulled the cursing bandit out of his reach. The other two grabbed Shaw by the arms.

"Mr. Sheriff," one of them said, "you must not interfere with our prisoners. When we put a man in jail, he is your prisoner, and not until then." The pair led Shaw down the street. Boyce was later taken to jail. Next morning he silently paid his fine, his wife there as usual to lead him home. All day long Ira felt a glum sense of futility as he conjectured what must be shaping up.

Rube Boyce was not one to take a pistol whipping from another man. Shaw's ill-advised action had canceled any chance of avoiding that showdown. The outlaw would demand an accounting.

On the night after the buffaloing Rube Boyce made another visit to the Ranger camp. His head was bandaged and smelling of strong salve.

"Hear you boys will be pulling out in a couple of days," he said. "Thought I'd drop over to have a last smoke and say good-by."

"Better not say good-by, Rube," Ira responded; "if you kill George Shaw, we'll be looking for you. And we'll find you."

Rube rolled a cigarette. His tense lips barely moistened the paper. Crumbs of tobacco flittered down on his trousers.

"Hell," he mumbled disgustedly, "I'm sure losing my grip." He jammed the sack of Bull Durham into his shirt pocket, then announced: "I'm not drawing on George Shaw."

Ira gaped in astonishment at Boyce. What was going on in that smart, bruised head?

Rube tossed a pebble at a scavenging field mouse. "I know what you boys are thinking," he said pensively. "That somebody the Rangers ran so long was just a tinhorn and not worth all the bronc dust. That it just took one taste of George Shaw's gun butt to make me call calf rope." The bandit was having trouble explaining himself to his equals. "It wasn't old George who laid down the law to me—'cause he ain't much law. 'Twas my wife."

The Rangers were silent. A man's relationship with his wife was his own business. You didn't pick him about it.

"Yeh," Rube continued. "After she put this bandage on, she told me I was gonna be a daddy."

"A daddy!" Ira repeated in amazement. Somehow a man who had robbed stagecoaches didn't stack up as a proper father.

Then, recovering himself: "That's good, Rube. Congratulations."

The outlaw had that sheepish grin of all expectant fathers. "Yep! Told me, too, that kid wasn't gonna live on the run like its folks. Said she was fed up to the craw on running. On running and on waiting, like she did those years I was in Mexico."

Rube Boyce rolled another smoke in hands now growing steady. He blew a slow, twining column of smoke from his nostrils before speaking again.

"You can't blame her. I reckon you can push a gun till you're dead. But you can push a woman just so far."

A Ranger asked tactfully, "Now that you're settling down, Rube, how do you intend to make a living for your family?"

Boyce removed the cigarette, holding it crosswise between two fingers. "Same way I've been doing lately—flipping the cards. She's not gee-hawing me on that so long as I don't play a six-shooter for trumps."

Smart gal, Ira thought. A woman, tired of running, might lure a maverick into a sort of working domesticity. But she didn't try to pen him up with a humdrum trade. Not unless she wanted to push him back into the brakes and the dry gulches.

"You know," Boyce observed, "a wife is like a bird mating. She'll fly fast with you for a long time. Then she starts picking up straws for a nest."

His eyes flickered slightly toward Ira. The Ranger caught the message emphasizing the pledge that the outlaw was giving with his lips: "If it hadn't been for you boys, George Shaw might have done me in last night. After you go, there won't be any shooting—not if George Shaw don't pick one to save his ugly face."

Ira arose from the campfire. "He won't, Rube. I'll see to that. You stay here till I get back."

Ira saddled his horse and rode into town. As he dismounted before the barred jailhouse, he was wondering what he would say to the local lawman. He tied the horse to a metal stake in front of the structure. He'd just tell him that he ought to call it square with a family man named Rube Boyce, like Ira had with a family man named Jim Epps.

Epps was a good citizen. Boyce never would be much more than a hobbled maverick. But even a maverick took care of its young, Ira reckoned.

*"If he should be an outlaw,
direct him by Thy mercy
into paths that are good."*

PRAYER ON DEVIL'S RIVER

Guns, according to the popular mythos, were the foundations of law and order in the Old West. That legend became furbished and distorted beyond all believable dimensions by lurid writers and overblown actors after the Colt forty-five six-shooter was nicknamed "The Peacemaker."

Ira Aten never subscribed to the dogma of the gun without limiting it by some very sharp qualifications. The West, of course, had gaudy star-flashers like Wild Bill Hickok who killed as frequently to show off as to enforce law. Some of these incarnated dime-novel "heroes" even drifted in and out of the Texas Rangers when times were rough and recruits were scarce.

Temperamentally and morally, Ira Aten had nothing in common with any of these men who, but for luck, might have been dodging posses instead of heading them. It was in no spirit of vainglorious boast that he stated he had "never been a saloon rounder," although his investigations often took him into booze joints and gambling dives. He was, and remained, the solid, substantial type of frontiersman who believed in strengthening the emerging institutions of a stabler society by conformities which balanced reason with rote.

He believed that one particular institution "made people do right more often than six-shooters kept them from doing wrong." Religion, in his mind, rated above both education and man made law.

Through religion, his preacher father had tried to persuade that prairie buccaneer, Sam Bass, into a deathbed repentance. Ira was never the pietist that his parent was. But those deeply instilled principles of his childhood were constantly reflected in his lenience toward wrongdoers when many lawmen of the other kind might have slain for a reward or to satisfy an ugly, self-conscious cannibalism.

And religion played its part in the most unusual arrest that he ever made during his entire career of riding for the law.

The year was 1886. The season was the usual hard winter of the vast Texas highland, covering a fifth of the state, called the Edwards Plateau. At the time Ira was assigned as sergeant of a Ranger detachment operating from Camp Wood in Edwards County, on the plateau's highest and most rugged summit.

Ranchers from Devil's River, a hundred miles away, came to this headquarters complaining of some unknown thief who was robbing their line camps of food and bedding while their cowhands and sheepherders were away performing their duties on the range. The offense, as such, was even more serious than horse stealing in this savage country. Most of the camps were seventy-five to a hundred miles from the nearest town, so that victims of the robberies might go hungry or freeze if their supplies kept disappearing.

Ira decided on a lone trip to search for the thief. Possibly the robber had henchmen. It would be useless, however, to try to take two or three extra men and pack mules through an area where roads were few and traveling so correspondingly difficult.

He mounted the horse that he rode all through his years of Ranger service. He carried along his compass to maintain his directions since even the keenly observant Seminole Indian scouts of the United States Army had been known to get hopelessly lost in that jungle of thorn and rock where he was heading. For bedding he carried a blanket, an ordinary slicker, and an oiled raincoat which could be used for a top covering in case of a downpour.

Ira set out westward along a very rough mountain road, paralleling the West Nueces River leading to the last camp

and watering place on the border of the Balcones Divide
between this stream and Devil's River. Beyond that point
was a nesting place for Mexican sheepherders. On the second day, around noon, Ira reached the sheep camp where
the Mexicans dined him on mutton and boiled pinto beans
flavored with chili peppers.

"You are making a big mistake to take such a trip, Mr.
Ranger," cautioned a herder who spoke English. "The next
water is fifty or sixty miles from here. You can die of thirst
unless you follow the deer up some canyon or strike some
temporary camp. And then"—the Mexican crossed himself—"you may find your self the guest of a *mal hombre*—
bad man."

Ira shrugged off the warning. He had come out to catch an
outlaw. From the shepherds he got as much information as
he could about the safest ways to cross the Divide—though
they could tell him very little. He spent the night at the
camp. Very early the next morning he started out again,
keeping a course that was almost due west.

Shortly Ira reached the point where the huge Divide inter-
sected the great Plateau. He saw no trails leading anywhere
after his careful horse had made a slow, cautious descent to
the lower altitude of the Divide. Immediately ahead loomed
piles of big flat limestone boulders that nature had piled
topsy-turvy in a weird jungle of rock.

Man and mount squeezed through grudging stone block-
ades. Their progress was maddeningly slow. Five hours later—and noon—it was when Ira guided his horse across the
last patch of rocky wasteland toward a stretch of smooth
ground bordered by runty mesquite trees.

He halted for the customary midday stop. His horse was
panting from thirst and from the tedious weariness of
crossing that inferno of rock. The Ranger looked vainly for
a spring or some piddling branch with a trickle of water, so
that the animal might drink.

Concerned for the pony, he began walking around, hoping
to find a barrel cactus whose stem could be tapped for its

liquid. He meant to let the stored water flow into his Stetson so that the horse might, at least, have a token drink from his hat.

Cactus of many species he saw growing in spiked, harsh patches, daring any intruder on two feet or four to enter. But not one solitary plant of the kind that would quench thirst. Ira then made what Texans call a dry camp—one without ample water. He took a drink from his own canteen, which he had filled at the sheepherders' headquarters, feeling ashamed as the horse neighed plaintively, seeing its master drink. Sitting on a rock, Ira ate his only food—a little jerked mutton that had been given him at the sheep camp. As he looked at the overtaxed horse and thought of still more unknown country to travel, he wondered if he hadn't used very poor judgment for a Ranger sergeant.

Acted like the romantic rookie he'd been three years before. Gone chasing off into this arid wilderness without even a pack mule to carry extra grub and water, thereby endangering the lives of his horse and himself. Flouted the well-meaning advice of the sheepherders because they were only poor, illiterate Mexicans while he was an officer of whatever law that existed in this raw wasteland. And all because he was so impatient to nab the sorry specimen who had been robbing the line camps, As if the thief wouldn't stay put as long as there were pickings—and until a certain impulsive sergeant had properly equipped himself for a chase.

Ira chewed angrily on the mutton. He was tempted to turn back to Camp Wood, equip himself with what he needed, then again take up the pursuit of that cussed robber. But could his horse stand up to a second trip across that torturous morass of stone and, afterward, to the hazardous climb up the Divide?

He looked at the animal. Flecks of dried blood stained its haunches from cuts inflicted by jagged edges of boulders. The answer was plainly no. Disgusted with himself, Ira climbed back into the saddle. The horse moved forward patiently. Its rider noticed tracks of timber wolves and mountain lions but no prints of boots or hoofs to indicate that men or horses had ever been here before.

Across lesser patches of rock and through scraggly groves of scrub timber tired man and weary horse continued what seemed verily a journey into nowhere. Toward evening he struck a long draw veering slightly to the southwest. Ira guessed hopefully that it was one of the many dry passages leading to Devil's River. Deer trails became numerous; Ira believed that they would guide him to water. The thought caused him to raise his canteen, which by now was nearly empty.

The horse was blowing hard. Its legs were treading the rough ground at a snail's pace. Ira feared that it might drop from exhaustion. Yet neither of them could stop till they found water—either the water of the river or that flowing in some spring frequented by the deer, now so thick and so ignorant of men that he rode through herds of them without their bounding away.

He stopped to let the pony rest and to shoot a couple of the bucks with his Winchester. As he took out his knife to skin the carcasses, he realized how foolish exhaustion had made him.

Without the salt that a pack mule would have carried he could not preserve the meat. Without the mule he could not carry it, for the horse was much too tired to bear any extra weight.

Ira kept coaxing the fagged animal down the draw. He struck a trail, which, though crooked, was smooth so that the going was easier on the horse. The path led him to a wide canyon. Ira noticed that the hills on each side were higher and more rugged than those that had bounded his course on this long, trying day.

Suddenly the horse stopped, standing as motionless as the stones it had braved. With the intuitive feeling of an outdoorsman for horses, Ira knew that his mount had reached its limit. All played out, it was. Nothing to do now but make another dry camp, one for overnight.

Ira slid from the saddle, feeling like a lump of stone himself. A night's rest would help both of them, he decided.

Even if they had no water. Come daylight, he might be able to trail the deer to their hidden watering place up this canyon or some other one.

Ira turned to glance at the brush ahead. He stood stock still in surprise when his eyes detected a gleam of light in the thick tangle.

Fireflies weren't making that glow. This wasn't the season for them. He knew he was seeing a campfire. He wondered if he had stumbled on the hideout of the thief he was seeking, or that of some other outlaw.

Ira eased up to the edge of the bushes, which were, fortunately, high enough to conceal him while he stayed in a half crouching position. Then he looked the spot over.

A small buckboard wagon was standing in a clearing. Two horses, hobbled for the night, were grazing nearby. Several water casks were around. The sight of them made Ira remember how thirsty his own poor mount was.

Beside the campfire sat an old gray-bearded fellow. He looked something like Santa Claus, with those whiskers flowing from cheek to belly. He was wearing a six-shooter strapped around his middle. A long-barreled rifle lay within easy reach on the ground.

Ira wondered if this venerable-looking stranger was his man. Nobody had ever caught a glimpse of the mysterious camp robber so there was no description to go by. The thief might be anything from a smart-aleck kid to a sin-steeped old rogue.

Ira studied the man's arsenal—the pistols he wore, the rifle lying handy. Just about everybody on the Texas border owned that kind of lethal hardware.

Those skillets Ira saw by the fire held out the hope of a hot meal. The casks spelled both a drink and a wash. Hunger and thirst made him decide to move in and ask to share the camp for the night.

He went back to his horse, remounted, and managed to get the animal in motion for those few remaining yards. Entering the camp on foot would be dangerous if the gray-

beard was a desperado. This would convince him that the
visitor was an officer prowling around. Riding in might give
him a different impression.

The old man grabbed his rifle, and stood tensely waiting
as he saw Ira ride through an opening in the bushes. It was
risky but he counted on bluffing the fellow out of a fight if
he seemed threatening.

"Howdy, friend," Ira said as he reined in beside the fire.
"Reckon I've got lost in these hills. I'm looking for a bunch
of steers that strayed from the Beaver Lake range over east
of here."

The bearded man hesitated, seeing that Ira's hand was
staying close to a revolver butt. "All right," he said at last
"Light down and I'll fix you some grub. There's water in the
barrels, and oats for your horse in the sack beside them."

The oldster eyed the younger man warily through a supper of fried venison, cold sour-dough biscuits, and hot coffee. As Ira ate, he noticed how close the hand of his host
stayed to that rifle.

"My suspicions about him grew stronger," Ira said later.
"But I made up my mind to make the best of things that
night, and to try to learn more about the fellow come morning."

Bedtime came after desultory talk between the two. The
guest spread his blankets to the left of the fire; the host
laid his to the right, then put a pistol on one side of the
pillow and the rifle on the other. Also prepared, Ira tucked
his Winchester alongside his right leg and laid his revolver
across his chest so he could wake up shooting if the occasion
demanded.

Ira had meant to let his host fall asleep first. But fatigue
got the better of him so that he dozed off in a few minutes.
An hour must have passed before he awoke with a start at
the sound of a voice.

Ira's first thought was someone, some partner in crime
of the old man's, had come sneaking in from the brush to
help take care of the uninvited intruder. He sat bolt upright,

his hands clutching his weapons. He wheeled around, pistol cocked and leveled, toward the opposite side of the campfire.

Then his finger froze on the trigger. A long second later, when he saw what was going on, he put his gun down. The old fellow was up and about, sure enough. But his hands were folded in prayer and not around a gun barrel. His talk was not to some partner in crime, but to God.

"O Lord," he was saying as he knelt by the wagon, "thank Thee for thy help and guidance. Thank Thee, too, for the game which Thou sendest me to sell for my needs."

Ira realized that he must be a professional hunter who used the wagon not only to haul his water from Devil's River, but also to carry deer and bear carcasses to the Rio Grande border settlements.

"Lead and bless the young wayfarer in camp." Now the prayer was for the visitor. "Thy servant trusts that he is a good man—" The old fellow's voice fell. The next words Ira heard made his face redder than the embers of that campfire. "But if he should be an outlaw, direct him by Thy mercy into paths that are good. Set his steps in ways pleasing to Thee so that he may no longer grieve his loved ones, whoever they are. This Thy servant humbly asks in Jesus's name. Amen."

"Amen," Ira echoed in a whisper. He lay back on his blankets and looked up at the sky. The old man returned to bed.

Then everything was quiet again.

"I felt ashamed of my fears and suspicions," Ira afterward told his Ranger comrades. "A man who could pray to God like that, out in the wilds with only the stars and the blue heavens above, could hardly be the low-down thief I was looking for. After listening to that petition, I kicked my rifle out of bed, laid my six-shooter at my side, closed my eyes, folded my hands across my breast, and said the little prayer I had learned at my mother's knee. I never slept better before—nor after."

Next morning Ira identified himself as a Texas Ranger in search of a camp robber. The old man proved to be Tom

Harris, native of Indiana, who had hunted buffalo till the great herds had vanished. Ira thanked him for his prayer. The two had a good laugh about mistaking each other for outlaws.

"I'm mixed up on my boundaries," Ira said. "What county am I in?"

"Kinney County," Harris answered.

Ira was pleased that he had not strayed from the county where the thief had often struck. He mounted his horse, now rested and spry as its rider.

"Camp robber..." Harris said reflectively. "Could be a saddle drifter named Ray Martin I've seen around here. He don't talk much about himself. I kind of think there's a lot of things he wouldn't want to let out."

"What does he look like?" Ira asked.

"Young, slim, light-complexioned. He's got a strong northern accent, so probably he's been in Texas just a short spell."

The old man paused for a second. "Try to take him without gunplay, Sergeant. So long as there's life, there's a chance that one day he'll start walking a straighter trail."

Ira had a strong hunch that Ray Martin was the man for whom he was carrying a John Doe warrant.

"I won't play rough unless he does," he promised Harris. He waved good-by to the old hunter and, on another hunch, headed his pony west to ward the Rio Grande.

A day later he picked up Martin, who had evidently spotted him beforehand, guessed he was an officer, and had fled toward the boundary stream, hoping to escape across it into Mexico. Martin made a full confession of the line-camp thefts, but Ira never revealed the details of the capture.

Never given to brag he simply recorded in his memoirs that he seized a frontier burglar "without much trouble." An interesting bit of Aten apocrypha declares that he outmaneuvered "the Yankee" by flashing a Bible which had purportedly been given him by Tom Harris. Martin—and the story has been told in many Texas revival meetings—was so flabbergasted by having a lawman produce such a "weapon" that he handed over his revolver without attempting resistance.

Whatever the truth of the legend, Ira took no chances when he had his prisoner remount a stolen bronc on a fifty-mile ride to Brackettville, the county seat. The hands of his prisoner were securely cuffed to the saddlehorn, leaving Martin just enough leeway to hold the bridle reins.

Captor and captive slept that night at another sheep camp, located on a rough country road leading to Brackettville. Before bedtime Ira said to the foreman of the herders: "I'll call you if this man gives me any trouble tonight."

But Martin slept resignedly beside the man who had caught him. Saddle blankets the two used for bedding, slickers for covering, and saddles for pillows, which "was the custom when nothing better was available." Ira cuffed his left hand to the prisoner's right. His pistol, his Winchester, and the key to the manacles he entrusted to the foreman who would have produced them immediately in case of emergency.

"Of course," Ira commented in his memoirs, "one doesn't sleep much the first few nights hooked up to a prisoner in such a manner. But when he goes on for a week or two, he gets used to it."

Ray Martin was delivered into the custody of the Kinney County sheriff a little more than twenty-four hours after being overtaken on a Texas bank of the Rio Grande. An alert officer, the sheriff dug through a pile of reward posters and found one with Martin's picture from Pennsylvania, where he was wanted on a charge far more serious than burglary. Texas authorities then surrendered jurisdiction to those of the prisoner's native state and Pennsylvania officers soon came to take him back under customary extradition processes.

Whether or not Martin genuinely repented of his sins, Ira never learned. But as he rode out after other fugitives, his conscience kept echoing that petition to the Creator he had heard invoked near that stream appropriately named for the Devil.

Next to his Ranger oath, nothing ever so shaped his fundamental character as a lawman or his total image of a swiftly
changing West.

Tom Harris, he reasoned, could have shot Ira Aten as a
suspected outlaw. Ira Aten, under a code commonly applied
in frontier justice, might have slain Ray Martin, indisputably
a wrongdoer.

A human being would have been annihilated without any
retribution of law, whoever shot whom. Ira Aten's bones
would have bleached under scorching summer suns and not
even a Ranger searching party might ever have found them
in this wild country. Or Ray Martin's extinction would have
gone unpunished after his slayer had made a perfunctory
appearance before a grand jury and been no-billed after testifying that the prisoner had "resisted arrest."

But maybe, Ira concluded, everybody was alive because
Tom Harris practiced the tenets of religion far from any
chapel. Believing his own life to be in danger, he had still
knelt and asked divine mercy for a suspicious-looking wanderer. Similarly, Preacher Aten had prayed for Sam Bass.

Then Ira began endorsing what the church members of
the West were always maintaining: that law officers were
sometimes in too much of a hurry about pulling triggers.
More and more church folk were using their votes and
their growing influence to eliminate professional gunmen
as wearers of the law badge. Even in communities where
they were not predominant, their counterchallenge, based
on stable social institutions, continued spreading to all the
bawdy, gunfire-christened frontier towns.

Ben Thompson hadn't lasted long as marshal of Austin
because the city's militant congregations had resented the
public safety's being in the keeping of a desperado. Any ar-
ticulate religious sentiment in Arizona had contributed to
the exiling of Wyatt Earp and the egregious Doc Holliday
after their celebrated massacre of some equally unsavory opponents at Tombstone. In a newly-organized Texas county
homesteading citizens had elected as their judge the notable

old buffalo hunter turned Campbellite preacher, Emmanuel Dubbs. Citizens of Chaves County, New Mexico, had turned down Pat Garrett for sheriff even if he had finished Billy the Kid while holding the sheriff's post in Lincoln County.

Throughout the West, Ira recognized, the transient, trigger-quick lawmen, offering their guns for hire, were beginning to fade with the era which had produced them. From this flamboyant element had come such as the Earps, and the Thompsons, wearing badges everywhere but having roots nowhere.

The church increasingly was becoming the main catalyst in the West's still unwon struggle against outlawry. Narrow and grimly uncompromising the little chapels might be in their attitudes toward all off-trail behavior, but the irreconcilable contrasts of frontier society afforded them scarcely any middle ground.

At the same time, the new type of civic consciousness created by religion brought forward new breeds of western officers who didn't retain lucrative illegal side lines after taking their oaths and donning their badges.

Except when it was absolutely necessary, Ira never again drew a pistol on anybody he arrested. "I figured," he commented once, "that something said in the Book might go for a lawman as well as an outlaw. He who lives by the sword, shall die by the sword. Guns hadn't been invented when the Lord made that remark. But I guess he meant it to cover them, too."

"The only prisoner I ever let get away."

BEAT TO THE DRAW

Every Texas Ranger had to meet very specific requirements of courage, endurance, and above-average marksmanship. Beyond that, his public rating depended pretty much on the personality make-up of the man himself.

Most Rangers were courteous, reasonable, and outgoing, like the majority of Westerners. They mirrored the best levels of an evolving society dependent for collective survival on unusually broad standards of give and take. These men knew that their job was not to create trouble but to quell it.

But there was a minority who were literal cameos of that society in all its vestiges of hardness and backwardness. They were ones whose only respect was for power—whether power embodied in their six-shooters or power symbolized by the dollar. Suspicion, arrogance, contempt for little people and racial minorities—such were the dominant character traits of these men. Their essential hostilities were, in fact, magnified by the commissions they carried. Sometimes their galling behavior touched off scandals casting unfair reflections upon the entire corps.

Ira Aten's humaneness and spirit of moderation made him one of the most popular men who have ever served on the gallant force. His name was never mentioned contemptuously in the Texas legislative halls when the question of Ranger appropriations was being debated. No legislative committee ever raised issues about his official behavior. Both of the governors under whom he served would have publicly vouched for his competence and his personal integrity.

Only veteran and unredeemable wrongdoers despised him for being an officer of the law. Many lesser offenders, whom

he routed to the penitentiary, felt that they were alive because Ira Aten was the Ranger who had arrested them. Always, as an elderly reformed horse thief told a Texas writer,
"Aten talked out something with you instead of putting you
on a spot where pride made you want to shoot it out. Many
offenders, cherishing a six-shooter spite against Rangers
as opponents, would wind up convinced by Ira that it was
cheaper to pay a debt to justice than live like hunted coyotes
in the brush."

Where leniency was merited by some extenuating circumstance, Ira never hesitated to ask it for a defendant who
had "come clean" with the court. As his knowledge of law
expanded from his police work, so did his consciousness of
how legal codes themselves should be implemented.

After his moving experience on Devil's River, he kept insisting that the dead letter of the law only made for more
dead men. Society, he felt, protected itself, far more than it
did law breakers, by tempering justice with mercy.

*Of the many prisoners I handled—you will never find one
man to say I mistreated him.* This is one of the very few brags
that slipped into Ira's memoirs. *A prisoner, being brought in
by me, ate out of the same frying pan, drank coffee out of the
same pot, and water from the same canteen as long as there
was a drop, whether this water came from a well, a babbling
brook, or a mudhole. He [the prisoner] would sleep in the
same bed, and be subject to the same conditions as myself.*

Even when arresting a known bad man, Ira would try
to be as considerate as possible—consideration being exercised through initial firmness on the part of the officer.
Rangers generally felt that a confirmed criminal "would be
unnerved and easy to handle—if approached in a determined way." Hard talk, too, had often to be a part of the
approach. A favorite salutation of theirs was "If you bat an
eye, I'll blow a hole through you big enough for a dog to
crawl through."

This greeting generally squelched any determination to
put up resistance on the part of a man being apprehend

ed. "Of course," Ira commented wryly, "such language, when used, had to be meant, and couldn't be said with a smile."

At the same time Ira was far from being a soft-head. He was proud of having never "really mistreated" a really bad actor, but he carried the customary leg irons to shackle prisoners "who wouldn't come in like gentlemen." If an officer gave a confirmed desperado the slightest chance of escape, the fellow was bound to run or fight. Ira, with his apt knowledge of criminal character, took necessary precautions to see that they did neither.

Actually only one law dodger ever "got the drop" on him during his many years as an officer. That man was, in Ira's chronology, "the only prisoner I ever let get away."

Ira had never meant even to be bothered about this offender who spoiled his record of "no escapes." With a Ranger patrol, he had been scouting for two fugitives believed to be holed up somewhere within a forty-mile radius of Eagle Pass. Before he left, the sheriff there had told him of another man named Rex Lawson, who was at large on a misdemeanor charge in the same area.

"Pick him up, Ira, if it's handy for you," the sheriff had requested.

After a search of a day or two along the Rio Grande, the Rangers spotted the two felons on a ranch overlooking that stream. The pair surrendered readily. The detail of officers started back toward Eagle Pass with them the next morning, intending to turn them over to the sheriff.

Captors and captives had traveled only a few miles when Ira remembered that Lawson, the petty culprit named by the sheriff, was reported as having been seen at a camp of migrants a short distance away. Ordinarily, Rangers didn't care to be involved in misdemeanor cases, which could generally be handled by the greenest deputy constable, but the sheriff involved was a friend and Ira wanted to oblige him.

"Ride on with these fellows," Ira directed the Rangers. "I'll pick up Lawson, then meet you at the Valdez ranch, ten miles ahead."

The morning was still early when he rode into the migrant camp. Three people whom he immediately recognized were sitting at a table—a middle-aged woman called Clara Carter, her younger son, Sammie, who was about sixteen, and Rex Lawson, the petty-offender fugitive. Mrs. Carter's eldest son, Eli, was unavoidably absent, being on the run from Rangers who wanted him for horse stealing.

The woman jumped up from the table when Ira halted his pony near the arbor. "I done told you Eli ain't here," she shrilled. "You've already been here three times lookin' for him."

"I'm not looking for Eli right now," Ira answered. "Fact is, my business here doesn't amount to very much."

She changed her tune. "Light down, Mr. Aten. You're just in time for breakfast."

Since Ira's meal had been scanty, he accepted. He dismounted, tied his horse to a tree, and took a seat next to Rex Lawson, who was sitting at the head of the table. Lawson, he noticed, was very nervous and kept glancing toward a canvas tent that housed this sorry clan, subsisting by casual labor and casual thievery.

Ira guessed that Lawson's weapons were inside the tent, but had no intention of letting him make a dash to claim them. As he drank coffee and ate hot corn-meal mush, he made small talk with Clara Carter and Sammie, sitting across the table from him. Rex Lawson, saying nothing, worried at his mush.

Ira turned and spoke mildly. "Lawson, there's a little charge against you up at Eagle Pass. Maybe you'd better come along with me and straighten things out."

"All right," the migrant answered tersely. Ira noticed that the man was getting more jittery; he would probably break down before a justice of the peace, whine for mercy, then passively accept any sentence handed out to him.

Probably, Ira thought, Lawson had already done more than one stretch in more than one jail for such minor offenses as raiding hen roosts or stealing sacks of meal from country grocery stores. He hoped he wouldn't be pestered again with such jacklegs.

Lawson gulped down the last mouthful of mush, got up from the table, went to a stove behind the woman, and rolled a cigarette. Ira watched him to see that he didn't bolt for the tent. Satisfied that the migrant would continue behaving, the Ranger poured a very hot cup of coffee, Texas fashion, into a saucer to cool it off.

He took a sip from the saucer. For one second it covered both his eyes. When he lowered it a rifle was pointing at him. The Ranger dropped the saucer. Behind the gun stood Rex Lawson. He was looking Ira straight in the eye.

Ira's mind worked quickly. He was just about to duck under the table into the woman's lap to have her between him and this surprising vagabond. Then he meant, with an upward shot, to wound Lawson in the hand and force him to drop the rifle.

But the migrant seemed to read his mind. "Wait, Aten," he said curtly. "I don't want to kill anyone. All I want is to get away."

Ira sighed, feeling foolish for underestimating the man. "All right, Lawson. You have the best chance in the world to get away."

The fellow slowly backed off into the brush, keeping Ira covered until he was out of sight. Then Ira stood up, feeling like an eagle whose wings have been clipped. He walked past the stove to a post of the arbor. Here, evidently, the gun had been parked where he couldn't see it. Possibly Lawson's repeated glances at the tent had been a ruse to throw him off the track.

Ira spoke angrily to the woman. "Clara, who is this man? Where's he from and how long has he been around?"

Clara Carter's answer did not impress the Ranger. "Don't know much about him, Mr. Aten. He's just somebody who stopped by. I gave him a bite of vittles just like I done for you."

Ira looked angrily toward the tent. "Reckon you also bedded him as well as fed him, Clara. So who is he?"

The woman's face reddened. These tribes of roamers were also casual sexually. Gossip claimed that half their children were born from caperings under the wagon covers.

"Don't know much about Mr. Lawson," she repeated testily. "He ambled by—now he's ambled on."

Ira raged inwardly; this crude woman was taunting him. *Want Lawson? Go find him.* So she was saying, though not in plain words. She'd been equally evasive—and as subtly sarcastic—whenever Rangers had come here inquiring after her horse-stealing older son.

A mortified Ranger lifted his Stetson to bid his hostess a gentlemanly good-by. In Texas, you tipped your hat to every woman except those who openly sinned for fun or hire. Ira rode off to join the waiting patrol at the Valdez ranch. For a couple of days he submitted good-naturedly to the hurrahing of his brother officers because he'd let a no-count wagon scamp like Rex Lawson get the drop and then get away.

Underneath the badgering Ira felt a nagging loss of face. He could have forgiven himself had the escapee been some man worth tangling with. But to have been outdrawn and outfoxed by a cheap ne'er-do-well! That rubbed him rawer than a saddle without a pad would have rubbed his pony.

But was Rex Lawson just a third-rate jailbird? The question started plaguing Ira after the joshing had died down. Why should a man, charged with so trivial an offense, have made such a calculated and dramatic break? A verdict of guilty would have probably cost the runaway no more than thirty days of compulsory labor on the Maverick County roads.

Adding it all up, Ira got no answers that made sense. Except one that scorched a Ranger's pride: that he'd maybe underestimated a man who looked and dressed like a bummy field hand.

On a day that was rare because Rio Grande outlaws were giving him a breath of rest, Ira dropped into the Maverick County courthouse. There he spoke to his friend, the sheriff.

"Got any record on that fellow, Lawson, who skipped out?"

The sheriff laughed. "Lawson's really mud in your craw, ain't he, son? When you've been lawin' thirty years like me, one little tinhorn more or less won't matter. You can't catch 'em all."

Ira kept hold of his patience. "I'd still like to find out if Lawson has a record, Sheriff."

The sheriff bit into a plug of tobacco. "Nope. No record, boy. That pollywog is a stranger in this county."

Ira thumbed through a pile of "wanted" circulars lying on the sheriff's desk. "You won't find Lawson's mug on any of them," he was assured. "He's not big enough to get his picture took."

The younger officer retained his misgivings. Through Ranger channels he had descriptions of Lawson sent, with requests for cooperation, to federal and local authorities in all the states and territories bordering Texas. A Ranger who was a Texas Mexican translated the data into Spanish and delivered it to the Rurales—Mexico's equivalent of the Rangers—across the Rio Grande.

If Lawson was a man with a rep, Ira reasoned, he had made for the Texas border so he could jump across to Mexico in case he got found out. If he was just a nobody with sticky fingers, the reports would show it.

Impatiently, Ira waited for replies to his query about the floater. Arkansas, Louisiana, and New Mexico had no files on the missing Lawson. In Mexico, the Rurales—always zealous when pursuing gringo wrongdoers—beat miles of chaparral trying to spot him. Had he been in their country, they probably would have hanged him summarily after giving him a swig of tequila, which was often their way of dealing with fugitives from the north side of the river.

Then one day there came a communication from a federal officer in Indian Territory. Ira was as happy as a kid at Christmastime when he read it.

The absent Mr. Lawson was widely, if not creditably, known in the Territory. There he had made an impressive record for speed, having outrun the Choctaw militia, the high sheriff of the Cherokee Nation, and several frustrated posses of United States deputy marshals. There were three murder charges outstanding against him. The same information listed the also-missing horse thief, Eli Carter, as Lawson's trigger partner.

Ira slapped his hand excitedly on his thigh. "By golly, we'll get that so-and-so now!" he told Captain Jones as they conferred in the headquarters tent at Eagle Pass. "Nab Eli Carter, and you'll pull in Rex Lawson, too."

Captain Jones quietly agreed. "Lawson probably hit the border to link up with Carter in some kind of horse-stealing deal with Mexicans across the river. But when he got here, he found that we'd made Carter jump and was scared to death that everything would come down around him if he surrendered to you on that misdemeanor charge."

Thoroughly, skillfully, Ira set about to vindicate a Ranger tradition and redeem his own pride. His first step was to see what could be wrung out of Clara Carter.

The woman and her younger son had vanished on the day after Ira's scrape with Rex Lawson. Ira knew, however, that the Carters had a fixed range over which they prowled. It covered seven or eight Texas counties, with San Antonio as the eastern pivot and Eagle Pass as the southern.

Every one of the sheriffs of these counties knew the sleazy family. Almost all of them had boarded Eli in his jail at one time or another. It was no trouble at all, after they'd been alerted, for one of these officers to grab Clara Carter and Sammie.

The sheriff, who knew them best, put the mother through the most relentless grilling she'd ever had to face. Spouting oaths, she denied knowing where either Eli or Rex Lawson was. Finally the sheriff threatened to commit her for life to the insane asylum in Austin. Clara asked for a box of snuff, took a dip, and talked.

Her story didn't quite confirm the suppositions of Captain Jones.

Eli, she said, had "high-tailed" it out of Indian Territory when persistent lawman attention had given him unpleasant forebodings of the rope. Lawson, by her account, had been making a forced journey out of the Territory at approximately the same time. Their trails had crossed, and the horse thief had asked the killer to take a "message" to his mother camped on the Rio Grande.

"Where is Lawson now?" the officer asked Clara Carter.

"New Mexico, I reckon," the woman replied after sulking a minute. "That's where he was meanin' to ride. It's closer than Arkansas or Louisiana—and no goddamn sheriff's got anything on him there."

Ira didn't give a hang about Eli Carter, but he felt a personal responsibility to bring in Lawson since he had let the murderer escape by failing to size him up correctly. He was preparing to go to New Mexico to track down his man when Captain Jones decided otherwise.

"Ira," the captain said, "we have to find Lawson and turn him over to the marshals of Indian Territory where he committed the real crimes." But he wouldn't let Aten go because Ira was the main prosecution witness—having been the arresting officer—in several cases that were being tried in different Texas counties.

Ira's disappointment was keen. But orders were orders—and lack of his testimony in court might result in setting loose a lot of vermin for the Rangers to run down again. So he requested Captain Jones to send his close comrade, C. W. Giffin, after Lawson.

Giffin went—and came back. Rex Lawson didn't. The Ranger "got his man" too literally, by shooting him. And, Ira wrote, "that was never quite satisfactory to me."

Lawson had humbled him and brought ridicule on him in the force. Killer he had been. Still, Ira felt, he would have been able to bring him back alive.

Years later Ira was asked how he would have acted in Giffin's place.

"I talked Lawson out of shooting me once when he had me at his mercy," the lawman replied thoughtfully. "I would have probably delivered him to the nearest New Mexico sheriff for extradition to Indian Territory. We had no felony counts against him in Texas and that misdemeanor charge wouldn't have been worth the trouble of bringing him back. Maybe Lawson's behavior might have been different if I'd been steering him toward a Territory gallows. Still, I'd have tried—tried the tongue before the trigger."

*"One bale of barb spelled
more trouble in Texas than any
ten outfits of bad hombres."*

BORN TO BUST BARB

Ira had served three years as a Texas Ranger. Adherence
to discipline and routine had earned him rapid promotion
from private to corporal, from corporal to sergeant. He had,
long since, put away those boyish fantasies of cleaning up
every tough town and locking up every bad man.

Except for occasional flare-ups of his old individualism, he
functioned with precision and intelligence as part of Texas's
only state-wide law-enforcement body. He was alert and re-
sourceful. He had shown that he could combine obedience
to orders with thoroughness and mature judgment in exe-
cuting them.

He had learned through shrewd, analytical observation
the characteristic habits of those who committed the crimes
common to that period. Train boarders, stagecoach robbers,
horse thieves—each group had its own occupational methods and left clues stemming from the nature of its particular "craft." Ira's mind became a broad catalogue of criminal
habits. Because he could mix so readily with any sort of people while keeping his own identity concealed, he was able to
move around handily and accumulate evidence that would
stand up in the loosely functioning Texas courts.

State authorities in Austin read his colorful reports and
saw his possibilities as a Ranger detective. When they were
confronted with a dangerous new type of outlawry, they
chose him to deliver law's first major counter-challenge.
During the summer of 1886 Ira was ordered to Austin for
special-duty assignment from the adjutant general. That official sat him down for a closed-door conference when he
got there.

"Sergeant Aten, you've heard of the fence cuttings going on all over the state?"

Ira nodded. Fence slashings had been rampant since the Supersalesman, John Warne Gates, had introduced the highly effective, and controversial, barbed wire to Texas eleven years before. Cowhands were being thrown out of jobs because fewer men were needed to handle cattle safely enclosed by fences. Some ranchers and farmers were retaliating with wire clippers and claw hammers to rip down the hated barriers that excluded their hungry stock from what had been traditionally open-range pastures.

The young Ranger replied that he had. He knew about the fence wars that were flaring up from Houston to El Paso. But it was his impression that the county sheriffs were handling them pretty well.

The adjutant general looked grave. "Up to now sheriffs and local constables have kept things under fair control—unless they owed their jobs to the votes of the rippers. But the situation is getting very much worse; the Rangers have to step in."

Ira had only one question. "What do you wish me to do, sir?"

He was instructed to go to Lampasas County. A great many fences had been cut on a large ranch there, as well as other fences in nearby counties. Ira was to find out if the same gang was doing it all and to get evidence against as many as he could. A conviction or two, brought about by the Texas Rangers, might put the fear of God into other fence cutters operating over the State.

A day later Ira entered Lampasas County, eighty miles west of Austin in the heart of the central Texas hill country. He talked with the rancher who had been the victim of the wire cutters, warning the man not to tell any neighbors that a Ranger was working on the case.

Then he went to Lampasas town, the county seat, and dropped word around that he was another broke cowboy retired by barb. Nobody questioned his story. Within a matter of hours he had become intimate with various citizens who despised fences and anybody unneighborly enough to put them up. He soon developed leads that implicated two teen-age youths and arrested them easily. They confessed to him that they had committed the crime, more for "notoriety" than anything else.

"Well, boys, I'm sorry for you," Ira said as he delivered them into the custody of the Lampasas County sheriff. "But fence cutting has to stop. And if it's notoriety you want, you're going to get plenty of it—by standing trial over there in that courthouse."

The case was brought to a quick hearing before a Texas district judge named Blackburn whose briefs obviously contained none for barbed wire. Ira, called to the witness stand in an obviously unpopular proceeding, was baited by the defense attorney.

"Ranger Aten," the lawyer remarked caustically, "you came to this county and deceived its good citizens by telling them you were a cowpuncher unemployed because of the fences and so forth. So didn't you tell a lot of lies while you were trying to catch these boys?"

Ira looked at the jury of Lampasas County men and then at the defendants, sitting by the attorney at a table near the witness chair. "Yes, sir," he admitted reluctantly, "I guess I did."

The lawyer turned toward the jury with a triumphant smirk that riled Ira. "Now tell me, Ranger," he asked mockingly, "are you still telling lies?"

Ira sprang from the chair. He shook his fist at the attorney and roared: "I want you to understand, sir, that there is a big difference between swearing to a lie and telling a lie to catch a couple of damned rascals!"

He stepped down from the stand and rushed toward the defense table, intending to leap across it and collar the man who had insulted him.

Judge Blackburn pounded the gavel loudly and shouted: "Ranger Aten, you're out of order!"

Ira halted, glared at the attorney, and turned to face the court. Judge Blackburn spoke to the district clerk sitting below the bench.

"Mr. Clerk, I fine this witness fifty dollars for contempt."

Ira swallowed hard. "Your Honor," he said, "I beg your pardon and ask you to cancel that fine."

The judge shook a bald angry head. "As a Ranger, you're an officer of this court. Such conduct from an officer cannot be overlooked."

Ira's misconduct, though provoked, probably contributed to the leniency shown the fence cutters by the jury. The boys got off with light sentences. Their captor left, smarting over the fifty-dollar fine, a big bite from a Ranger's small pay.

Disgusted, Ira hoped that he would never be sent out again on such a thankless task. But he had no sooner gotten out of the Lampasas County affair than he was again summoned to Austin by the adjutant general—and once more assigned to run down fence cutters.

This assignment involved risks of life and limb he hadn't been required to face while rounding up a couple of mischievous youngsters. The work required would have taxed the mettle of a veteran range detective such as Charlie Siringo or John Poe. The section was the Jim Ned area of Brown County, once a main hunting ground of the Comanche Indians and next door to McCulloch County, where Ira had helped erase the maverick brands.

Fence cutting had been rampant for several years in this locality, lying between a seventy-mile-long stream called Jim Ned Creek and a wide lake with sinister associations named Pecan Bayou. Several people had been shot in a continuing vendetta between fence raisers and fence rippers. Many men on each side were openly carrying arms and gunning for each other. Cattle stealing and horse stealing were natural results of a conflict that county officials were giving the hands-off treatment. A dozen or so detectives had been sent in at various times by associations of stockmen. None of them had produced any evidence on which prosecution could be based. Several had barely escaped with their lives.

"The people around Jim Ned are very suspicious of every stranger," the adjutant general told Ira, "So you'll have to be more careful—and a lot smarter—than any other investigator who's ever nosed into their doings. You are to contact the fence rippers and do whatever they ask you to do so that you can get their confidence. Drop me a line whenever you can—but mail nothing out of Brown County."

When Ira left Austin he traveled by train across the Texas hills to Coleman, thirty miles west of Brownwood, the Brown County seat. At Coleman he bought a pony and saddle. Then, wearing a pair of batttered old chaps, he set out for Jim Ned settlement, sixteen miles north of Brownwood. Since he was still in his early twenties, he decided to pose as a wandering range kid, who had been kicked around from pillar to post and wasn't much interested in anything—not even work. At the Jim Ned general store he parried suspicious questions by saying that his name was Bob Benton and that he had started roving after the death of his parents.

The story aroused some sympathy, though most residents were still chary of the ragged young stranger. For several nights Ira slept in haystacks or wherever he could find shelter. Then one afternoon a man named Jim Worsham approached him at the store.

"Why don't you get a job, boy?" Worsham asked. "You can't be a saddle tramp for the rest of your life."

Ira answered, "Don't seem to be no jobs, mister. Least, nobody has offered me one."

Worsham gave Ira a keen second look, then said hesitantly, "Well, son, I ain't got much work to do on my little ranch and can't pay you much. But if you want, you can go home with me and take whatever I can afford."

Ira accepted, concealing his exultation. As a hired hand he would have an excuse for staying in the community with its festering hostility toward outsiders. He knew he would have to play his role very skilfully: one slip might land him at the bottom of Jim Ned Creek—where dead men, weighted down with stones, were still being found as late as 1914.

His employer still seemed a little suspicious as he began his duties. Pretending not to notice, Ira chopped wood, milked cows, fed chickens and pigs, conducting himself in general as just a handy boy around the ranch. Worsham's wife plainly sympathized with the "orphaned" saddle tramp, since the couple had no sons or daughters of their own. Taking advantage of this, Ira helped the woman with her chores, drawing bucketfuls of water for her wash tub, sometimes grabbing a broom and sweeping the house to relieve her of the labor.

Ira's gawky gallantry pleased the rancher. The man's fears were quieted and he soon became friendly. When neighbors called, the hired hand didn't force himself into their company and seemed to have no interest in anything they said. Often, as he was doing his work outside the house, he could hear visitors discussing him pro and con. Some believed that he was nobody but a rambling simpleton. Others argued that, as an outsider, he was potentially dangerous and ought to be "taken care of"—Ira interpreted this, no doubt correctly, as "killed"—or, at the least, run out of the country.

Through the usual casual introductions, "Bob Benton" had learned—and memorized—the names of all the rancher's friends. In every instance, those who meant him harm were self-revealed fence cutters. Without ever betraying himself by one question or one nervous gesture, the drifter listened to them brag of their crimes. Stowed in his head were the details of every ripping and-rustling spree they so proudly remembered.

But he kept wondering whom they were talking about when they kept referring to somebody designated only as "the Boss." Whoever the Boss was, they were careful to protect his identity. Ira did no fishing to find out. Time would provide the answer if he kept ears peeled and lips locked.

Eventually, Jim Worsham stopped making any bones about his side trade. It was then that Ira realized, to his deep satisfaction, that by fantastic good luck he had landed right under the roof of a leading figure in Texas's most destructive ring of fence cutters.

Night after night the hired hand watched Jim Worsham ride away, saddlebags bulging with clippers to cut wire strands and pliers to yank fence nails. A bleeding quarter of fresh beef would be tied behind the saddle when its owner returned. Next day some of the gang might show up to ask Worsham jokingly "if the meat tasted like wire." Then there would be more brag about the steers they had slaughtered and the fences they had cut to get at them the night before.

They talked, too, about the Boss—the Boss had ordered this or forbidden that. Ira kept hoping that they would let their leader's real name slip. If they did, then his stay here might be shortened. The more they mentioned their headman, the more curious Ira became, while maintaining his pose of simple-minded indifference.

Ira realized that he was becoming increasingly accepted by the community, although there were some who still believed him to be "no good." He was asked to attend neighborhood square dances and now and then some girl tried to "spark" him when he went shopping for Mrs. Worsham at the general store. He never inquired for any mail but that of his employer's at the post office. This confirmed, to the residents, his original tale of being a wanderer without family or connections.

One night, as Ira lay on his cot in the attic of the ranch house, he overheard a heated argument about whether he should be taken into the gang. This was just what he had been waiting for ever since arriving in Jim Ned. He got up and posted himself behind the attic door, straining his ears to catch every word.

The debate was long and loud. Some of the men stoutly and profanely maintained that all "outsiders" should be excluded. Then Ira heard the voice of his employer ending the argument.

"That kid ain't no outsider any more. He's good to my wife—he does anything I tell him to do without no sass. We need another man to skin—and if I hand him a knife, he'll skin."

Ira went back to bed, knowing that he was in. That he was about to be accepted as a member of one of the toughest bands of desperadoes that the cattle country had ever known should have given him pause. Ira felt only satisfaction.

At sundown one evening thereafter, a group of the wire cutters rode up to the ranch. One dismounted and entered the house, where Ira was sitting with the Worshams. The fellow greeted the couple, then spoke to the hired hand.

"Howdy, boy. Wanta go for a hoss ride tonight?"

Ira looked at Jim Worsham, as if asking permission. Worsham said, "Come along, son. I need your help on something."

He walked outside with Worsham and the other man to the spot where the gang sat waiting in their saddles. He mounted a good horse they had brought along for him. One man handed him a skinning knife; another tossed him a pair of clippers.

The band rode down a series of dim roads leading from Jim Worsham's unfenced ranch to a larger enclosed one. There Ira Aten, a Texas Ranger, became a thief in order to catch thieves.

At Jim Worsham's command the fence cutters dismounted and went to work. Ira seized his clippers and cut a long strand of wire, which fell to the ground. Others also cut or pulled lengths of wire from posts with hammers and pliers, cursing when the barb retaliated with cuts and scratches.

Twenty yards of the fence came down. The men got back into saddle and rode toward a herd of cattle. Lassos swung, six shooters roared. Steers went down, bleeding.

Cattle escaping the slaughter were sent scattering in all directions across the ripped-down fence so that their owner would have plenty of trouble rounding them up. Ira dismounted.

"Go over there and help the boys skin," Jim Worsham directed.

"Yes, sir," Ira answered humbly and drew his knife to begin the job of slicing the hide off a carcass. At that moment a man he hadn't seen before rode a horse across the slashed wire.

Ira glanced up. His heart nearly stopped beating. In the moonlight he saw something bright gleaming from the man's chest. It was a badge.

Here was an officer, Ira thought, who had caught up with this crowd and come to have it out with them. It would tip Ira's hand to a showdown he didn't want, but when he drew on this outfit, Ira would back him and let them know who he was. They were in for quite a surprise!

Then the rest of the bunch saw the lawman. Ira expected them to shoot or run. What did happen made his jaw drop and the knife slide from his hand.

"Hello, Boss," Jim Worsham called out to the man with the star. Then Worsham beckoned to the saddle bum.

"Hey, Bob Benton, come over and shake hands with our headman."

Ira always wondered how he got through that meeting without betraying himself. But it made known to him the identity of the mysterious Boss of the Brown County fence cutters: Constable Buck Harlow of Jim Ned precinct.

Ira had seen Harlow often around the store and post office but had said little to the officer, not wanting even another lawman to know who he actually was. Small wonder the county had been so torn by plunder and depredation, with the leader of the outlaws a turncoat lawman!

After the raid, Ira decided to bring his investigation to a speedy finish. He knew that he might go on fooling the majority of Buck Harlow's henchmen, but the renegade constable looked far too sharp to be hoodwinked indefinitely.

Next evening after supper Ira pleaded weariness to Mrs. Worsham as an excuse not to sit and listen to the hymns that she played on a squeaky parlor organ. He went to his room in the attic, then wrote down the names of known fence cutters, with Constable Buck Harlow heading the list. He drew a rough chart showing the ranches where the fences had been ripped. Before blowing out the kerosene lamp, he put the data in a pair of old workshoes and hid them in the eaves of the attic till he could figure out his next move.

That night he slept little as he tried to figure a way of getting his evidence, in the shortest possible time, to the adjutant general at Austin. His explicit instructions had been not to mail anything from Brown County. Sending it from the Jim Ned post office would probably be signing his own warrant of sudden death, for Ira had no doubt that Harlow had every piece of outgoing mail scrutinized. Anything addressed to the capital city would be cause for suspicion, and a letter directed to the principal commander of the Texas Rangers would be opened and read.

Although Ira now had the clinching evidence in hand, he could not think of trying to leave the county in a fast lope. That would be a fatal move, for both Worsham and Harlow would quickly draw the correct conclusions about his riding out after just one raid undertaken as an apprentice of the ring. Men on fast horses would be started immediately in determined pursuit.

He wouldn't get to the county line, Ira told himself. They would butcher him like one of those steers, then pitch him into Jim Ned Creek.

At 5 A.M. Ira awoke from a restless sleep to begin the customary labors of a hired hand. He split wood into kindling and larger stove sticks, carried dripping buckets of water from the well into the house, then shucked ears of corn before pitching them into the feed trough for Jim Worsham's horses. Work generally made him eat a big breakfast but this morning he only picked at the fatback and fried eggs as he joined the couple for the meal.

Because he wanted to be completely alone, he begged off from some chore that would have meant being with Worsham and went off to weed the vegetable garden behind the house. Midmorning it was when his employer's wife approached him, holding an empty bucket that had once contained sorghum molasses bought from the general store.

"Bob," she asked, "would you mind pickin' me a mess of Okra for dinner?"

Ira took the pail from her, but did not immediately begin snapping off pods of okra. He sensed that she wanted to talk, and this was her excuse.

"Yes, ma'am," he answered. "But I'll have to go up to my room and get my gloves or the prickles on that okra will sting my hands like netttles."

Mrs. Worsham looked at him in a worried way. "No big hurry, Bob, okra don't take long to cook." She took a tin box of snuff from her apron pocket and whiffed some of it into her nostrils.

"I noticed you didn't make out your meal at breakfast. I sure hope your feet ain't started itchin' to leave Jim Ned."

Ira answered her in the vernacular of West Texas: "No, ma'am, I ain't got nothin' to complain about. Jim Ned folks have been mighty good to me—'specially you and Mr. Worsham."

The gaunt woman looked relieved. "I'm proud you feel that way, son. It didn't please the good Lord to bless me and my old man with young-uns. But we look on you as if you was our own boy."

Ira, touched even while appreciating the irony of it all, could find no reply.

Mrs. Worsham's voice was motherly and compassionate. "Jim and I want you to know that you'll never have to be on the road again. You got a home with us so long as we got a crust to share. Now, I'm gonna go and kill one o' them yaller-legged pullets for your dinner."

Ira stood watching her lean figure, topped by the inevitable sunbonnet, torn between the maternal projections of this lonely, childless woman and his sworn duties as an undercover man for the law. Mrs. Worsham couldn't help her husband's trade and couldn't do anything about it. Women had to go along with whatever their menfolks did—good or bad. And Jim Worsham had to go along with Buck Harlow because that was the way things were set up around here.

Ira was swept by a wave of blind hatred toward the constable who had disgraced a lawman's badge. Harlow was using his star to show his contempt for law. The poor suckers who rode and raided with him thought they were being protected because he wore it. They were little people, caught between push and shove, because of the change-over from free range to closed range. They ought to be shown lenience in a court—but that damned sidewinder ought to be strung up!

At dinner Ira managed to do justice to the chicken, forcing himself to down the big helpings that Mrs. Worsham kept heaping on his plate.

"Thank you, ma'am," he said when he finally had to refuse still another helping. He excused himself: he had to go mix some worm medicine for that heifer that was sick. As Ira prepared the remedy, his conscience began troubling him again. He might be dead right now if Jim Worsham hadn't spoken up for him. There were men around here mean enough to kill a stranger just for being a stranger. And it was going to be mighty tough on Mrs. Worsham when she found out the boy she'd been mammying was a Texas Ranger out to lock up her husband.

It was late afternoon before Ira had resolved this most acute conflict of his life. He'd ask the judge to go easy on Jim Worsham, he decided after much mulling. When the trial came up, he'd tell the court that he ripped and stole, but didn't kill or maim. It was the least he could do as a man, and as an officer of the law.

During the next week or so Ira went on several more cutting and raiding parties, obeying orders but managing to avoid more than the minimum of conversation with Buck Harlow, the Boss. Each sortie with clippers made him more uneasy.

If this gang wasn't smashed soon, it might extend its operations all over West Texas. Harlow was foxy enough, and greedy enough, to see to that. Already fences were being cut in Coleman County, just over the line, and Ira suspected that Harlow probably had a hand in it.

Ira was careful to show no more restlessness before the Worshams. Kindly Mrs. Worsham would gossip worriedly to the neighbor women if he let her see his impatience to leave. And that might revive the suspicions of the men who at first had wanted his neck for being an outlander.

Ira discarded plan after plan to vanish as being both unsafe and impractical. His concern grew when he heard that Buck Harlow was talking of running for sheriff of Brown County in the next election.

Victory for this strutting renegade would place the county's thousand square miles of hills and prairies under the control of a well-organized outlaw combine. Swaggering wire rippers would become Harlow's deputy sheriffs. They would utilize badges as well as their tools to starve out and run out law-abiding ranchers and farmers. Brownwood would become a center of thievery and hell raising, like certain Rio Grande border towns whose lawmen openly protected killers and wideloopers.

He was a Ranger—he had to squelch this, Ira kept reminding himself. But how? How could he without undoing what little he had been able to do already?

On Ira's last "job" the gang stole horses, instead of butchering steers, after slashing the fences. Next morning he glumly went with Jim Worsham to a council of the gang held in a ramshackle farmhouse on the outskirts of the settlement. The host was short of chairs, so empty barrels had been dragged in from a barn to provide more seating.

Buck Harlow paid no attention to Ira as the Ranger entered the house with Worsham. The constable curtly stated the purpose of the meeting.

"We have to dispose of those horses—somewhere across the county line." The question was where—because Ranger patrols and antihorse-thief associations were getting mighty active.

Jim Worsham made a suggestion. "Let's sell 'em in Belton. It's a hundred and sixty miles from here." The farther the distance, the harder it would be to trace the brands to Brown County, he said.

Belton used to be the best market in the state for rustled saddle stock, another wire cutter commented. "But who's gonna drive 'em there?" he demanded. Belton had recently hanged several men who were caught stealing horses.

There was an uneasy silence and a troubled shifting of eyes. Ira saw that his chance had come, and took it.

"I'll go," he said timidly after realizing that nobody else meant to volunteer.

Buck Harlow lashed out from the barrel where he was sitting, "You'll go! What makes you so ready to risk a noose, kid?" Ira's face flushed. He wanted to leap on the crooked constable and strangle him. But he answered with calculated mildness.

"Then maybe you ought to drive 'em, Mr. Harlow. You're wearing that badge and any posse would ride on when you flashed it."

The desperadoes guffawed. Their leader glowered. Ira suddenly felt stark fear. Had he, after all these months of being so guarded, made a fatal slip?

"Kid," Buck Harlow said, "I ought to take my horsewhip and whale the tar out of you for that."

Then Jim Worsham spoke quietly. "You got the boy figured wrong, Boss. Look how handy he's been with the cutters and the skinnin' knife. And he's took orders like a kid born to bust barb."

"All right," Harlow snapped. "If Benton gets back, he can have half the horse money for his risk. If he gets hung, better it'll be a saddle bum than one of us."

The parley adjourned. Four picked men, including the constable, had been chosen to cut the fences of a ranch near Pecan Bayou, two weeks from that day. Ira went back to the Worsham place to get ready for his trip.

A little after dark two men rode up to the house, each leading an unsaddled horse behind his own pony. Ira met them at the gate.

"Boss thought that two horses would be enough to start you out on," one fellow said. "Better make a hard ride tonight and get out of this county so these broncs won't be recognized, come daylight."

"I'll waste no time," Ira promised. He tied lead ropes to the stolen horses, intending to hold the hemp with one hand and the reins of his mount with another. Tucked in his pockets were, the documents he had removed from the brogans. Along with this evidence was a note he had scrawled, informing the adjutant general in Austin about the impending raid at Pecan Bayou. Stuffed in his wallet were his private funds, which he had kept hidden in a safe spot in the attic.

Once mounted, Ira rode rapidly, forcing the led horses to keep the pace. He avoided main roads where he might encounter strangers. He had no intention of landing in Belton, where a Texas Ranger might be hanged as a horse thief without being given the slightest chance to prove his identity. Instead, he headed for Lampasas County and to a ranch owned by a friend there.

It was a fifty-mile trip that he made by sunup that next morning. The horses were lathered with sweat when he finally reached his friend's ranch. Ira was ready to drop from the saddle but he insisted on riding into Lampasas town and mailing his evidence to the adjutant general before sprawling on a bed for a rest.

For several days Ira remained in Lampasas County where the fences were unbroken and the herds untouched after his work there. Each morning, when he awoke, he felt happier at being out of Brown County, relieved to be eating his meals with honest people.

Every day he rode out into his friend's pasture to see how the two stolen horses were faring. Later, after the Brown County gang had been crushed, it would be necessary to trace them through their brands and return them to their rightful owner. Then he realized that his concern for the horses masked the much greater problem that was plaguing him.

Should he return to that county to place a little more tempting bait on the trap he knew the Rangers would start laying after receiving his communication? Knowing Ranger methods, he was sure that a company would be slipped in without fanfare to the territory of the wire cutters. Probably this would be one of the most seasoned and shrewdest outfits—the one commanded by Captain William Scott, whose permanent headquarters was the nearest to Brownwood. They would move at night, like their quarry, the wire cutters, without making their presence known till they were ready to pounce.

But suppose that Harlow's band became impatient because that fool kid, Bob Benton, hadn't returned with the money for the stolen horses? They might assume he'd been caught and hanged or else had drifted on to some other place with all the cash. But what might happen if Buck Harlow sent somebody out to check on the missing saddle tramp, only to learn that he hadn't been seen in Belton or any nearby place where stolen horses were accepted articles of commerce?

Then they would get suspicious and figure he might have been an investigator, Ira concluded. That would start them nosing around, looking for other strangers who might be lawmen. But if he went back and handed them some money, that would keep them off the scent...

Ira knew that he could return to Brown County or report back for duty at Camp Leona as he chose. Rangers, on detective assignment, were given wide latitudes of decision. It was characteristic of him that he made his decision in terms of the Ranger company that would be moving in to restore law. To cover up what he knew would be their preliminary operations, he went back to the danger zone.

Leaving his own horse at the ranch with the stolen ones, he boarded a train from Lampasas to Brownwood, carrying his saddle with him. When he arrived in the Brown County seat, he ran into a wagoner who carried him and the saddle to within two miles of Jim Worsham's ranch.

Lugging his saddle, he walked the rest of the way. The Worshams greeted him with open arms when he knocked on their door. Ira pulled out a handful of money—his own money.

"Here's what I got for selling them two hosses," he said. "What I got for my own bronc I'm keeping—or what's left of it after riding back on the train."

Jim Worsham beamed and handed back some bills to Ira. "Here's your half. Wait'll the Boss sees our half! Any chance to sell any more broncs in Belton?"

Ira grinned. "Best bronc market in the state if you can fetch 'em more like them two."

Worsham laughed. "We'll fetch 'em all right. I'll see that you git some to take in every couple o' weeks—and you'll make on it, too, since I ain't never been able to pay you a nickel of wage money."

On a crisp moonlit night of November, 1886, four men rode stealthily to the ranch whose fence line bordered Pecan Bayou. They dismounted and pulled clippers from their pockets. Walking along and leading their horses, they began cutting the wires between each post. Then a voice rang from a dense thicket across the road: "Halt! Surrender!"

The surprised desperadoes wheeled around, revolvers drawn, as a company of Texas Rangers plunged from the thicket. The demand for surrender was answered with burning gunpowder. The Rangers returned the fire. After the gunsmoke had cleared away, two of the lawbreakers were found dead; two more lay dying by the fence line.

Of the pair who had died instantly from the Ranger volley, one wore a badge that gleamed ironically in the pale autumn moonlight. A bullet had torn into Constable Buck Harlow's chest just below the emblem he'd dishonored.

It marked the end of Brown County's fence-cutting crime wave. No postscript of legal proceedings would be necessary, for this was a classically Texas way of crushing lawlessness. Ira, feeling sorry for little people, may have influenced the decision to end the matter there.

Ira never revealed whether or not he was with the Ranger outfit that, in his own words, "mowed down that bunch like wild ducks roosting on the Bayou." He was as chary as a soldier about admitting to killing men, even when killing was a regrettable matter of public duty. It was something that a modest Western officer didn't boast about. Without his patient, hazardous job of detection, however, the fence cutters might have carried on for several more years.

Nor did Ira ever describe his final leave-taking of the Worshams. Probably he just disappeared, with poor Mrs. Worsham tearfully concluding that even fried chicken was no cure for itching feet. But Ira forever regretted having had to spy on the Worshams after they had taken him in and "given him a home."

"I'd have felt mighty flustered to have faced Jim Worsham from a witness stand," he once said. "And troubled worse on Mrs. Worsham's account if the road kid she befriended had sent her husband to the rock pile."

"Bring those murderers in dead or alive. Dead would suit me best."

BUTCH CASSIDY'S RIGHT BOWER

In Wyoming—northern rim of the great West—arose one of the most aggressive and durable criminal combines in American history. In Texas—Southern edge of the vast region—men of deadly trades were lured by the new enterprise, with its promise of fat pickings. North by west, along a secret outlaw trail, they rode to enlist under a new master of frontier freebooting.

Called Butch Cassidy, he was born George Leroy Parker. The former Utah cowhand was just twenty-one in 1887, when the Rangers began hearing about him from drifting saddle toughs. Operating from a roost in a broad, hidden valley guarded by wild, gaunt peaks of the Rockies, the place accessible only through a narrow, tricky gorge called the Hole-in-the-Wall, Cassidy directed the widespread operations of his long-riding riffraff, gathered from every part of the West. A sizable number of that notorious "Wild Bunch" were recruited from the frontiers of Texas.

Among the pack's Texas guns were silent, taut, moody Tom O'Day, for whom the Rangers had out murder warrants and reward offers; Blackjack Tom Ketchum, mad at the world because a girl had jilted him; Deaf Charley Hanks, son of a drunken whore, on the run after raping and pistol whipping a rancher's daughter. Ben Kilpatrick, with the cruel, pale yellow eyes—"a prime shot" and "absolutely fearless," according to the archives of the Pinkertons who spent a fortune hunting him.

Another Texan among them, whom Ranger Ira Aten got to know, was a tomcat and a trigger man called by many names, but identified on Ranger "wanted" circulars as Judd Roberts. Butch Cassidy was still serving a brief apprenticeship as a Utah horse thief when Ira's trail first crossed the crooked one of Roberts, the gun slinger. In 1885, while still operating on his own, Roberts had led a gang of four men who robbed and killed an old ranchman named Brautigen in the German-speaking settlement of Fredericksburg, west of San Antonio. Ira, then still a rookie, had been a part of a Ranger squad dispatched by Governor Ireland to hunt down the killers.

In a short time the Rangers had captured two of the gang, one being Roberts, the leader. Feeling against the sorry pair had run very high in the tidy, ordinarily peaceful little town. Since the local jail was a flimsy old structure of rock and wood, the state officers had moved their prisoners to a new, reputedly lynch-proof, escape-proof lockup in San Antonio.

Afterward a Fredericksburg posse caught a third member of the murder quartet and threw him in their ancient calaboose. As Ira wrote, "This building almost immediately and mysteriously burned down upon the prisoner," roasting him alive. Within four months Roberts and his remaining partner had broken out of the stout San Antonio jail, much to the embarrassment of the Bexar County sheriff and the annoyance of the Texas Rangers.

The same Ranger squad had trailed these two in their old haunts around a section called Travis Peak on the Colorado River, west of Austin. Each time the fugitives had dodged capture. Finally the detail lost track of them altogether and went back to headquarters in Uvalde County.

During this period Roberts probably made his way over the outlaw trail to the Hole-in-the-Wall and to Butch Cassidy, then accumulating more manpower along with more loot. His actual stay in the rendezvous must have been short. He soon turned up at a southern outpost of the Wild Bunch in an almost unpopulated section of the Texas Panhandle, just across the Canadian River from Indian Territory. Horse stealing became his trade, murder and robbery of solitary travelers his occasional side line.

Rounding up Judd Roberts and any of his cohorts became Ira's first individual detail. This chance to prove himself as an investigator, which he had wanted since joining the Rangers, came through coincidence but Ira gladly embraced it.

Judd Roberts had been born and brought up in Williamson County, where he still made furtive visits to see kinfolks. Ira had been reared there, and he knew every boulder that an outlaw might use as a barricade, every cedar-brake shanty where one might den.

Ira was stationed at Eagle Pass, on the Rio Grande, when he received orders to report to the adjutant general's office in Austin. "Special duty, Corporal." Captain Jones laughed. "I know you've been wanting it. But don't kick up your spurs too much till you know what it is."

Pleased and nervously expectant, Ira pressed and brushed his blue-serge suit till it was as immaculate as a Boston drummer's. Adjutant General King treated him with a new deference when he arrived in the capital. There was no more fatherly talk of the kind that had been directed at an eager, imaginative boy three years before. Instead, the general greeted him with the easy informality of one knowledgeable lawman receiving another.

"Good work you did there in Llano." General King chuckled. "Rube Boyce is behaving himself—and I hear that Sheriff Shaw is catching up on sleep."

Ira grinned. "I sure thought they might be putting each other to sleep."

General King looked at him wryly. "Don't get chummy with the man you're going after, as you did Rube Boyce. Shoot him like a snake."

Ira asked who that man was.

"Judd Roberts," General King replied. "The one who broke out of the San Antonio jail while awaiting trial for the Brautigen murder in Fredericksburg. You've run him before. But go to Governor Ireland for your special orders."

Ira went to the governor's official quarters. The same bored gray-haired clerk was acting as receptionist in the outer office. The Ranger corporal remembered the bare tolerance with which the old fellow had treated him when he had come there as a bumptious recruit. More politicians were slumped on chairs. More red-eyed mothers were there to beseech pardons for erring sons. But this time the clerk jumped to his feet and came forward with outstretched hand when he saw Ira.

"Welcome, Ranger Aten! Mister, you're really making a record. I'll take you in to the governor, right this minute."

Governor Ireland looked deeply concerned when the two entered his sanctum. Ira learned later that he was feeling acutely worried about losing the support of the sizable Texas German element, which was demanding that the slayers of Brautigen be caught.

"Aten," he said crisply, "you're going to Williamson County because you know it. Judd Roberts has been seen a lot in the hills there. I want you to bring him to account—Roberts and, if possible, his partner who broke jail in San Antonio along with him."

"Yes, sir," Ira replied.

"Bring those murderers in dead or alive," the governor ordered. "Dead would suit me best."

Ira had never heard any superior speak in such a sharply mandatory tone. Impressed, he exchanged a hurried handshake with the governor, then rode northwest through the remembered hills of Travis County to the familiar ones of adjacent Williamson. He felt a deep, glowing pride in his first individual mission. But confidence was overshadowed by caution when two and a half hours after leaving the governor's office he crossed a boundary into his home county.

Everybody in this mountainous third of it would be knowing Judd Roberts, the Williamson County boy who had gone off to join Butch Cassidy's outlaws. But, equally, everybody would be knowing Ira Aten, the Williamson lad who had left to join the Texas Rangers. When it came to a numerical count of supporters, Roberts held a clear advantage. He was kin to a quarter of this primitive, individualistic community and the friend of another half of its potshooting, whis-ky-drinking wood haulers and charcoal burners.

Ira decided to lie low by day and scout by night. He felt that Roberts and his partner, being fugitives, would do most of their visiting and frolicking after sundown in the eve-nings. Only to a few close personal friends did the Ranger, come home, reveal his presence. One of these was George Wells, who ran a ranch at Long Hollow near the line of Bur-net County.

For many nights Ira searched for his quarry's hide-out. He crouched in woods outside cabins where dances were being held, to recognize almost everybody but never to catch sight of the two wanted men. He prowled around caves, to find them tenanted only by varmints.

His friends kept unobtrusive watch on cabins occupied by Roberts's kinsmen. It was a big group, continually visiting back and forth. But Judd Roberts, its prodigal, was never seen entering one or another of its clapboard shanties.

Ira got word that a man resembling the killer had been seen in a Burnet County community called Mahomet, al-though the residents were God-fearing Baptists. There he found the "suspect" sitting on a barrel in the general store, munching crackers and cheese, begging every rancher who came in for a sheepherding job. Ira gave him a quarter and wished him luck.

"Hell!" the disgusted Ranger remarked to a local deputy constable before leaving. "That poor tramp does look a little like Judd Roberts. But you could scare him with a lightning bug on a corncob."

It was late afternoon when Ira reached his rough beat in Williamson County. Tired and dejected, he decided to lay off the chase and get a good night's sleep at the home of George Wells. There, too, he had often rested by day.

He rode up to the Wells place and turned his horse loose in the rancher's big corral. For about an hour Ira and his friend swapped talk in the back yard while waiting for Mrs. Wells to announce supper. About sundown Wells stepped into the front yard after hearing a clatter of hoofs echoing from the road.

"Ira," he called excitedly, "there's a man riding here mighty fast! Can't make him out yet. But he's sure got business of some kind!"

The guest sprinted into the house. The man might be just a neighbor needing help in some emergency. He might also be a neighbor friendly to Roberts and one who would recognize Ira as the Ranger from Williamson County.

A few seconds later Wells entered the room where Ira was concealed. "It's your man," he said tensely, "that sidewinder, Judd Roberts, himself."

Ira checked his revolver. He felt none of the tension that was obviously gripping his friend. "George, go back to the porch. Carry on a conversation till I make a surprise appearance. Then jump—jump quick—out of the line of fire."

George Wells did as directed. Ira took a position just inside the closed front door. The hoof sounds and the accompanying tinkle of tiny silver bells from Roberts's fancy Spanish bridle drew nearer. Ira wondered why the desperado's partner wasn't along.

Seventy-five feet from the door, Roberts reined in, his face, as Wells afterward described it, a mixture of hard sensuality and manic fury.

"Hello, George!" he bellowed to the rancher. "I've come to do a little killin'."

Ira heard Wells's nervous reply: "Reckon you've come to the wrong place, then."

Roberts's answer was a snarl. "Don't guy Judd Roberts, because he don't take it! I know you're harborin' that cuss-fired Ranger from Round Rock, Ira Aten. I want that trigger sprout worse'n he wants me."

George Wells's voice had a shakiness that surprised Ira. "Who told you that Ira Aten was here?"

The desperado was getting impatient with this palaver. "Who told me? Even the damned rocks around here got eyes that see for Judd Roberts. I'm goin' in there to bring out Aten's carcass. Step aside, you—"

Ira flung open the door. He jumped to the porch, pistol drawn and cocked. "Hands up, Roberts!" he shouted.

Roberts went for his six-shooter. He and Ira fired in the same thunderous second, as George Wells leaped to the side of the porch and took shelter in a grape arbor. The desperado's bullet thudded into the wall of the house. Then Judd Roberts screamed; the Ranger's shot had hit the trigger finger of his right hand.

The killer's gun dropped to the ground. He put spurs to his mount and flattened out on its neck as he sped away. Ira took another shot at him. The shell pierced a large limb of a tree above Roberts's head as he ducked under it.

Before Ira and the rancher could fetch their ponies from the corral, Roberts had escaped into the dense surrounding brush. For an hour or so the two scouted along a small creek hoping that the outlaw might have halted briefly on its banks to wash and bandage his wounds. But no evidence was to be found either in the form of bloodstains or hoof tracks. Then Ira had a hunch he decided to act on.

"Where's the nearest doctor, George?" he asked the rancher.

"Thirty-five miles up the Colorado River, in Burnet County," was the answer.

"There's where we'll ride," Ira said. "Roberts may be going there to get his hand fixed."

All night long the pair traveled, heading due west along the sand-encrusted shores of the Colorado. The sun was just rising when they reached the doctor's residence. They knocked on the door. An elderly, worried-looking man invited them into a room that served as an office.

"Good morning, Mr. Wells," he said, recognizing the rancher. "I don't think I know your friend."

Wells made the introductions. "This is Ranger Aten, Doc. He's trailing a mean son of a bitch you may have seen."

The doctor's face went white. "Please—please," he begged. "I'm a medical man, not a lawman. If I can't help you gentlemen professionally, please excuse me."

Ira had been studying the upset physician. "Doctor, you look like you need some medicine yourself. I think you've had a big scare—and not long since."

The doctor laughed weakly. "No—no; you're—you're mistaken. It's just the strain of practice and—and—"

"And," Ira interrupted, "having to pick a bullet out of a filthy skunk who paid you with threats."

The doctor's lips trembled. "My—my relations with my patients are matters of professional confidence. Now please leave me alone."

Ira was firm. "Doctor, I don't want to embarrass you nor hurt sick people who need you. But if you don't tell me about *this* patient, I'll have to arrest you for shielding an outlaw."

The doctor was near collapse. "No—no, I—I don't want to be disgraced by an arrest. But"—tears were running down his wrinkled cheeks—"I don't want to die either."

Ira's tone was kindly. "Did he threaten to come back and kill you if you told anybody about your doing surgery on him?"

The doctor nodded weakly.

"Don't worry," Ira assured him. "Nobody will ever know but me and Mr. Wells. Was the bullet in his right hand?"

Another nod. "The forefinger."

"Did you know the man?"

"Yes," the doctor mumbled. "Everybody in these hills knows him—Judd Roberts."

"How long has Roberts been gone?"

The doctor was getting a grip on his nerves. "Just about half an hour, Ranger. His whole hand is in pretty bad shape. It will be months before he can do any more shooting. I hope to God somebody shoots him in the meantime."

"I don't," Ira answered.

He thanked the doctor and left with George Wells. As they mounted their horses, Ira felt an exultation that made him forget the fatigue resulting from the long ride. But Wells had a tense, harried look, like the one that had been on the face of the doctor.

"Ira," he said apologetically, "I hate to pull out on you now. But I can't help you chase Judd Roberts any longer. I do have my stock to look after."

"That's all right, George," Ira answered. "I'm not going to do any more running of that cutthroat right now."

George Wells was surprised. "You're going to let him get away when he's only got half an hour's start on you?"

Ira's hand touched his pistol butt. "No, I'll never let him get away." His eyes were smoldering. "I want to meet him when that trigger finger is working again."

"I'm a Texas Ranger. I'm looking for an outlaw named Judd Roberts."

TWO ON A TRAIL

Ira went back to Camp King and rigorous duty on the Mexican border. Judd Roberts went to God knew where. But the Ranger felt, with the sure intuitiveness of the born lawman, that the two would be meeting again, to conclude the unfinished duel.

When they met, there could be no considerations of quarter or of any spurious, theatrical gallantry on either side. That sort of thing was for the dime novels and for the tent shows touring America. It was, by implication, what General King had warned Ira against on the day he had reported for initiation into the Rangers.

Ira had felt some friendliness toward Rube Boyce. But within the visible gradations of outlawry, that boisterous trigger hoodlum was of a different sort from Judd Roberts, who killed because he liked to see men kick. Roberts gave himself no margin of mercy, and no jury would accord him any if he ever stood trial. "I won't, either—if he doesn't get me first," Ira promised when he reviewed that preliminary stage of a still unended quest with Captain Jones.

Letters from friends in Williamson County told Ira that Roberts and his partner hadn't turned up on that common ground. Probably, Captain Jones thought, the two had temporarily parted for mutual protection. As Ira kept analyzing the pistol thug, he believed that his man would remain within convenient saddle distance of the county. Roberts at this time could hardly afford to venture beyond the shielding bounds of the Texas hills. With his shooting hand out of commission, he would not want to risk a long ride to the open prairies of the Panhandle in search of Butch Cassidy's southern contingent.

Shelter would be almost nil for a fleeing bad man in that treeless, sparsely-populated section. The hazards of travel would be multiplied for Roberts, with his wounded trigger finger, if he ran into some roving Ranger patrol. Starvation would face him since he would be unable to shoot quail or jackrabbits. Days of solitary riding might pass before a wayfarer spotted a ranch house or a cowboy chuck wagon. Even then, a visitor with a crippled trigger hand would be self-identified as a fugitive.

Roberts, Ira reasoned, would find himself a wench and a shack in some secluded strip of the hills. "He'll stay there till his trigger finger heals," the Ranger predicted to Governor Ireland, still raising Cain about two uncaught killers. "Then that finger will be pointed toward me."

Ira's deductive powers were developing. Actually, as was learned later, Roberts holed up in a six-shooter community in another mountain county. There he found a trollop who had borne three different children, being reared by her parents, to three different sires. The outlaw moved into her log shanty after she offered him hot biscuits and certain other attractions. She poulticed his hand with some herb nostrum to draw out the infection. It wasn't long before Judd's trigger finger unkinked.

Ira had been gone three months when he got written word that Roberts and his partner had returned to Williamson County. He requisitioned a new gun and a fresh horse from Ranger headquarters. This time he meant to resolve a challenge finally. Quietly he slipped back into the county. Naturally, he looked up George Wells, only to get a frosty reception.

"I can't help you do outlaw running, Ira," his old friend said coldly. "And I'd be obliged if you wasn't seen too much around my place."

It was no more than Ira had expected, after the sand had started seeping out of the rancher's craw at the Burnet County doctor's.

"All right, George," Ira answered. "I wouldn't ask any man to take a risk he figured was too much. What happened to you after we chased Roberts? His kin fire your grass?"

George Wells shook his head. "Not yet. But a deputy from Georgetown came out to warn the law-abiding folks about Roberts's connection with Butch Cassidy. We just ain't big enough to take on anybody who rides with the Wild Bunch."

Damn that deputy, Ira thought. As scared of Cassidy's henchmen as were the settlers he was supposed to protect. Passing on his fears to good people instead of rallying them in the continuing fight for law. But George Wells was a bellwether of the decent element in this generally lawless neighborhood. If he refused to back a Ranger, it was unlikely that any other honest citizen would.

Ira felt deserted, isolated, and a little sick. By their coward ice, the law-observing ranchers and farmers were making him a marked target for Judd Roberts to shoot at.

"Tell me, George," Ira asked gravely, "is there anybody around who wasn't scared when the Georgetown deputy gave that warning?"

George Wells studied for a moment. "I reckon you could count on John Hughes. He had trouble with Cassidy's crowd in New Mexico."

Ira asked him where Hughes lived. George Wells jerked a thumb toward the little stream where he once had scouted for Judd Roberts. "He's got a mustang spread a little way down the creek—a few miles from Liberty Hill settlement." The rancher hesitated, then said, "Don't tell nobody I sent you to him—it'd get back to Judd Roberts for sure."

"All right, George," Ira promised, annoyed. "I won't tell anybody. So long."

Ira rode till he reached a fenced enclosure of about seventy five acres centering around a neat-looking frame cabin with half a-dozen wooden corrals off to the side. The pens were full of ponies. Ira guessed that this was John Hughes's place. A tall serious-faced man, in his early thirties, came forward to greet him.

"Howdy, sir," he said in a Midwestern twang that reminded Ira of his father's. "My name's Hughes. Get down and
come in."

Hughes probably noticed that his guest seemed disturbed,
but he waited for his visitor to broach his business. After
they had threshed over random subjects for a while, Ira got
down to brass tacks.

"Mr. Hughes," he said, "I'm a Texas Ranger. I'm looking
for an outlaw named Judd Roberts and his partner. Roberts
being a pal of Butch Cassidy, nobody around here will lift a
hand to help me. But I've heard that you've already tangled
with the Wild Bunch, so I thought maybe I could call on you."

With his left hand Rancher Hughes tapped thoughtfully
on the kitchen table where the two sat. Ira had already noticed that his host's right arm and hand had an awkward
stiffness. And the visitor guessed that the permanent lame-
ness had come, like Judd Roberts's temporary one, from gun
trouble.

"I didn't tangle directly with the Wild Bunch," Hughes answered after a minute of pause. "But a couple of New Mexico
officers I drummed up shot four rustlers when I trailed them
there after they lifted some Williamson County broncs last
year. Two of them were Butch Cassidy's personal friends and
two were Robertses who left here with the horses. So," John
Hughes concluded mildly, "Mr. Roberts wants to even accounts with me—for his kinfolks, and for Mr. Cassidy."

Ira hoped that he had won an ally. "Roberts is looking for
me, too, Hughes. So let's go find him.

John Hughes answered without a second's hesitation. "All
right, Ranger."

Ira related his own history with Judd Roberts. Ranger and
mustang hunter agreed to pursue Roberts and his partner
until one or both of the outlaws should be dead. Hughes
requested a few days to make arrangements with his neighbors to take care of his stock.

That night Ira slept in John Hughes's cabin. Hughes, as had
been his custom since returning from New Mexico, spread a

pallet of blankets about two hundred yards from the corrals. He was determined to lose no more of his stock to prowling horse thieves.

Ira removed his boots and stretched out on the bunk. At daybreak he was awakened by a stealthy creak of the door. He jumped up in his sock feet and crept toward the bolted entrance.

There was another push at the door. Fingers were fumbling at the outside latch. A voice uttered a low "Damn" when the door remained closed.

The prowler must be looking for John Hughes, and Ira reasoned that there was only one man who would be seeking him at such an hour without announcing himself. Ira drew his forty-five with one hand and loosened the inside bolt with the other.

Again the groping hand outside pawed at the latch. The door eased open. Standing silhouetted in it, his gun raised, was the man Ira had expected to see. He spoke from the darkness.

"Roberts, you're under arrest."

A healed finger pressed a trigger. The shot whined past Ira's head, to tear a hole in a tin stovepipe. The Ranger fired as the killer wheedled back from the open door. As Ira groped in the dark for his boots, he heard several quick gasps of pain, then the clatter of receding hoofs.

Jamming on his boots, Ira rushed outside. Splotches of blood on the ground led toward a low cluster of hills overlooking the ranch. But Ira, on his horse, lost the trail after riding a quarter of a mile through a big patch of tall weeds and cockle burs. Hughes knew the country around here better than Ira did. He'd have to go back and get the mustang hunter.

John Hughes was standing with a drawn rifle by the cabin door when Ira returned. "I heard the shots," he said, "then found you gone. If you'd stayed away much longer, I'd have started looking for you."

Ira wiped sweat from his forehead. "Whew! That was a close shave. Judd Roberts came looking for you—and found me."

The two made a foot scout of the weedy jungle. Finally, Ira picked up a black Stetson hat with a bloodstained brim.

"Looks like you plugged him in the head," Hughes commented. "He must have dropped from the saddle before getting very far if you did. So maybe we'll find his carcass lying somewhere around."

All day long the men searched for a corpse. They scoured ravines and the banks of three creeks. Once a hovering flock of buzzards drew them to a particular spot. They hurried there to find a dead mustang but no trace of a dead man.

The sun was beginning to set. Roberts had made another getaway. Ira concluded that he had scored another hand hit on the outlaw, and the blood had stained the hat when he put his hand to it.

Hughes agreed. "What I think, too. But we'd both better sleep outside tonight. Roberts might come back with his partner to burn the cabin and roast you alive."

That night Ira spread blankets near those of the rancher's. The two alternated in sleeping and standing watch. But nothing disturbed the night's stillness except the restless snorting of captive ponies and the moaning howls of the little black wolves on the hilltops.

After breakfast Hughes agreed to Ira's proposal for a quick pursuit of Judd Roberts. The rancher left to talk with a neighbor about the care of his place. Within two hours he returned with an understanding negotiated. Also he had news to give. Judd Roberts had been seen riding north that morning, apparently favoring an injured hand. His partner had been with him.

"North," Ira repeated. "Toward the Panhandle. I don't know that country very well."

John Hughes did, he said. He had driven trail herds and traded with Indians there. The two man-trailers bought supplies for a long journey at a country store.

Another morning found them riding north. For some days they followed intersecting back roads and stretches of different cattle trails. Ira reasoned that the desperadoes would also avoid main roads and all but the most inconsequential settlements. Here in the back country they would find the isolated ranches and the Kansas-bound trail outfits from whom they could expect a hospitality both casual and safe.

Clues found along the way convinced the two that they were on the right track. Once a couple of bent, small bells that had adorned a Spanish saddle of the type ridden by Judd Roberts. On another day a discarded bandage soiled with dried blood and stuffed in an empty tobacco can. But no rancher or trail crew reported having seen two men answering the description of the law dodgers.

John Hughes made a reflective comment to Ira. "You gave Roberts only a flesh wound—probably in the palm—when you plugged his hand. Both our men are sneaking along while they're still in country where people grow crops. They can shoot game and steal from the fields without needing to light down at any house."

Ira agreed. No farmer was going to miss a dozen roasting ears from his corn patch. Hughes's keen observation made Ira feel more admiration for the modest, serious-faced stockman: a native of Illinois, like himself. Never had the Ranger corporal worked with a civilian volunteer who showed such balanced judgment and such innate good sense. This man's left-handed marksmanship was sure, whether the target was a running deer or a stationary object, such as a tin can set on a stump. His mind functioned with the tested precision of a fine pair of scales. Like Ira, he disliked squandering money or loafing in saloons.

What a fine Ranger John Hughes would make, Ira began thinking. A fine Ranger because he was a fine citizen...

Ten days after leaving Williamson County the two reached the Cap Rock: that wide, long promontory of Texas separating the High Plains from the rest of the state. The Texas–Oklahoma Panhandle is a part of this immense subregion of the West. Once they were on these windy mesas, it was Hughes who took the lead because he knew so well this little-known and barely mapped section.

Trails were few, roads practically nonexistent in an area where a man had a clear and unobstructed view in all directions for miles around. Yet the monotony and the sameness never confused John Hughes. He was a mariner on saddleback navigating, without compass, an ocean of grass bewildering to his companion. But confidently, surely, he guided the Ranger from water hole to water hole. The fugitives would also be following the water line.

Now and then Hughes would dismount at some spot that seemed no different from any other vast splotch of grass to Ira. "Here's where I swapped blankets for buffalo hides with the Comanches," he would say. Then he'd dig around with a hunting knife till he came up with a handful of arrowheads overgrown by the grass. Or "here's where the Osages pitched their tepees." And somewhere the rancher would uncover a crumbling old tent stake.

The pursuers found more substantial traces of the desperadoes on the South Plains. Here in bare, unfarmed country they'd had to make halts for food and shelter. At ranch after ranch Hughes and Ira were told that two men, one with a scarred palm and finger, had stopped for a night's rest and grub.

The trail became hotter as the man-hunters entered that northern half of the Texas plains called the Panhandle. In this section the two pursuers became warier. They represented themselves to be wandering cowboys, taking a look at new range now opening after the recent extermination of the buffalo.

Three weeks after starting the chase they reached the remote, thinly settled country where half of the men camping or settling were supposed to have one or another connection with the expanding Cassidy organization. Safety, while getting the lay of the land, was the first requisite for the pursuers. So they hired out as cowhands at the county's most isolated ranch: a spread bordering on the Canadian River and overlooking Indian Territory.

Bunkhouse gossip told them that a man resembling Judd Roberts was courting a girl living on a ranch at the other end of the county. The hunters then quit their jobs to put this place under surveillance. They managed to establish a hideaway from which they could watch the ranch house unseen. Several times they caught sight of the girl. But no man was around except an elderly one, probably her father.

Ten days passed. Ira was impatient and worried. The bunk-house talk might have been a false lead. Or some friend of the Wild Bunch among the cowboys might have guessed the true identities of Hughes and himself, and carried or sent a warning to Roberts and his saddle partner.

But the fearless assurance of John Hughes gave him courage. "Roberts is probably over in the Territory stealing horses from the Indians," Hughes surmised. "If he's laying up with that girl he'll be back."

Two more days of frustration ensued. Horseflies tortured their horses. Beans were running low in the saddlebags. They were ready to give up, bored and discouraged. At sundown on the twelfth day the hunters saw a solitary horseman riding up a trail leading to the ranch. They could hear the tinkle of bells from his saddle.

"Roberts, I'll bet," Ira declared. "Let's head him off."

He and John Hughes scrambled down a hillside bordering the trail, half-crouching to keep themselves concealed behind boulders and bushes. Two hundred yards from the ranch house they stationed themselves behind a broad, towering clump of sage. Pistols drawn, they awaited the approach of the lone rider.

The horseman drew nearer, having slowed his mount to a walk. Ira looked toward him and winked at Hughes. It was Judd Roberts.

The Ranger waited until Roberts was within a dozen feet of the sage clump. Then he jumped out, followed by Hughes.

"Roberts, I want you!" Ira shouted.

With a lightning-like motion, the outlaw tilted his pistol holster and began shooting through its open end. One of his shots ripped a hole in Ira's jacket, barely missing a lung.

Dust from his bullets churned around the boots of his challengers. But he was dying when he fired his last round.

Six shells apiece from the two dismounted men had shattered his body from chest to groin. As he tumbled from the saddle, Ira and his friend rushed forward. Hughes went to summon help from the ranch, and the outlaw was carried there in a one-horse spring wagon to die, with touching dramatics, in the arms of his hysterical sweetheart. But before he gasped out his last good-by to her, Roberts confessed to the killing of Brautigen, and to other crimes that could now be closed in the Ranger files. His partner, the desperado said, had ridden north to Wyoming.

Ira left the corpse for the girl's father to bury, after first having the old man sign a statement that Judd Roberts had died resisting arrest. Then he and John Hughes rode away, satisfied with a job well done.

"Where'll you go now, Ira?" Hughes asked.

"Austin," Ira replied. "To report to Governor Ireland."

Hughes smiled. Liberty Hill was just thirty miles from Austin, he said, so they'd have another long ride together.

Ira answered with studied carelessness, "Maybe a longer one."

Hughes came erect in his saddle. "No, sir, Ranger. No more chases for a while. I've got a ranch to tend."

Ira's eyes were twinkling. "You won't have that ranch long, John. Butch Cassidy will send one of his gunmen down from Wyoming to bushwhack you after what happened in New Mexico, and now this. And he'll keep sending them till one gets the drop. So if you're going to be shot at anyhow, you might as well join the Texas Rangers and get paid thirty dollars a month for it."

Hughes's lips tightened. He said nothing until they had ridden another two miles. Then he turned and said with casual matter-of-factness: "I'll take you up on that, Ira."

Ira was with him when he took the Ranger oath after their return from the man-chase in the Panhandle. August 10, 1887, it was when John Reynolds Hughes was sworn in as a private by the district court clerk at Georgetown.

One great Ranger had recruited another, who proved his equal as a lawman and his closest friend. The taciturn, dignified plainsman was destined to surpass all records for tenure by serving twenty-eight years, and to become one of the force's most illustrious captains.

Thousands of Texans came to know John Hughes. But Ira Aten was probably the only one who ever plumbed all the depths of that resolute, semi-solitary man.

"I knew a little about handling dynamite and its dangers."

BARBS SPROUTED BOMBS

Fence wars kept breaking out here and there in Texas as barbed wire kept lacing across the dwindling open range. Cattle and horses were caught in tangles of the cut wire, sometimes to bleed to death. Tempers were red hot in many counties where Fence Men and Free Grass Men found no grounds for truce, nor sought any. Only one element of the state's population profited from the chronic conflict: the merchants. Barbed wire and the tools to cut it could be bought at many general stores and all hardware shops.

Peace officers tried to stem a social convulsion by enforcing various laws ground out of the legislative mills at Austin. But the fence cutter was a wary man when he unslung his nippers. Probably, as Ira once estimated, twenty went uncaught for every one who was nabbed.

If there was one Ranger task he despised, it was hunting wire rippers. He loathed the job even though his brilliant work in the Brown County Fence War had earned him a reputation as the shrewdest undercover man of the force.

During the summer of 1888 a bristling fence feud came to a head in Navarro County, sixty miles south of Dallas. Miles of wire had been cut, including that strung by one of the county's largest ranchers, Judge Samuel R. Frost. A man named Humphries had been given a two-year prison term for fence cutting after having been betrayed to Sheriff West by a reward-hungry barmaid known as Flirting Nell. But Flirting Nell's greed had only magnified a whole crisis. Free Grass Men were threatening to march on the county jail at Corsicana and release a friend or two of Humphries who were still awaiting trial. Fence Men had already held one mass meeting on the courthouse lawn and announced that they were ready to counter any attempt at rescue.

Reading about the trouble, Ira hoped that his superiors would forget all about what he'd done in Brown County. Now serving his second enlistment as a Ranger, he was proud of his sergeant's rank. He hoped there would be no need for his services in Navarro County, which was in the more populated eastern half of the state where legal institutions were better developed and Rangers seldom assigned.

His hopes proved in vain. When Sheriff West and Judge Frost requested that state officers be sent to help, Governor Ross assigned Ira and a younger Ranger called Fiddling Jim King to make an investigation and effect all possible arrests. Working with a fiddler posed certain problems for Ira, as it would have for any other man of his essential solidity. He would have much preferred staid John Hughes who had helped Captain Jones put down a fence war on the border.

Ira was therefore pleased to find, when the two got to Navarro County that Jim's fiddle made friends for them in their role of wandering farmhands looking for cotton-picking jobs. The two located at a village called Richland, destined later to become a tough little oil town after having been a tough little farming and ranch town. This community, south of Corsicana, was main headquarters for the fence cutters. Soon the pair of Rangers got to know every suspect on a list furnished them from Austin. It was August and the cotton-picking season had started, so there was a lull in that nocturnal outdoor sport of wire ripping. Ira found that the ring consisted of small landowners, with farms averaging about a hundred acres, who depended on cotton for an annual cash crop and who had been used to running small herds of from fifteen to two hundred head of cattle on the open range. Most of them were members of pioneer families in the county. They bore a bitter hatred for the Grangers, as they called more recent settlers who had come in after the Civil War and, later, put up the despised fences.

Several weeks passed. Jim King sparked the Richland girls and played the fiddle for the Saturday-night dances. Ira, dragging a heavy cotton sack up and down the rows in the blazing hundred-degree heat, became increasingly restless. His new acquaintances told him that they were too busy in their patches now to cut fences, but promised to "lay them low" at the end of the picking season.

Cotton picking was disgusting, miserable footwork for a man used to the beat of the hoof and the swing of the stirrup. "I'd long since left the old plantation never to return," Ira grumbled in his memoirs. He was wondering how he could stand two months of it when fate, in the person of the loose-tongued sheriff, presented him with both a release and a risk.

The sheriff knew from Governor Ross that two Ranger detectives had been sent into the county. Indiscreetly, he told somebody and that somebody else passed it along till the information was buzzing along the grapevine. Suspicion naturally fell on the two young strangers, since every resident of Navarro County knew just about every other resident and his business.

Ira and his fiddler hurriedly threw up their cotton-picking jobs and hired out as cowhands on the Love Brothers ranch, two miles west of Richland, after first revealing their identities as state lawmen to the owners. Just before their arrival in the county, the Loves had had three miles of fence cut and it was still down.

Ira instructed the brothers not to restring the fence immediately. Such a move might confirm the suspicions of the wire smashers about Jim King and himself. As he wrote to his original commander, L. P. Sieker, who was now adjutant general, "the rascals would smell a rat" and would cut no more fences until the strangers were dead or out of the county.

Ira's caution brought results. By mid-September ring members who had finished picking their cotton pulled out their nippers and started razing fences again. The two Rangers

stationed themselves at an excellent watch point called the
Cross Lanes where pastures converged. At night, as they lay
on the ground listening, they could hear the sounds of wire
being snipped and it echoed mockingly in Ira's ears.

He attempted no arrests because a pitched battle with
the ring then would have been premature. A Ranger had to
know when to fight and when to be impatiently patient. "I
want to take the villains without killing them," he wrote
General Sieker. "But I think a little more of my life than
theirs, and I will stand a trial for murder rather than stand
up and be shot down like a fool."

As the vandalism continued, Ira considered various plans
to stop it. None seemed to be practical. Meantime, the in-
cidence of wire cutting grew till all of the Navarro County
fences on the western side of the Houston & Texas Central
Railway had been destroyed by what he called "the wild and
woolly wire cutters."

The solution on which he finally hit was a ticklish one.
It alarmed Governor Ross and threw the adjutant general's
office into an uproar. Even today there are arguments about
its merits among chroniclers of Texas. But grim situations
sometimes demanded grim solutions in a land so unused to
compromises as the Old West.

Ira proposed to place small bombs, made of dynamite
stuffed into concealed shotgun barrels, at suitable intervals
along the fences. The mechanism would not explode unless
set off by tampering with the wire to which it was attached.
Ira felt that the setting off of just one of these homemade
contrivances would end fence cutting by the psychological
aftermath of fright.

"When one of my bombs explodes," he wrote General
Sieker, "all fence cutters will hear of it most likely." Then all
a pasture man would have to say to secure the safety of his
fence against these midnight depredations would be: "I have
dynamite bombs on my fence."

Ira ended this proposal, written to General Sieker, on Octo-
ber 15, 1888, with an admonition to "Keep your ears pricked.

You may hear my dynamite bomb clear down there—if I get blowed up, you'll know I was doing a good cause."

Back came an urgent instruction to Ira, picked up in his mail at the Corsicana post office. He was to manufacture no bombs, but to report to the adjutant general's office in Austin as fast as a train could bring him.

Purposely, wilfully, Ira disobeyed the order—probably the first time in his Ranger career that he ever flouted a major instruction. He had no intention, as he wrote General Sieker, of spending two or three years by a fence line to catch a few rippers. He ordered Jim King to return to Ranger duty on the Mexican border. Then Ira boarded a train to Dallas, where he purchased fifty pounds of dynamite and two dozen dynamite caps.

He put the caps in his vest pocket and checked the dynamite through as luggage. He did not know then that he was violating a federal law against transporting this explosive on a train. "Any one of the caps would have blown me to pieces had it exploded," he said in his memoirs. "But I knew a little about handling dynamite and its dangers" so "was taking chances as Rangers always did."

To his credit, Ira planted all the bombs and took all the risks. He returned to the Richland vicinity, but kept himself carefully concealed from the fence cutters while instructing their rancher victims how to use them. Then, and only then, did he comply with the order to report to Austin.

In a masterpiece of understatement Ira wrote that General Sieker "frowned" upon his undertaking, then sent him to Governor Ross. The Ranger remembered that the governor's bald head "got redder and redder" when he heard the story. Ira was expecting to be "court-martialed and then shot."

Finally, however, the two reached a compromise. Ira was to go back to Navarro County and remove the bombs. Instead, he followed what he considered to have been one act of justified disobedience with another. As he said in his memoirs, "I exploded the bombs, and they were heard for miles around."

People came from all over the county to the Love Brothers ranch. They learned. They saw. And, so declares tradition, the Navarro County Fence War came to an abrupt halt.

Nor did Ira Aten get fired from the Rangers as he fully expected he would be. For Sul Ross was something of a pragmatist, as western governors had to be. A Ranger had gotten results. And that the governor appreciated, having been a Ranger himself.

*"Mexicans signed a peace
treaty with Texas Rangers
where they never signed
one with Sam Houston."*

VOTING AT HELL'S BORDER

United States citizens of Mexican descent kept crossing
to the south bank of the Rio Grande to fight for or against
Porfirio Díaz. Mexican nationals kept swimming the river
and voting for Díazista or anti-Díazista candidates on the
north bank.

The Rangers might have intervened to halt nonresident
suffrage anywhere outside of the state's "Little Mexico"
stretching from inland San Antonio to scores of fiercely ir-
redentist hamlets on the Rio Grande's edge. But the natural
associations of a people living under two different sover-
eignties formed a hard cultural monolith that would only
begin to be dented during generations after Ira's.

Ira kept his ears tuned to the raucous politics of the border, as every Ranger had to do. He soon learned, however,
that election patrol meant curbing bloodshed rather than
checking ballots. The resident voters on the north bank
had scarcely heard of the Treaty of Guadalupe Hidalgo that
made them American citizens. The visiting voters from the
south bank were equally uninformed about the agreements
of dead diplomats and regularly paddled over to swell the
polls.

Between elections, partisans of both groups waged warfare that left men bleeding from bullet wounds or knife
slashes on each bank. Sometimes Rangers were able to halt
feuding before it got further than abusive verbal exchanges.
Often they failed. Ira never forgot one incident that flared
suddenly during his early period as a border officer.

The company was camped at its headquarters in Uvalde
County. One sundown a man rode in wild-eyed on a spent

horse from Carrizo Springs, halfway between Laredo and Eagle Pass. Bandits, he gasped, had crossed over from the Mexican side of the river, run off a bunch of cattle, and killed the vaqueros tending them.

The Rangers were soon ahorse, to make a non-stop ride of sixty-five miles. When they reached Carrizo Springs, they could confirm no reports of thieving invaders across the border. But Captain Jones was told that a large body of Mexican horse men was gathered at a certain crossing, with guns pointed toward Texas.

The Rangers sped to the crossing, arriving there shortly after dawn. They sighted a number of riders milling around on the Mexican side. The band wheeled in battle formation, rifle barrels gleaming in the early morning sun, when they saw the Texans on the opposite bank.

"Close your ranks, boys," Captain Jones ordered his command. "Keep your guns cocked. I'll see what these hombres are up to."

The captain shouted across the narrow channel: "Good morning, señores. Why do your guns threaten our soil?"

A rider on the south bank edged his horse forward. "We have no intention of harming Americanos in Texas, señor," he yelled back. "But we have political differences with Mejicanos there."

Ira understood then what this commotion was all about. Another of Old Mexico's boiling political ruckuses was about to spill over to the Mexican communities of Texas. These men were probably planning, with the tacit consent of officials in their country, to massacre a batch of anti-Díazista refugees.

Captain Jones moved closer to the water's edge so that he could be heard. "We are all Democrats in Texas," he called. "You fellows fight out your politics in your own republic. Don't cross over here to settle your squabbles."

The Mexican leader took off his sombrero and made a sweeping bow to the captain. "Nevertheless, we insist on crossing, señor. This is an affair of honor that—"

Captain Jones was getting impatient. "Nevertheless, you insist on getting your damned heads blown off!" he interrupted. "Now pull leather and pull out or we'll be doing the crossing."

The Mexican said something to his men. They raised their rifles. Ira and his comrades matched the move. The flowery one bowed again to Captain Jones.

"Before we fight, señores, may we have the privilege of knowing whom we are fighting?"

Captain Jones signaled to his men. They drew around him, their Winchesters still at ready, the hoofs of their horses all but touching the water. "You'll know damn well who we are when we cross that river!" the commander flung out. "But I don't mind telling you now. We're the Texas Rangers!"

"*Rangers Tejanos*—Texas Rangers!" Ira heard the words echoing through the ranks of the would-be invaders. He saw their guns lowering. Some of the group were turning their horses and quietly easing away.

The head politico said something to his men. Then he cupped his hand to his mouth and called: "*Rangers Tejanos*— American soldiers, we will not fight. Therefore we propose a peace treaty."

"Agreed!" the captain called back. Don Porfirio's punitive expedition needed something to save its collective face, and a "treaty" was as good a way as any of ending the affair.

Negotiations began with a man from each side riding into the middle of the stream. These two served as couriers to carry notes back and forth from Captain Jones to the Díazista chieftain. Each emissary held his carbine high over his head. From each gun muzzle a white handkerchief fluttered as a flag of truce. Ira and several other Rangers slipped into a marsh at the river's brink as the parley began. From that concealment they kept their rifles aimed at the Mexicans, ready to protect their outfit against any sudden aggression.

As water oozed down his boot top and horseflies stung his skin, Ira watched the solemn farce. A dozen pieces of paper were handed back and forth. The spokesman for the Mexicans wanted all sorts of flowery stipulations in the script. Captain Jones, putting teeth in tomfoolery, bluntly insisted that the "treaty" just cover one point: Texas forces wouldn't cross the river for battle if Mexican politicians stayed off Texas territory with their grudges and their guns.

An impasse of two hours developed while swarms of insects clustered on rifle barrels. Ira sensed that the Mexican leader might have a rough time explaining a pact that was turning into a formalized ultimatum from Texans. His cohorts, in whatever town he came from, wouldn't like it.

But blunt as Sam Houston, Captain Jones would grant no more and discuss no more in this impromptu negotiation. And the alternative would be a crossing of the river by Texans geared for battle.

Ira saw how embarrassed the Mexican leader was becoming with each increasingly emphatic communication from Captain Jones. His force might indeed have risked a skirmish with regular United States troopers had odds been in its favor. Such episodes usually ended with protests from Washington to Mexico City and perfunctory apologies from Porfirio Díaz. But Texas Rangers had a well-grounded reputation for taking the counteroffensive when invasion was threatened.

Finally, after some more exchanges of paper, the Mexicans reluctantly agreed to Captain Jones's one-point non-aggression pact. Still protected by the truce banners of the messengers, five men from each group then rode into the river and put signatures to a document made in two copies, each written in two languages—English and Spanish. Then the session ended cordially with the two armed forces exchanging military salutes and the Mexicans disappearing into the brush that lined the south bank.

Ira arose from the marsh with the rest of the hidden guard. His boots were full of rancid water; his arms were flecked with blood from insect bites. He asked to see the pact.

"Here it is, Ira," Captain Jones laughed, "the first and only peace document ever signed saddleback in midstream between Americans and Mexicans."

Ira read the paper whose legal effect, at the very best, was highly dubious. For what it was worth, Mexicans had signed this peace treaty with Texas Rangers, where Santa Anna never had signed one with Sam Houston.

For a time political bickering subsided on the Lower Rio Grande. But through the years "Little Mexico" kept reacting to every civil convulsion south of the border. All the dilemmas of a dictatorship kept mounting for Don Porfirio, and their international repercussions let few Texas Mexicans remain neutral.

Commercial relationships across the Rio Grande gave the small elite among the Texas Mexicans a vested interest in maintaining the iron regime of El Presidente Porfirio. They spent money and distributed judicious bounty to promote the candidacies of Spanish-speaking sycophants who could curb the dominant anti-Díazista sentiment among their dark-skinned semi-peons.

Anti-Díazistas, on the other hand, found it advantageous to elect border magistrates and peace officers who would look the other way when men or munitions were smuggled over the river to bolster different companies of revolutionary guerrillas. Each faction rallied every ballot and every bullet it could from either side of the river for elections that were too often accompanied by bloodshed.

Ira had no sooner returned from the Navarro County fence war than he found himself involved in another threatening tilt of Mexican politics. Elsewhere in the nation, citizens were trying to decide whether they should re-elect Grover Cleveland as president of the United States. But in a seething Texas border town, the residents were stewing over the question of whether Porfirio Díaz should continue as president of Mexico.

Roma was the name of the place. It was located right on the Rio Grande—"so that you could holler across to Mexico." Its population was three-fourths Texas Mexican; the only American flag ever seen within its limits was the faded, shabby one flapping over the courthouse. An Anglo judge had recently been shot off the bench there for trying to bring peace according to the legal forms of a state whose rulers enjoyed scant respect among the Spanish-speaking Indios who were only accidentally United States citizens. Both pro-Díaz and anti-Díaz factions were running candidates in a bitter campaign that showed every promise of ending in a showdown slaughter on election day.

The community had already separated into two armed camps when Captain Frank Jones arrived with five Rangers, including Ira, three days before the balloting. Each party had entrenched itself behind high adobe walls with the only entrances being heavy double-iron doors, supposedly bullet-proof. Drums were banging, harmonicas blaring. Trigger fingers presumably were itching inside each armed citadel.

Ira looked toward the river to see hordes of peons swimming across. Some to back up Don Porfirio in Mexico's lost colony of Texas. More to take a thrust at him in a Texas ballot box when they didn't dare whisper a word against him on a Mexican hacienda.

As soon as one of the state's visiting electors set foot on its soil, he went to the fortress of his party. There he gorged on tortillas, beans, coffee, and mescal. Outside those barricades a Mexican couldn't get a bite or a sup.

The furor mounted as Díazistas and anti-Díazistas kept coming across the river. As each new batch of recruits reported to its stronghold it was greeted with a fanfare of bands and a salvo of drums. "You'd think it was enlistment day for the Mexican War," Ira remarked to John Hughes. Empty mescal jugs began piling up in ominous little pyramids before the adobe barriers.

Two days of almost sleepless duty passed for the Rangers. On the morning before the election another legion of anti-Díazista partisans forded the river. The Rangers turned no contingent back because their concern was not with how many voted, but with how few got shot. By noon rows of gun barrels were poking menacingly across the walls of each fort. Mescal jugs were being thrown tauntingly into the main street; jeering songs were being sung; drums were being pummeled, the beat seeming to speed up with each burst of rolling sound. One shot—just one— fired drunkenly from either wall, and Roma might be made a miniature of the shambles that Porfirio Díaz had made Mexico.

The Rangers started riding up and down the street, saying nothing, only riding. "Six of us," Ira recalled with pride and eloquence, "keeping a thousand men from blasting out each other's guts. Our lives dependent upon any mescal-soaked peon who might take a notion to try a potshot at some patch of hair sticking out above a Winchester muzzle on the opposite wall. That would have set off a crossfire, wiping us out like clay pigeons."

But from main base to outpost the Rangers kept riding. Riding for hours, back and forth from the hitching stake that marked the nearest limits of the street to the one indicating its farthest.

Noon came. Bells rang for dinner in each of the war camps. Guns disappeared from the grim mud turrets. The patrolmen relaxed with sighs.

Captain Jones muttered hoarsely that if this had been a warm-up, the town would need a regiment of undertakers, not a squad of Rangers, tomorrow. He turned to Ira. There was just one way of heading off a massacre when those damned polls opened, he said. That was to keep the two sides from tangling on the streets.

"Right, Sergeant Aten?"

"Right, Captain," Ira agreed. "That—and cutting down on the mescal."

The commander agreed. "Good idea. Aten, escort the Díaz leader here. Hughes, bring in the anti-Díaz one."

Ira rode to the Díaz fortress. Hughes went to the anti-Díaz stronghold. A few minutes later the feuding chieftains were facing the commander. They bowed suavely to each other: foe men on their best behavior before strangers. Then each shook hands, too cordially, with the Anglo come to spoil a good fight.

"I understand," the captain began dryly, "that Roma with five hundred people casts one thousand ballots and fires two thousand bullets in every election. I'm not here to check the qualifications of voters. But the governor of Texas asked me to tell you that the picnic is going to be peaceful this year."

The rival bosses flashed each other a look—a "let's-stick-to-gether, to-hell-with-this-gringo look," as Ira recalled it.

"You do not understand, mi Capitano Jones," the Díaz man replied. "With all due respect to el señor Gobernador, this is an affair between Mexicans." His words were pleasant, but edged with all the hatred of all the Aztecs for all the conquerors from Spaniards to Saxons.

The captain's eyes blazed. "*With all due respect to you, señor!*" he stormed, "the ground that you stand on is Texas. Whatever candidates win the election will have to swear oaths to administer their offices according to Texas law. And that's what I'm here to enforce. Texas law, señores. Every damned word and syllable of it!"

The anti-Díaz leader winked at his opponent. What two rivals couldn't conveniently speak with their tongues they were telling each other with their eyes. This new breed of conquistador wasn't telling the border how to run its business.

"You disturb yourself unnecessarily, Capitano," the anti-Díaz man said smoothly. "We—"

"Shut up!" the captain roared. "I'm running things here." He calmed down a little. "I'm authorized to tell you fellows that the election will not be held except under certain conditions."

"The conditions, señor?" murmured the Díaz leader.

Captain Jones's gaze fixed on them. "One bunch votes in the morning and the other in the afternoon, with each side staying behind its walls while the other is marking its ballots. One drink of mescal—just one and no more—under the belt of a voter, and no gun at his belt. The losing side to accept the decision of the majority. After the polls close, everybody scatters."

The two politicians glanced at each other. Plainly these rules upset preparations for the rowdiest and goriest election ever seen on the border.

"These are hard conditions, amigo," one said. "What if we refuse to accept them?"

"Then, señores, if one peon, whatever his side, so much as gets a bullet scratch, I'll hound the both of you to hell or Mexico City—even if I have to trade draws with Don Lucifer or Don Porfirio to do it."

Next morning the sun lazed up bright and hot over the Rio Grande. The Díaz faction marched out, bound for the voting place. At their head the leader rode a handsome black stallion. Flanking him, two color-bearers waved the Mexican and American flags, the Eagle and Serpent perhaps flaunted just an inch or two higher than the Stars and Stripes. Right behind armed guards sat gleaming silver-mounted saddles decked on beautiful prancing horses. Then came the musicians, blaring their loudest. Bringing up the rear, the poor cheering rabble kept step, on feet either bare or wrapped in Indian straw sandals, to drumbeat and hoofbeat.

Afternoon saw the same kind of glory march, with all the trappings, staged by the anti-Díaz party. Evening came, and the Rio Grande was once more a teeming passageway of men returning home, on stomachs that would not be as full again until next election day in Texas.

Not a shot had been fired. Not a dare had been passed. After it was all over, Captain Jones began congratulating his men. Ira, too tired to listen, flopped down on a bench in front of a store, satisfied that the town had barely missed being turned into a slaughterhouse.

He had been through a tough three days, "with politicos making the Rio Grande sizzle hotter than hell's lake." Which side won, he never remembered. It didn't matter much to him. But he had seen Roma hold its first peaceful election. That gave the whole border country some kind of precedent.

"I made up my mind to
hang that saddle tramp."

ROCK & A ROPE

The Rio Grande was an international cemetery as well as an international boundary. Corpses were constantly being fished out of the stream during all the years that Ira was on border detail. The bodies were usually those of bullet slain solitary males, and generally recognizable as those of bad men presumably rubbed out by criminal competitors.

Border officials were stumped when the body of an elderly woman was found floating in an eddy, twelve miles above Eagle Pass, during the latter part of February, 1889. One by one, during the next week, three more corpses rose to the surface. Two were female—a woman of about thirty and a girl of possibly sixteen. The fourth was a male—a youth in his early twenties.

Gruesome evidence indicated that all had been murdered by the same killer or set of killers. The skull of each victim had been crushed, evidently by blows from a heavy, blunt instrument. Large stones, lashed by strands of rope, had been used to sink all four bodies.

Maverick County Sheriff W. N. Cooke could secure no identifications for any of the victims, though hundreds of citizens viewed them at an Eagle Pass undertaking parlor. Finally the sheriff recorded the descriptions of the four dead strangers and had them buried at public expense. Public opinion through out the state seethed with indignation at one of the most revolting mass murders in Texas history, and newspaper pressure mounted as editorials demanded a solution of the series of grisly crimes.

After some weeks Ranger Captain Jones ordered his two best troopers, Ira Aten and John Hughes, "to take up the matter and stay with it, regardless of time or trouble." The two bosom friends suspended an investigation they were making near Barksdale and rode immediately to Eagle Pass, ninety miles away.

The mystery was the most puzzling one that either man had ever tried to unravel as a frontier detective. Ira was disappointed when he read the descriptions of the victims furnished by Sheriff Cooke. The front teeth of the youth were widely spaced. The thirtyish-looking woman had worn dentures, and her feet were marked by bunions. Nothing in particular distinguished either the elderly woman or the teenage girl.

Sheriff Cooke, however, had retained the tangible items of evidence—the stones and the lengths of rope, which resembled those used for plow reins by many Texas farmers. Ira felt that the strands had all been cut from the same length of hemp. Moreover, they looked new, as if they had been freshly bought from one or another general store.

"We'll try to find that store," Ira said to John Hughes. "But first we've got a long hike along the river to see if we can find rocks matching the composition of these. Wherever we find them might be the murder spot."

For one hot, baffling day the two Rangers tried to find boulders like those which had been used as "sinkers" for the corpses. They picked up hundreds of rocks on the Texas bank of the Rio Grande, only to toss them away in disappointment after examining them. That night, by the campfire, Hughes lapsed into one of his thoughtful silences, which lasted until Ira could contain himself no longer.

"What are you mulling about, John?" he finally demanded.

"That redheaded drifter we arrested at Barksdale a couple of weeks ago," John Hughes answered. "The one who went on a spree and tried to shoot up the town."

Ira recalled him. Dick Duncan, a mean-looking hairpin. He had come to the company camp shortly afterward, asking about Rangers he claimed to know and dropping the names of various gun slingers as though they were all old sidekicks of his.

"I saw Duncan again the day after that visit," Hughes remarked. "And this time he had company with him." Then he told of having met Duncan with a party of travelers on a road near the Nueces River. Three women had been riding in a new green Mitchell wagon, driven by a youth whose description fitted roughly that of the dead boy who had been pulled out of the Rio Grande. Duncan and another horseman, whom he had introduced as "Picnic" Jones, had been riding ahead of the vehicle as if guiding the passengers toward some destination. Hughes remembered also that the wagon bore the name and address of the merchant who had evidently sold it: *J. S. Clark, San Saba.*

"Funny," Ira mused. He had taken Duncan for a typical saddle tramp when they arrested him in Barksdale. But the man had produced plenty of money to post for the peace bond that the judge made him put up.

After much reflection, Ira decided to let Private Hughes keep scouring the riverbank for rocks while he went to San Saba to check on the redheaded wanderer. A stage took the Ranger sergeant from Eagle Pass to the central Texas hill town. There Ira learned that "Picnic" Jones was the alias of a cattle rustler, Walter Landers, whom he had once kept under detention. The local sheriff didn't know the whereabouts of Landers. But, surprisingly, Dick Duncan was a voluntary prisoner in San Saba County jail.

"How did that happen?" Ira asked in surprise.

The sheriff, a farmer wearing a star, laughed. Duncan had banged on the jail door last night. He had seemed mighty upset because people were accusing him of a murder and he said he wanted to be locked up till the sheriff cleared him. Ira stared at him. "What murder, Sheriff?"

The local officer bit into a plug of chewing tobacco. Well, Duncan didn't say, but the sheriff reckoned he was thinking about "them folks who got killed at Eagle Pass. Some people around here were saying they might be Miz Ida Williamson and her family."

Ira pricked up his ears. "Mrs. Ida Williamson—tell me

about her."

The sheriff related that Mrs. Williamson had, until recently, owned a small ranch near San Saba and that Duncan had lived on her place. Her family had consisted of a thirty-year old daughter, Mrs. Lavonia Holmes, widowed like the mother; a younger daughter, Beulah, who was sixteen; and Ben, her son, who had just reached twenty-one.

"Anything peculiar about the teeth of Mrs. Holmes or Ben?" Ira wanted to know.

The sheriff spat expertly into a cuspidor. "Come to think of it, there was," he said. "Ben had gotched teeth that a doodlebug coulda crawled through. Ira asked more questions and learned that "everybody in San Saba knew that Miz Holmes wore false teeth and that she had bunions that sorta made her limp."

A few weeks earlier, the sheriff said, Duncan had bought Mrs. Williamson's scrub ranch for four hundred dollars, giving her two hundred dollars in cash, vendors' lien notes, and a new Mitchell wagon purchased from dealer Clark in San Saba. Other ranchers had heard that the aging widow had meant to settle with her family on a spread she aimed to buy in Old Mexico. Reports had also spread that Duncan and Landers, alias Jones, were planning to escort them to their prospective home.

One morning, at daybreak, the family had left San Saba County with their two guides. Then, puzzlingly, Duncan had returned a week or ten days later to ask San Saba's blacksmith, Tom Hawkins, if he knew "what had become of the Williamsons."

The sheriff casually wiped some tobacco juice from his lips. "Why, everybody here thought that old boy had rode on down to Mexico with the Williamsons. So they just naturally started talking, like folks would, after they read about them corpses turning up in the Rio Grande. I'm sure glad you came, Ranger," he ended.

Ira was boiling with suppressed fury. "I'm glad I'm here, too, Sheriff," he said with forced politeness. Why hadn't this old fool wired or written the authorities at Eagle Pass when Dick Duncan was cutting such suspicious didoes? And why was he accepting almost at face value Duncan's gesture of becoming a voluntary prisoner to free himself of suspicion?

So far, of course, Ira's feelings about the redhead were only suspicions. But sometimes the very fears of a murderer were his own undoing. The Ranger asked the local lawman to hold Duncan for a questioning that Ira meant to conduct. Then he made a rapid canvass of this town that was doing so much tongue buzzing about Dick Duncan.

Everybody, Ira discovered, knew Duncan. Nobody had very much that was complimentary to say about him. He had long been a town hoodlum and was a cousin of the Ketchum brothers—Sam and Blackjack Tom—notorious bandits both. Walter Landers, his partner, bore only a slightly less unsavory reputation, and Landers's brother-in-law, living under the assumed name of Thompson, had fled to Old Mexico to escape prosecution for rustling.

Ira found a dentist, Dr. A. E. Brown, who had made the dentures for Lavonia Holmes, and who remembered Ben Williamson's gapped teeth. Tom Hawkins, the blacksmith, verified Duncan's strange query about the whereabouts of the family. Finally the Ranger went to the suspect's cell and let him talk glibly, pretending to believe every word that was said.

"Where are your friends now, Dick?" Ira asked casually.

The prisoner answered carelessly: "Don't know, Ranger. I left them when we crossed the Rio Grande and headed on back here to my home town."

"Guess we'll locate them through the Mexican rurales," Ira answered easily. "And what became of your friend, Mr. Landers, that you call Picnic Jones?"

Duncan shrugged his shoulders. "Oh, Picnic went on into Mexico with that family. Seemed kinda sweet on Lavonia." The prisoner winked.

Ira returned the wink. "Well, a man can get sweet on a gal —even when she's got false teeth. But tell me, Dick, as a friend of the Williamsons, do you think that those people buried at Eagle Pass are them?"

Dick Duncan studied a minute. "Might be. Some Mex might have killed 'em for that two hundred bucks I paid for their ranch."

Ira's suspicions about the redhead increased. The murder victims had been his closest friends and they had treated him as if he'd been a member of the family. Yet he showed no concern over the possibility that they might be the people lying in the Eagle Pass graveyard. No concern. No worry. Only casual speculation.

"Thanks, Dick," he said. "I hope you'll be out of here soon." He shook hands solemnly with the prisoner, then went out to try to weave more threads in what seemed a gathering net of evidence.

Clark, the storekeeper, confirmed selling the wagon and harness to Duncan but insisted that the town tough had bought no rope. Other San Saba merchants also informed Ira that he had purchased no rope from them—"Though," said one, "I'd gladly donate enough to hang him."

Back at the sheriff's office Ira found a hasty letter written by John Hughes and brought by the stage from Eagle Pass. The methodical private had found what he believed to be the murder scene while puttering over rocks. It was a secluded, unoccupied ranch house, twenty miles above Eagle Pass and near the little town of Spofford. Bloodstains, probably not more than a month old, were on the walls. Rickety, overturned furniture indicated that a struggle might have taken place. The house was approximately eight miles from the Rio Grande eddy where the first corpse had come bobbing to the crest.

Ira instructed the San Saba sheriff to book Dick Duncan on a technical charge of vagrancy so that he could be legally held for any possible further action. Otherwise, a voluntary prisoner might decide to leave voluntarily. He and Hughes then went before a Maverick County judge to obtain a court order for the exhumation of the bodies. Ira wired the San

Saba sheriff to come to Eagle Pass and bring Dr. Brown as well as other people who had known the Williamsons.

At an inquest conducted by a justice of the peace, the sheriff and several friends of the San Saba family viewed the corpses. These witnesses were almost positive that the bodies were those of the Williamsons but would not say so under oath. Dr. Brown, however, made the identifications that started winding the rope around the neck of a suspect.

"This is Lavonia Holmes," the dentist said, after examining the dental plates in the decaying mouth. "These are the teeth I made for her." He turned to the corpse of the youth. "And I'd know Ben Williamson anywhere by his buck teeth."

Dr. Brown signed some necessary affidavits. The corpses were laid to a second and final rest. At Spofford the two Rangers uncovered additional evidence. A storekeeper named George Hobbs remembered selling rope, like the strands that Ira showed him, to a man whose description clearly tallied with that of Dick Duncan. The customer had been carrying a Winchester with a barrel that was badly bent—Duncan had said—from "handling" a stubborn burro that had balked at crossing the Rio Grande. However, a rancher, W. W. Collins, who had been in the store at the same time, had seen the man with the burro on the very next day, and it bore no marks of having been beaten with a rifle.

Ira felt now that he had a case. Duncan must have bent that gun barrel while using it as a murder club on the four victims, while they were all making overnight "camp" in the abandoned ranch house. The missing Landers might have been an accomplice—or Duncan might have made a fifth casualty of him. In that sparsely populated country the killer could have then loaded the corpses in the wagon where they would have been concealed by the arching top covers, then sunk them in the murky river. Whatever became of the wagon Ira never learned definitely. However, the case seemed complete enough without the wagon. Ira made up his mind to hang the saddle tramp.

He went back to Eagle Pass and obtained an indictment of murder in the first degree against Duncan. During the first week of December, 1889, the San Saba man was brought to trial before District Judge Winchester Kelso in the Maverick County courthouse. Jurors, bringing in a verdict of guilty, decreed that the rope artist die by the rope.

Duncan fought to save his neck by pleas to a federal court and to the state court of criminal appeals in Austin. That two year fight brought him nothing but denials of writs and motions. He then begged Governor Hogg for clemency. But on September 17, 1891, the governor wired Sheriff Cooke in Eagle Pass:

After careful investigation, I decline to commute Dick Duncan's sentence. Let the law take its course. Inform him of his fate so that he may prepare to make peace with God.

Dick Duncan died the next day as gamely as his cousin, Blackjack Tom Ketchum, would die on a New Mexico gallows a decade later. He ascended the traditional thirteen steps at a public hanging in the Maverick County jailyard, "the coolest man there," Ira wrote later. An eyewitness, Ira remembered the "last handshakings" and how, the final words asserting his innocence over, the noose was adjusted, the trap was sprung. The tall figure, "with a bunch of flowers making a gay splash of color upon his breast," dropped from sight.

"You had to be quick on the draw and ready to kill your own brother if you ran for office in Fort Bend County."

WAR ON THE SALT GRASS

No scars left by the Civil War healed more slowly than those in Texas, with its fierce divisions between the dominant Secessionists and the bitterly resisting Unionists. Several of the state's bloodiest feuds had their origins in that tragic conflict.

As in Missouri and Kentucky, so in Texas. Little wars kept popping for a generation after the big war. One such smaller imbroglio erupted during Ira's service with the Rangers. And, ironically, it was a Ranger, northern born but reared in the Confederate tradition, who was chosen by the government of the Lone Star State to become its final instrument of southern Supremacy.

The scene of conflict was Fort Bend County on the Texas coastal plain near Houston. Here all the Civil War paradoxes were being recapitulated in their classic form. No other county had been more fiercely Secessionist and more politically sacrosanct than this one, with its nine hundred square miles of sugar plantations and rich ranges of salt grass nurturing thousands of humpbacked Brahma cattle. Not a single ballot had been cast for the Union when Texas voted on the question of joining the Confederacy in 1861. Ninety per cent of the white males between sixteen and fifty had then enlisted in the southern armies or engaged in some auxiliary military service—such as dragging out Union men hiding in the South Texas cane brakes.

Even after Lee's surrender, the fire-eating ranchers and planters had assembled to resolve that they would never submit to the damyankees who had "placed an ocean of blood between us which can never be crossed nor dried."

Another thunderous declaration had urged the Confederate armies west of the Mississippi to carry on in the spirit of Fort Bend and keep slaughtering bluecoats.

By some process that reeked of cosmic irony, Fort Bend was still governed by a coalition of its enfranchised former slaves and incoming white Unionists for more than a decade after the collapse of the state Reconstruction government at Austin. Cavaliers, their spurs jingling angrily, had to pay their taxes and file their litigation in a courthouse run by hated "black Republicans" at Richmond, the county seat named for the tradition-encrusted Virginia city that had been the Confederate capital. Negroes, at one time or another, had held every office, including the one of local representative in the Texas legislature. But by the late eighties the balance began shifting with the ousted neo-Confederates determined to wrest with guns what couldn't be won with votes.

The young native whites organized themselves as a quasi military branch of the Democratic party. "Jaybirds," the Republicans in the courthouse nicknamed them derisively. "Woodpeckers," the youthful Democrats dubbed their opponents. Each faction proudly adopted epithet as title. And soon the two sides were having at it in the good old Texas custom of bushwhacking.

Several Jaybirds and several Woodpeckers were assassinated during a number of election campaigns. Corpses gaped at the tranquil blue skies of Texas from cane patches and Brahma ranges. The Republican or Woodpecker majorities started dropping after Negro cowhands and cane reapers were warned that they would be fired and sent out to starve if they continued the annoying habit of voting. By 1888 the Woodpeckers still maintained a tenuous hold on the courthouse. But so many Negro politicians had been murdered that colored citizens were very reluctant to run for office. With their mass base dwindling, the white Republican leaders were finding it increasingly unsafe to stay in the county where some hotheads were daring to dream of a new Confederate rebellion.

Matters reached a climax on a turgid day in adjoining Wharton County, where both Jaybirds and Woodpeckers had strong and bloodthirsty allies. Kyle Terry, Fort Bend tax assessor and leader of the Woodpeckers, chanced to meet Ned Gibson, a chieftain of the Jaybirds, on the streets of Wharton town, the county seat. It seems probable that Gibson had followed Terry there to kill him. Anyway, Terry was "laying" for the Jaybird with a double-barreled shotgun in a saloon patronized by Woodpecker sympathizers.

Terry aimed as Gibson passed the saloon, fired. Gibson dropped, dying instantly as the heavy shells splattered his innards on the sidewalk. This shooting started the Fort Bend Court feud. Its convulsions shook the state.

Ira was hurriedly ordered to proceed from his station of Realitos, on the border, to attend Terry's trial at Wharton and prevent a threatened pitched battle in the courthouse. When the trial opened, his detachment of Rangers searched every witness and every spectator for firearms and confiscated enough of them to equip a military company.

The trial passed off with surface quiet because the Rangers were there. But Ford Bend County rumbled like a volcano getting ready to erupt when the judge postponed action on the case and released Terry on bond.

Jaybirds left their plantations to congregate day and night on the streets of Richmond. Kyle Terry was despised more than any of the Woodpecker leaders for being a scalawag—a native white who had forsaken the loyalties of his respected patrician family for political gain based upon the votes of Negroes. His uncle, David S. Terry, gunman and jurist, had slain California Unionist Senator David Broderick after leaving Texas and getting himself elected to the supreme court of his adopted state. Still another member of the family had organized a famous outfit, Terry's Texas Rangers, to maintain order in the state during the Civil War.

The Jaybirds declared that Terry should be killed by inches and forced to drink his own blood till he died. Eyewitnesses fanned the flames by telling how the scalawag had behaved after shooting Gibson—how, gloating, he had looked down on the man he'd just murdered; how, with the lordliness of a conqueror, he'd pulled a silk handkerchief from his pocket and fastidiously waved away the smoke wreathing from the barrels of the shotgun; how, afterward, he'd bowed courteously to the sheriff of Wharton County coming forward to arrest him, then handed the weapon, butt first, to that officer.

The slayer himself was keeping on the move, alternating, so it was said, between Houston and Galveston. At the Fort Bend courthouse a Woodpecker deputy assessor was fulfilling the duties from which Terry had taken an abrupt leave of absence. Later, Terry's case would be transferred for final trial on a change of venue to Galveston.

Ned Gibson had two brothers—both crack shots—living in Richmond. They were swearing to write their own verdict in Kyle Terry's blood.

Governor Sul Ross, a former Ranger captain, feared that the feud might spread into every other county of the rich Brazos Valley. Earlier in the year he'd gone to Richmond, trying to arrange an armistice till the next election, due in fifteen months. The leaders of both sides had wined and dined the governor, promising that Jaybirds and Woodpeckers would keep the peace in their common nest of Fort Bend. They had even swapped handshakes all around in his presence. But the wheels of his train had barely rolled across the county line before the same hands were once again busy oiling triggers.

In this new postlude to the Civil War Governor Ross acted firmly and quickly. He ordered Texas's most courageous Ranger Sergeant, Ira Aten, to move into Richmond. Ira was ordered to pick three men of proven bravery as his aides. Four strong, the state officers entered the little county-seat town on a scalding day in August.

Everything was quiet on the surface when the detachment rode down Main Street. Nothing more exciting was happening in the sluggish Sun than a fight over a bone between a couple of cur dogs. But as soon as the Rangers pitched camp on the outskirts of town, they sensed that they were astraddle a powder keg that might explode any minute.

Maybe it was just the flicker in some Jaybird's eye when he passed some Woodpecker who'd beaten him for constable or school trustee. Perhaps it was the bulge of concealed pistols in every pair of pants. Grudges were festering into what was shaping up as a shooting crisis. Ira, as a farseeing law enforcer, hoped to keep tempers under control while patching up some kind of truce that would last.

Politically he was a Democrat, like the Jaybirds and Governor Ross. His pressing concern, however, was to prevent either group of partisans from touching off a slaughter, bullets being so impersonal about whom they hit.

With two Rangers, Ira began patrolling Richmond's streets from dawn till midnight. His third man was out of commission, malaria having stricken him as soon as the detachment had hit this swampy stretch of Texas. When Ira wasn't standing guard duty or waiting on the sick lawman, he was talking himself blue in the face, trying to work out terms the furious members of both sides would accept.

Then he found out that the role of the peacemaker is often hard. The Gibson brothers, speaking for the Jaybirds, would hew to no truce so long as Kyle Terry walked the earth alive. Sheriff James T. Garvey, "King of the Woodpeckers," showed himself more interested in keeping office than keeping order by rejecting all of Ira's proposals for a collective disarmament to be supervised by the Rangers as an impartial body.

There was one thing both sides agreed on enthusiastically: that the state officers should evacuate the town and let them write their own intimate sequel to Appomattox.

Ira had never seen men so utterly hell-bent on killing each other. Many times Jaybird leaders told him, "Someday we're going to march on that courthouse and kill 'em all out"— meaning the Woodpecker officeholders. Woodpeckers were equally vehement in their threats against the out group.

Patiently, tactfully, Ira kept trying to pour oil on waters "so troubled they'd have drowned old Noah." When appeals to Fort Bend's conscience fell on empty ears, he tried appealing to its pocketbook.

He kept reminding both sides that the county was losing huge sums of money with so many men, needed to herd Brahmas and reap Sugar cane, wasting good work hours in target practice. Indeed, the county's economy had slid to a virtual standstill. Nobody was doing much labor except the industrious Negroes who were packing no guns and issuing no ultimata.

After a while Ira realized that he might as well be pleading with the lampposts lining Main Street. The few peacefully minded white citizens brought him continual reports of secret Jaybird war councils disguised as "beach parties," and of Woodpecker delegations stealing off to Galveston, supposedly to confer with Kyle Terry and to stock up on firearms from the hardware stores there.

The Rangers had been in Richmond two weeks when the sun rose on the scorching morning of August 16, 1889. The day began quietly and drowsily with no more than the usual forebodings of trouble. Yet Ira was to remember it more than any other comparable span of hours he'd spent in his whole life.

As usual, Ira and his two aides hit the streets right after sunup. By 8 A.M. stores started opening and the sidewalks filling with people. Nobody was saying or doing anything that could be pinned down as overt. The street crowds were still "behaving" as the scalding day wore on. But they began showing signs of restlessness that no experienced officer could fail to detect.

Feeling harried and worried, Ira instructed his men to be extra watchful for gunplay. Toward evening he hurried back to camp for a quick visit with the sick Ranger who'd been alone since breakfast.

Ira was measuring out a dose of quinine in a glass when a gunshot roared, like a single crash of thunder, from the direction of the town. The glass dropped from his hand. Ira

sprinted toward his pony, leaped into the saddle, and gal-
loped toward the courthouse.

He reached the intersection of Main Street and the public square. There he saw Sheriff Garvey and his deputies,
marching with drawn rifles through the south gate of the
courthouse yard. Down the street from the direction of the
Brahma Bull Saloon a long line of armed Jaybirds was moving in military formation toward the building.

Other men were stepping from the sidewalk to join the
cheering Jaybird ranks, led by Volney Gibson and Henry H.
"Red Hot" Frost, proprietor of the Brahma Bull. Woodpecker adherents were rushing to the Courthouse gate to hoist
Winchesters with the sheriff's crowd. Ira's men—Rangers
Alex McNabb and Frank Schmidt—were in their saddles
doing their best to hold back the oncoming Jaybirds. The
effort was futile, for the surge of armed men was blowing
them along like chaff before a whirlwind.

"Go on" a Jaybird sympathizer yelled from a store.

"Come on!" a Woodpecker deputy shouted a challenge.

Ira spurred his horse toward Sheriff Garvey. "Back into
the courthouse, you and your men!" he ordered. "I'll take
over from here."

The sheriff hoisted a rifle. "I didn't ask you Rangers to
come here and start undermining my authority."

Ira looked around. The Jaybirds were coming nearer. Nearer to a showdown—and a massacre.

"Nobody's undermining you, Garvey," Ira answered. "The
Wharton County sheriff was glad to get our help when—"

"The Wharton sheriff asked your help," the Woodpecker boss interrupted. "I didn't. I'll handle this situation. You
keep out."

Ira turned his pony and sped to the Jaybird column. "Mr.
Gibson—Mr. Frost," he entreated its leaders, "go back—back
into the saloon. Don't shoot up your own community."

The Jaybird chiefs made no reply. Ira reached down from
his saddle to grasp the barrel of Gibson's rifle. Gibson jerked
it away and pointed the weapon at the Ranger.

"I don't want to hurt you, Aten," he said coolly. "But you can't take my gun or stop this crowd. We're going to clean them all out of that building this time."

Ira wheeled his horse to block Gibson's progress. He reminded the Jaybird leader that men in his line would be shooting uncles and cousins of the Woodpecker force.

"Your own cousin, Bill Wade, Mr. Gibson. His uncle, Judge Parker."

"To hell with that!" Gibson shouted. "They stopped being our kin when they turned scalawag with Kyle Terry. Move aside!"

Hoofs yielded before the pressure of feet as the surge of humans in the rear kept pushing Ira's horse forward. "Wait, Gibson!" Ira begged, desperation in his voice. "Parker—Wade —they're still your own flesh and blood—you can't—"

"I damn well can, Ranger!" The hubbub of voices was so loud that Ira could make out Gibson's words only by reading his lips. "Me and my brother, Guilf, have already decorated *Uncle Parker* with one slug today. Then we ran him to this courthouse meaning to finish him off."

Then Ira knew that one of two men had fired the shot which he'd heard in camp: either Volney Gibson or his brother, Guilf, the hotspurs of one more southern-descended family which had refused to be "reconstructed." Judge J. W. Parker had run to the sheriff's office for protection after having been badly wounded by a Gibson bullet. And now the war was on.

Ira saw that rifles were being cocked to shoot on the Jaybird side. He signaled to McNabb and Schmidt, who wedged their ponies close beside his in a last useless effort to stop the deluge of kill-hungry men. The human tide broke through the Ranger blockade like swirling waters overwhelming a weakening dam. Within a minute each officer had been hemmed in by advancing, grim-faced men. The eyes of the three were blurred momentarily by the glint of the blood-red setting sun on dazzling, newly polished Winchesters.

A shot came whizzing from somewhere in the Jaybird ranks. The guns were saying that the time for tongue talk was past. An answering volley ripped out from the cordon of Woodpecker riflemen.

In a few uproarious seconds shooting became general. Bullets bounced off the stone walls of the courthouse, ricocheting to shatter the windows of Woodpecker officeholders. Jaybird snipers opened up from strategic corners and the second stories of buildings in the square. As Ira put it, "Hell was puking!"

Outnumbered, the Woodpeckers wouldn't be outshot. They let go with a blast that momentarily halted the attacking Jaybirds. Sheriff Garvey stepped a few feet ahead of his followers—Red Hot Frost moved out from the Jaybird ranks. A few tense Seconds they stood, glaring past the Rangers at each other.

"Sheriff—Mr. Frost!" Ira Shouted. "Don't fire! Call off the fight. Then we three will have a talk!"

Garvey and Frost each stepped a few inches farther. Guns clicked on both sides, being readied. "Gentlemen!" Ira called hoarsely. "You'll both answer to the law if—!"

His words were drowned by a sharp volley from each side. Through the whirling tempest of gunsmoke, Ira caught a glimpse of Garvey and Frost furiously pumping shots in the direction of each other. Then, as if by prearrangement between mortal enemies, each side concentrated its fire on the chief of the opposing faction.

Jaybird gunsmoke enveloped Garvey in a thick, pungent cloud. Frost stood manfully receiving the concerted fire of the Woodpeckers, their bullets cutting off swatches of his clothes and slivers of his flesh. Shots and screams drowned out the abuse that the two principals in this collective duel kept hurling at each other.

Garvey staggered and fell against a hitching post. Frost slumped to the street at the same instant. Both were badly wounded. But they kept firing at each other till their arms sagged and their guns dropped.

The sheriff who had refused to let the Rangers take charge lay dead in front of the courthouse. From somewhere a man with a black bag came hurrying forward and, risking the barrage of Woodpecker bullets, bent over Frost.

The Jaybird leader shook his head feebly. "I'm a goner, Doc. Just leave me die." Painfully, he sat up. "Go on, boys!" he gasped to his nearest followers. "Go on and fight."

His face twitched in a spasm. Blood spilled from his mouth. He was dead when two of his men dragged him to a sidewalk curb.

Then Ira called his first and only retreat as a Ranger commander. The detachment had either to pull out of this crossfire or be slain as so much good riddance for both sides. By seeking cover now, the officers would be in a position to take necessary actions after the guns were stilled.

He looked around to see that his two companions had got separated from him in the melee. Alex McNabb was about six feet away and still trying to stop the two battling mobs. Frank Schmidt was nowhere in sight.

"Save yourself, boys!" Ira shouted.

Alex McNabb raised his gun to indicate that he had gotten the message. Ira spurred his pony across the street, hoping that Frank Schmidt, wherever he was, had heard, too. The horse jumped a board sidewalk, gunpowder blistering its belly as it made the leap. Ira guided it with a quick jerk of the bridle toward an opening between two buildings. Then he turned in his saddle for a safer view of the battle.

Triggers were snapping. Muzzles were blazing. Lying in the middle of the street where he might be trampled to death by the charging boots was a man whom he recognized— Ranger, Frank Schmidt.

Ira jumped from his horse and ran back into the street, crouching low. Schmidt was groaning painfully; his trousers were soaked with blood.

"Easy, Frank," Ira said. "I'll take care of you." He picked up the wounded Ranger in his arms and rushed with him to a laundry emptied of customers and employees by the shotgun spree. Ira carried him into a back room and laid him on a table.

"Frank," Ira asked, "where are you shot?"

"Right through the stomach," the Ranger answered feebly. Ira ripped open Schmidt's shirt. He saw a big blue spot about the size of a half-dollar on the skin over the pit of his stomach. A lead ball must have hit the ground and then, flattened, bounced up to strike the Ranger.

"It was a spent ball, Frank," Ira said in a relieved tone. "It didn't go in." His tensions broke in a gust of laughter. Frank Schmidt tried to say something, but only a great, wheezing sigh came from his lips.

"Are you hit anywhere else, Frank?" Ira asked anxiously.

"My right—leg seems paralyzed," Schmidt said between grimaces of pain. Ira jerked off Schmidt's trousers and underpants. There was a gaping hole extending around the thigh of the Ranger's right leg. Blood was oozing out steadily. A Negro woman, fearful and wild-eyed, ran into the laundry at that moment. Ira called to her:

"Go get a doctor quick! I've got a wounded man here."

Another series of shots rang out. "I'm too scared, Mr. Ranger," the woman screamed, and she ran out shaking with fright.

From a pile of freshly laundered clothes Ira snatched a white shirt. He tore a long, wide strip from it and made a tight bandage around the wound. Then he rolled the stricken man a cigarette. Frank Schmidt puffed it between clenched teeth.

Outside, the gunfire continued. Ira heard a sharp, piercing cry: someone was hit. Shots rattled off the minutes while he tended Schmidt and wondered if his other Ranger, Alex McNabb, was lying dead somewhere.

Schmidt asked for a drink. Ira brought a glass from a cooler of ice water in the laundry. Then he sat down gloomily on a stool to worry about his men.

Four Rangers had started duty in this patch of hell. Now the active force stood at two. Maybe only one, since Ira had no accounting of Alex McNabb. Even so, Ira determined to finish the job they had come to do. If he had to carry on alone, he'd give it his best.

At last, calm was descending over the public square. Men of each side moved about, quietly picking up their casualties. The final shot of the battle, Ira later learned, had been fired just as the sun went down.

Outside, Ira found his horse and mounted. He reined up several times to make inquiries of different groups about Alex McNabb. None could give him any information about the missing Ranger. On the courthouse steps Ira saw Chief Deputy Sheriff Tom Smith. Smith was standing alone, rifle in hand, apparently ready to renew hostilities.

Ira hallooed to him. "Smith, don't shoot any more. This town's a morgue already."

Smith lowered his gun. "I won't shoot if them damned Jaybirds won't."

Ira rode closer to him. "I'll guarantee they won't. Now get on back into the building. This time the Texas Rangers are taking over."

Tom Smith gave his foes a last defiant look, then turned and stalked inside. Ira stood erect in his stirrups, scanning the streets for Alex McNabb.

Then to his great relief McNabb came walking out of the courthouse, where he had taken cover. He reported to Ira that he was unscratched although he had been venturing out under fire to drag fallen feudists inside the building.

"Frank Schmidt is lying badly hurt inside the laundry," Ira told him. "Go over there and take care of him till I get back."

As yet he had no idea of how many had been killed or wounded. He rode rapidly to the depot of the Houston and Texas Central Railroad. The station agent there was also the town telegrapher. Ira scrawled a telegram to Governor Ross in Austin. It read:

> STREET FIGHT JUST OCCURRED BETWEEN THE TWO FACTIONS.
> MANY KILLED AND WOUNDED. SEND MILITIA.

Another wire was addressed to the commander of a militia unit—the Houston Light Guard: HOLD YOURSELVES IN READINESS.

Ira paid for the telegrams, then said to the station agent, "Contact your officials in Houston right away. Be sure that they have a special train ready for the guardsmen."

Darkness had now descended over the town. The silence seemed sepulchral. Not a man was to be seen on the streets. Wooden store signs were pitted with bullet holes and piles of shattered glass were all that was left of shop windows.

Ira went back to the laundry to find that Alex McNabb had located a doctor for Frank Schmidt. The two men left the wounded Ranger in the physician's care; then, carbines drawn, they began patrolling the streets.

They had meant to keep crowds from reassembling and beginning another round of battle. The streets remained deserted and silent. Ira, as he later admitted, "had a creepy feeling" during that vigil, "expecting to be pierced by bullets at every turn."

But no more shots came to echo the hundreds that had been fired earlier under the waning sun of that tragic day. Lights were burning low in some houses as Ira looked out over the town. Dried scarlet streaks stained the plank sidewalks. Stray cats prowled by, subdued and furtive, sniffing at street refuse, then uneasily padded on.

Midnight brought the special train and the militiamen from Houston. With quick military efficiency the troopers occupied the community. Armed squads took up positions on the courthouse lawn. Special guard details were placed around the homes of leading Jaybirds and leading Woodpeckers. Daybreak brought a second company from Brenham, another county seat in the Brazos Valley.

Richmond awoke to find itself under tight martial law. By proclamation of Governor Ross, all civil officials, save those excepted by the militia provost marshal, were relieved of their functionings. The edict suspended from office all local peace officers, including constables, the town marshal who had done nothing to stop the fight, and Chief Deputy Tom Smith, who had automatically become acting sheriff on the death of his superior, Garvey.

With the help of a militia officer, Ira made a check of the casualties. Four people were dead, including a young Negro girl caught by a stray bullet as she was trying to escape the lethal streets. Another Woodpecker lawman, Deputy J. W. Blakely, had died with Sheriff Garvey. Woodpecker Judge Parker was in critical condition. Many more of each faction, including Volney Gibson, had been wounded—exactly how many more nobody has ever known definitely.

Governor Ross himself came to Richmond on the following day. His entourage included an assistant state attorney general who immediately asked a district judge to impanel a special grand jury for any necessary indictments.

The two officials from Austin went into immediate conference with the Ranger Sergeant.

"What happened here was just what I expected," Governor Ross commented. "I suppose that it just had to happen." Turning to Ira, he added that the sergeant and his men had done a good job. A fine, courageous job that would always be remembered.

Ira's face reddened with embarrassment. "I'm afraid we did a very poor job, Governor. We didn't stop those mobs."

Governor Ross answered, with a grave chuckle, "Sergeant, you know the old saying about one Ranger being able to handle one mob. But nobody ever demanded that two Rangers be able to stop two mobs."

Ira felt better. "Yes, sir," he replied soberly. "There were just two of us after Frank Schmidt got shot. But now that the troops are here, how much longer do we have to stay?"

Governor Ross handed Ira a cigar and lighted one himself. "The other Rangers will be leaving within a few days. I'll ask the legislature to vote funds for the care of Frank Schmidt. But you're going to be here for a long time, Aten."

Puzzled, Ira asked the governor if that meant he was to be here on indefinite detail.

The governor shook his head. "Yes, Aten, but a different kind of detail. I've told the county commissioners that I won't pull the troops out until they appoint a sheriff who can command the respect of both factions. On my nomination, they chose you."

Ira felt his personal and private world crumbling around him. That world was the Texas Rangers. It seemed to him that his duty had been performed in Fort Bend County, and he was already sick to his guts with its rankling furies. A girl in Austin had been pressuring him to lay down his badge for a farmer's plow or a ranchman's branding iron. She was a growing influence in his life. But by temperament and choice, Ira was a career Ranger like Bill McDonald, Jim Gillett, and others to whom the force represented the highest form of public service.

The governor's voice broke through Ira's fog. "A local citizen named Clem Bassett has been proposed by the Jaybird organization to succeed Sheriff Garvey."

Ira nodded, seeing a chance to extricate himself. "Mr. Bassett is a good man from a fine old Texas family. I hope you'll approve him."

Governor Ross shook his head. "I have no personal objection to Mr. Bassett. But it is my considered opinion that only an officer from outside—and only one with Ranger background—can keep the lid on after the soldiers leave."

There was no point in further argument with the man who had been one of the state's most distinguished Ranger captains.

As Ira gave his consent, he was remembering all the local law enforcement positions he had declined, all the officials who had given him both hints and offers.

"All right, Governor," he said quietly. "I'll take the job."

Six and a half years as a Texas Ranger had ended in five confused minutes.

"Vol Gibson is here with a gun and ought to be disarmed."

COURTHOUSE KILLING

A few days later Ira was sworn into his new office. At twenty-six, he was Texas's youngest sheriff, if not the youngest in the entire Southwest. Shortly afterward Governor Ross restored civilian authority, then left with the troops and the Ranger detachment, including wounded Frank Schmidt.

The man who stayed felt deeply depressed as he walked back to the hotel where he had rented a room. As he put it, he had been "left alone a stranger in a strange land."

The citizens of Fort Bend County might consider him an interloper foisted on them by Austin. He wondered whether he could measure up to the confident expectations of Governor Ross and end this feud that had its roots in a period before he had been born. Such doubts were taunting Ira Aten as he closed the door of his room and slumped on his bed.

However, he did not allow himself to indulge too long in these bleak conjecturings. After shedding a few tears of self pity, he said a prayer and wrote a long letter to Imogen Boyce, the girl in Austin.

His natural good spirits returned as Fort Bend County's most substantial residents showed, by words and cold cash, that they were supporting their new sheriff. A fifty-thousand-dollar surety bond was required of Ira under Texas law. These prosperous ones obligated themselves, without question, for this amount. It showed their confidence in his ability to fulfill what was for him an entirely new role as an enforcer of law.

As a Ranger, he had been at various times warrant server, diplomat, and quasi-judge. As sheriff of a county pulling out of calamity, he must also be a small-scale statesman, taking the lead in everything from stamping out the embers of the feud to rebuilding the county's ravaged economy. First, the embers must be stamped out till none was left to blaze up into another holocaust.

Quiet had descended upon Fort Bend County. Both sides had buried their dead and were nursing their wounded. Neither faction was claiming any proud victory as a result of the battle. Old enemies passed each other warily on the board sidewalks of Richmond but they carefully avoided each other's hangouts, and no challenges were being issued in any part of the county.

Ira meant to enlarge that tacit truce into a permanent peace. A day after he took office he fired all the gun-toting deputies who had served under his predecessor, Sheriff Garvey. Shorn of the authority that went with badges, they quickly left the county. Other Woodpecker officials, seeing the handwriting on the wall, resigned their offices one by one, to be replaced by appointees selected by the victorious Jaybirds. Kyle Terry, still awaiting trial in Galveston, was considered to have vacated his post as tax assessor, and a new commissioners' court of Jaybirds chose one of their faction to succeed him.

The Republican clique began crumbling after Judge Parker, currently a member of the legislature, recovered from his wound and exiled himself from the county. The special grand jury requested by the assistant attorney general convened in Richmond and indicted a Woodpecker politician for the assassination of J. M. Shamblin, a landowner who had tried to organize a Jaybird faction among the Negroes before the coming of the Rangers. Later, the man was tried, found guilty, and hanged.

Normalcy began returning slowly as Ira kept a tight grip on the county's affairs. Schools opened, as usual, in September, the month after the battle, although few children of Woodpecker families were enrolled by their parents. Men stopped carrying hidden revolvers to church, but one visiting preacher found himself severely grilled by an armed group that surrounded him on a Sunday following services.

"Brother," a man declared solemnly, "we couldn't make out from your sermon whether you're a Jaybird or a Woodpecker."

"Jaybird or Woodpecker?" The minister was startled. What kind of question was that to ask a servant of God, he demanded.

"Brother," was the answer, "you got to be either a Jaybird or a Woodpecker in Fort Bend County."

The preacher scratched his head, then told the group: "Well, since I have to be some kind of a bird I'm a turkey buzzard, and it'll cost you a ten-dollar fine if you shoot me!"

A mild coastal winter followed a pleasant autumn in Fort Bend. Saturday-afternoon crowds in Richmond were once more friendly and jovial, in the accustomed fashion of Texas rural folk. Drunks and fist brawlers gave Ira some extra work on weekends, as did off-duty cowhands squabbling over bets placed on horse races. To the relief of everybody, the town moralist moved away with the henpecked parson who was her husband. Her name was Carrie Nation and she afterward acquired a reputation as a militant champion of virtue by chopping up saloons with her hatchet.

Ira was beginning to think that a sheriff's job was a boringly tame one when a delayed legal proceeding led Fort Benders to load their guns again.

On a Saturday afternoon in mid-December he stepped from the courthouse to make his usual Saturday-afternoon patrol. Store windows were decorated with tinsel and red paper Christmas bells. Trade was brisk in that annual pre-holiday shopping season. But Sheriff Aten detected a certain touchy unrest among the crowds congregated along the sidewalks.

Little cliques of whispering men grew silent when they spotted him. A woman of a Woodpecker family swept nervously past Ira, ignoring his lifted hat. Negroes were leaving the streets and boarding wagons to return to plantation shanties. Here and there, as Fort Bend's sheriff kept walking, he heard muttered oaths. Too many customers were coming out of a hardware store in the middle of Main Street. Bulges in their jacket pockets told Ira that their purchases were boxes of cartridges.

He stopped one man leaving the place. "What's up, Lou?"

"Buy a paper and find out, Sheriff."

Ira went into a confectionery and bought that morning's edition of the Galveston *Daily News*. His eyes widened as he read a headline:

KYLE TERRY, FORT BEND SLAYER, FACES TRIAL HERE JANUARY 21.

Ira knew that trouble would now be brewing, both in Fort Bend County, where he had labored so hard to restore peace, and in Galveston County, where the banished chief of the Woodpeckers would finally be facing justice for the brutal killing of Ned Gibson.

Half of Fort Bend County would show up at Galveston for that trial, Ira thought. They'd be there with guns—and the biggest guns would be carried by Volney and Guilf Gibson.

Showing a calmness he didn't feel, Ira started taking swift precautions against renewed violence. He sought out the Gibsons at the Brahma Bull Saloon, asking for their word as gentlemen that they would precipitate no violence at the trial but let the law take its course.

They listened to him with the studied correctness of blue bloods. Then Volney Gibson spoke:

"We appreciate your position, Sheriff. But as a gentleman, you should know that this is a matter of personal honor. Kyle Terry killed our brother, so—"

Volney Gibson left the sentence unfinished, but Ira Aten and every other man in the saloon could have supplied its ending.

Ira did secure a promise from the Gibsons that they would stage no personal vendetta against the other Terrys, all of whom had remained loyal neo-Confederates except Kyle, the neo-scalawag. Declining the drink that Volney Gibson offered to buy, Ira hurried from the Brahma Bull to seek out leading members of the Terry connection.

He found them to be almost as obstinate. Kyle Terry might have disgraced the clan by his political switch and his soliciting of Negro votes, but still he was a member of the family, entitled under the feudal code to its collective protection, whatever he'd done. Blood ran deeper in Texas than all the waters of all its rivers.

At last, however, he received their grudging promise not to wage a preventive war on the Gibsons. By narrowing the range of conflict, Ira felt that he had made progress; raging family feuds could be even more devastating than raging political ones in this volcanic state. Now he had to insure that the trial of Kyle Terry would not be punctuated with violence after the district judge pounded the gavel in Galveston County courthouse.

Ira hurried to Galveston city, eighty-five miles southwest. There Sheriff Pat Tiernan made light of his fears.

"You're a young country officer, son," he told Ira patronizingly. "This is a big town, where people don't pull any monkey shines in the courthouse. Besides, Kyle Terry has been here for months—and the Gibson boys have known it. Why haven't they been over looking for him before?"

"I don't know," Ira answered. "But it's the future I'm worrying about, not the past."

Sheriff Tiernan laughed. "Young man, Galveston County and the future are my worry."

Ira made no headway when he begged Tiernan to appoint special deputies for the trial. After he returned to Fort Bend County, he thought of writing Governor Ross and requesting that Rangers be sent to Galveston for Kyle Terry's bout with justice. But protocol kept him from doing what unhampered good sense would have commanded. When the sheriff of a particular county wanted Ranger help, he had to make the request himself. No outside lawman could do it without incurring the suspicion of every other officer in the state. Ira had always tried not to arouse rivalries that would cripple his own efficiency as a law enforcer.

Remembering Tiernan as an amiable jackass, he went back to his own jurisdiction, still hoping that he could prevent a blazing sequel to the Battle of Richmond.

He talked with every Fort Bend County man who would be going to Galveston as a witness. All happened to be Jaybirds, but all promised that they would travel to the island city unarmed and would not join the Gibson brothers in any gunplay.

Just when Ira felt that he had everything under reasonable control, the press began giving heavy coverage to the situation. Reporters from out-of-town papers began badgering him in his office at the courthouse. They tried in vain to elicit any blood-curdling statements from the young sheriff, but they got enough from the townspeople to satisfy their desires. Then the Galveston *News* ran a number of editorials abusing Fort Bend County for letting its fracases spill over into a "respectable" community (the city was plague-spotted with gin mills and bawdy houses).

January 21, 1890, was another day that would remain indelibly etched on Ira's calendar of memorable events. Another trial consumed the morning in the courthouse at Galveston. Ira arrived at the building around 10 A.M., to see the first and second floors jammed with Jaybird factionalists from Fort Bend. He shook hands pleasantly with everybody, not forgetting to remind them of their promises to behave. Kyle Terry, out on bond, had not yet put in an appearance, but somebody told Ira that Kyle's brother, Dave, namesake of the two-gun uncle, had come in from California for the trial.

The Fort Bend sheriff looked around for the Gibson brothers but found only Volney. Guilf Gibson had apparently stayed home, for reasons of his own. Ira sensed that Volney Gibson was carrying a concealed revolver but, having no authority in Galveston County, he could not disarm the somber-looking rancher.

"Vol," he said, after calling him aside, "I'm putting you on your honor that you've talked about not to start anything with Kyle and Dave Terry."

Volney Gibson's reply was dyed-in-the-wool Old South: "I cannot accept that obligation you place upon my honor, sir."

Ira went forthwith to the sheriff's office on the second floor. There he made a second appeal to Sheriff Pat Tiernan. "Pat, I don't want to pester you—but Vol Gibson is here with a gun and he ought to be disarmed."

Sheriff Tiernan gave Ira a fatherly pat on the shoulder. "Don't worry, sonny. Just leave it to me."

"Sonny." A hell of a label for a fellow sheriff!

Ira strode up to the third floor and entered the district attorney's office. "Judge," he said, addressing the prosecutor by the complimentary title given most Texas lawyers, "Volney Gibson's here and he's aiming to shoot Kyle Terry before you get a chance to try him."

The district attorney looked at Ira calmly. "Have you discussed this with Sheriff Tiernan?"

Ira replied that he had. The prosecutor answered with patronizing reassurance:

"Pat Tiernan's a very competent officer, Aten. Don't worry."

A blast of gunfire echoed from the floor below. The sound of excited voices followed. The district attorney ran out the back door of his office and down a private flight of stairs leading to the courtroom. Ira took the front stairs in descending leaps, to land beside a dying Kyle Terry.

Terry lay sprawled on elbows and knees across the last three or four steps of the stairs leading to the sheriff's office. Ira guessed that he had been shot by Volney Gibson as he was ascending the steps. A shaking pistol in his hand was pointed diagonally toward the sheriff's door. Though his eyes were already glazing over, he was desperately trying to cock the trigger.

The pistol dropped from his hand as Kyle Terry died. Ira realized that he had been trying to aim it at Gibson, who had followed the code by surrendering to the sheriff after getting his man.

Ira picked up the six-shooter and opened it. All the half dozen shells lay unexploded in their snug cylinders. Kyle

Terry had died without firing a shot. The voices in the sheriff's office grew loud and hilarious. Ira knew that the Jaybirds were congregating around Volney Gibson to congratulate him on the vengeance slaying.

Two city policemen came running up the stairs. They had heard the shots from the street. Ira asked their help in lifting the corpse to the landing. An undertaker came a little while later to carry away the remains of Kyle Terry, who had inexpediently turned scalawag when the Reconstruction period itself was at an end in a reviving era of white supremacy.

Terry's death rolled down the final curtain on the Republican party in South Texas. An inquest showed that Volney Gibson's bullet had punctured his heart. Sheriff Tiernan had unwittingly provided Gibson with a post-murder claque by herding all the Jaybird witnesses into his office while Ira had been conferring with the district attorney.

To the surprise of no one in Texas, Volney Gibson was never prosecuted. The classically western state of the American Union was unfailingly southern in its mores.

Ira took only reasonable precautions against a repetition of the feud after returning to Fort Bend County. He realized that the Woodpecker faction was finished, with its last leader dead and its Negro-based support now meaningless.

Dave Terry reportedly went back to California. Other members of the family migrated to the western half of Texas, where their descendants became prosperous, leading citizens. Most of the Woodpecker clans had drifted into Fort Bend County after the war; now they began drifting out.

The Jaybirds consolidated themselves into a permanent Democratic political organization, using its power to disfranchise the Negroes. From that time on, Fort Bend became one of the bulwarks of political conservatism in Texas though, paradoxically, it would keep producing Negro cowboys who starred in rodeos throughout the country.

Ira, trying to maintain his independence, became more of an outsider for the remainder of his term. Nevertheless,

Fort Bend citizens spoke admiringly of him as "our Texas Ranger sheriff," and he could have stayed on, perhaps to become a rich man, with all the opportunities that would have been his for the taking.

In that last year of his tenure, however, he wanted only to complete the task assigned him by Governor Ross, then move on.

*"You called me a liar not
long ago. Do you still
say it?"*

DUEL AT DIMMITT

The year 1890 came, opening a new decade that heralded a dawning new century. The West was already taking on the symmetry of the future as railroads kept expanding and smug little towns bearing prettified names kept replacing the godless old trading posts.

With Bibles and plows and washtubs, the inevitable puritans were superseding the nomadic breeds who had lived by dare and by chance. The colorful drifting cowhand knew that the corrals and the bunkhouse could not outlast the pigpens and the cabins of the virtuous; anchored nesters. The gambler was yielding to the parson. The dance-hall strumpet was disappearing before the eternal wife, doing more than anybody else to speed the process.

Everywhere change was manifesting itself in that impersonal arrogance of history. The epoch of Anglo-Saxon colonization and settlement, begun in the valleys of Virginia during the early seventeenth century, was drawing to a somewhat less than elegiac close on the prairies beyond the Mississippi in the late nineteenth. Except that these final frontiers had been made, by fences and railroads and post offices, smaller than those ancestral ones.

A new election was approaching in Texas. Thanks to an alert young sheriff, Fort Bend County would be conducting its first peaceful poll since the Civil War. During the summer, leaders of the Jaybird Democratic Association visited Ira in his office at the courthouse.

"You're the best sheriff Fort Bend ever had," a spokesman said, "even if you've served only an unexpired term. We'd like to put you on our ticket for a full term."

Ira asked for two weeks to think it over. After the delegation had left, he found himself torn by an internal debate. It revolved around Imogen Boyce, who was so sensitive to change and, like most frontier women, gladly welcomed it.

Eight years as a law enforcer were behind him. Eight years singed with gunpowder and accented by risk. Six and a half of them had been spent as a Texas Ranger, almost two more as sheriff of this county, which, until his coming, had characteristically combined the violence of both South and West.

His taming of Fort Bend County had given him stellar rank among western officers. From Dallas to Denver men regarded him as an outstanding professional lawman and expected the badge to be Ira Aten's constant, whatever authority it represented. Attractive offers were being made to him as his term of office in Fort Bend was nearing its close. He had received strong nibbles from Oklahoma, whose federal marshals were preparing the territory for statehood by exterminating the last outlaw bands. Town marshals, strong of will and resolute in action, were needed in New Mexico and Arizona, also faced with the necessity of making healthy transitions. Different Texas cities, including Houston and Dallas, would gladly have given such a seasoned and noted officer one or another top job in their police departments.

"Boy, I want you back in the Rangers," Governor Ross told Ira when he had visited Austin to pay a courting visit to Imogen. "You'll return as a lieutenant. Either you or John Hughes will be the next captain commissioned in the Frontier Battalion."

That bid had been the hardest for Ira to reject because it had been the most tempting. But the thought of competing with his recruit and best friend, John Hughes, stopped him from re-entering the force. Hughes, meantime, had done his sponsor and the state of Texas proud. Step by step he was advancing up the ladder of promotion, each time succeeding a superior who had been killed in action.

Anywhere in the West there would be employment opportunities for peace officers of Ira Aten's caliber. Yet Imogen

Boyce kept reminding him that he had not been shaped in that fundamental mold of a breed destined to vanish from the face of the West—the foot-loose lawman.

"You come from a refined religious home like I do," she had told him during one hectic session in which courting had given way to disputation. "You sometimes forget it because of all the glory you've won. But I don't forget it about either of us. I'm not going to trail a gun for the rest of my life—nor try to make a home behind a gun."

Ira kept being haunted by that set-to as he mulled over the invitation extended him by the Salt Grass political machine. With emphasis, tempered by a woman's gentleness, she had told him that marriage was conditioned on his pledge never again to hold public office nor to accept appointment as a lawman.

"So," Ira had asked, "it's lay down my badge before you'll accept my ring?"

And she had nodded yes.

A week passed in Fort Bend County. Within another week Ira would have to give his answer to the Jaybirds. He decided to make another quick trip to Austin in the hope of working out some sort of compromise with a woman whose determined strength so evenly matched his own.

"Fort Bend County's simmered down," he told her on the porch of the big farmhouse where the Boyces lived. "We'll buy a place there in Richmond. A lot of the folks are planters like yours, and they'll respect you as the sheriff's wife."

Imogen had no patience with such reasoning. "I don't want to be a Ranger's wife—a marshal's wife—or a sheriff's wife. If I did, I'd be in Richmond right now, and you wouldn't be living in a hotel."

Another impasse developed between Ira and the girl. In the end, it was a member of Imogen's family who broke the deadlock, and swayed the decision that he had to make in Richmond.

The mediator was her cousin, Colonel Albert G. Boyce, general manager of the three-million-acre XIT ranch in the

Texas Panhandle. He asked Ira to take a ride with him to the Austin hills. After they had stopped to roast a potted rabbit, Boyce hesitantly spoke what was on his mind.

"Ira, you're a stubborn cuss trying to marry a stubborn girl. Maybe you ought to be more considerate of her viewpoint."

"How's that?" Ira asked.

Boyce tried to be tactful. "The hitch is that you're still wanting to build a reputation, but Imogen wants to build a home."

Ira was silent. Colonel Boyce went on.

"You've got your reputation, Ira, and men will be writing about you years after you've hit the last trail. But do you have a home?"

Ira chewed over that thought for a moment. Then he stood up and whistled to his pony munching on the mountain grass.

"That question answers itself, Colonel. Let's ride back. I'm going to make Imogen that promise."

When they reached the city, Ira dismounted in front of Joe Koen's jewelry store. The jeweler was a man who admired Rangers, so that the ring a capitulating Ranger took to a strong minded woman was a handsome one, sold at a drastically reduced price. Imogen joyfully accepted token and pledge, then began figuring how many more sheets and doilies she should load in her hope chest.

Ira went back to Richmond and called in the Jaybird chieftains ahead of time. "I have to say no, gentlemen," he said. "I'm moving to the Panhandle and, afterward, getting married."

None of their attempts at friendly persuasion could change his mind. In November Fort Bend County elected a new sheriff. Ira turned over his accounts and records to his successor. December 1, 1890, found him spading ground for a dugout on a homestead claim in Castro County, fifty miles south of Amarillo. The XIT spread extended into this county. Imogen's cousin had recommended the location as one where he might start a small and profitable stock farm.

Eight hundred miles lay between him and his old Ranger comrades on the Rio Grande. Castro County was a lonely strip, just beginning to fill with nesters, and Ira's first months there were solitary ones. Imogen willingly would have gone with him to share the hardships of this new frontier. It was a matter of pride to Ira that he first have a place prepared for her, so the marriage had been deferred until he had made his start.

Ira knew not one person in Castro County when he located there. Yet no more than a former outlaw can a former lawman blot out a record he has made. The "Texas Ranger" label soon followed him to the Panhandle; more and more nesters coming in knew him by reputation. And once a Ranger, always a leader. Within a few months Ira found himself becoming the natural spokesman for one of two groups tussling for ascendancy.

Castro was an unorganized county, administered with other counties like it by the officials at Amarillo. This system was a sort of a subterritorial one, set up by the Texas legislature, to provide some framework for settlement and for law till the barren spaces would have enough population to justify the establishment of regular local governments.

Ira knew that the county where he had located would probably be organized within a few months. A town called Dimmitt had already sprung up within its borders. Logically, the community looked forward to becoming the county seat. But trailing the homesteaders was the usual clique of land agents and grasping émigré politicians who started running for office the minute they landed in the Panhandle.

Two slick adventurers had chosen Castro County for fat living in a lean land. Leading a nascent political ring was Andrew McClelland, a glib lawyer who had announced for county judge in the first election, still to be called. Paired with him in a booming real-estate business was his brother, Hugh. The McClellands were recent arrivals from Tennessee, and had never cast a vote in Texas. Grouped around them was a crowd of nondescript drifters hungrily anticipating posts in a courthouse yet to be built.

Ira was outraged when he estimated the sky-high profits that the brothers were making from the sale of lots in Dimmitt. Their sales pitch was Dimmitt's prospects as a county seat, and they intimated that it would outstrip mushrooming Amarillo once the railroad had been extended into the county. Their prices were extortionate for this section, where ground had been literally dirt cheap.

Many citizens were opposed to the highhanded McClellands but up to now none had dared try to organize a counter faction; the brothers' marksmanship was understood to equal their ambition. All that was changed when an authentic Texan, with a Ranger record, joined the ranks of the nesters.

Ira's fellow settlers made him a sounding board for all the developing antipathy toward the brothers. He was in a quandary, not wanting to begin any course that might alter his pledge to Imogen. But complaints against the McClellands piled up from nesters who hunted him down when he was branding calves or breaking broncs. Ira's sense of civic responsibility, nurtured by those years in the Rangers, eventually forced him to act.

"Damned if I could sit still and see that ring take over a county where poor homesteaders were investing their sweat and their last dribbles of cash." So he afterward described his reactions. Maybe Imogen wouldn't mind if he called a raw turn with something besides a gun. So suddenly, calculatedly, a former Ranger struck at land hogs in their most vital spot: their pocket book.

With funds realized from the sale of some steers, he bought a tract of ground and had it mapped as a town site he christened Castro City. Ira offered lots to settlers at much lower prices and on longer time payments than could be had from the McClellands in Dimmitt. At the same time, he announced that Castro City would compete with Dimmitt for the county seat when the election was called.

The reaction of the brothers was pained and quick. They called a public meeting in a schoolhouse to denounce Ira Aten as an irresponsible Johnny-come-lately. Ira boldly attended, listened to their abusive harangues, then took the floor to expose the McClelland clique for what it was.

In the middle of the former Ranger's speech Andrew McClelland jumped from a bench, ready to burst out of his neat black broadcloth suit.

"You're a liar, Aten!" he shouted.

The audience gasped. Call a man a name in Texas and be prepared to back it with fist or trigger. Every eye was fixed on Ira. Andrew McClelland's fingers were gripping a gun butt.

Ira knew that, if he touched his own pistol, Castro County would suffer havoc before it held an election.

Two minutes of taut silence. Women were fidgeting nervously. Then from somewhere in the crowd came the wail of a little girl who had seen her father die in a six-shooter duel. It served to sway Ira Aten.

"Neighbors," he said to the audience, "I did more fighting in the Texas Rangers than I ever want to talk about. But no Ranger ever started a fracas where women and children were present. Mr. McClelland has publicly called me a liar. I'll be asking him to repeat that statement—after the election."

He strode out of the schoolhouse, mounted his horse, and rode back to his dugout. Next day Potter County officials met in Amarillo to call an election for Castro County. Heartened by Ira's example, the anti-McClelland forces nominated a ticket headed by a settler named Gough for county judge. Ira, resolutely keeping his promise to Imogen, refused to accept the designation for sheriff. After he had declined, the citizens put up a cowboy whose tongue was quicker with a joke than his hand was with a draw.

During the campaign Ira spoke and electioneered for the slate. If the McClelland ring won, it would formulate public policy and fix public tax rates to the further enrichment of the brothers. Ten days before the poll some worried residents of Dimmitt came to Ira's dugout.

"Aten," one of them said, "we want to make you a proposition. Our town is already built; yours is something on a piece of paper. If you'll withdraw Castro City from the county-seat race, we'll back the Gough ticket against the McClelland one."

Ira answered immediately. "All right, men, that's a fair trade. Castro City's buried before it was ever born."

The settlers went to the polls on a blustery day in November, 1891, eleven months after Ira's arrival in the county. They gave the ring candidates the worst electoral trouncing ever suffered by any clique of roving politicians in the Panhandle.

Gough, the homesteader who subscribed for nine newspapers, crushed Andrew McClelland in the race for county judge. The joke-cracking cowhand was elected sheriff, with Ira wishing that his friends might have found a stronger man.

By the democratic way of the ballot the settlers had squared some collective accounts with the McClellands. But a more personal account of his must be evened with them if he was to keep the respect of his neighbors.

Ira waited till he was informed that Castro County's first officials had been sworn in by a district judge from Amarillo. Then he buckled on his forty-five and rode to Dimmitt. Imogen certainly would differentiate between an affair of honor and shooting done for salary. At least he hoped so.

He saw Andrew McClelland standing in front of a store when he entered the county seat. As he drew near, Ira saw that the lawyer's holster was empty. McClelland's face flamed red when he saw his enemy dismount and walk toward him.

Ira halted within a few inches of the discredited office seeker. "Andrew, you called me a liar not long ago. Do you still say it?"

The lawyer's hand went to the empty holster. "I still say it, Aten!" he spat. "But I have to say it unarmed."

"Arm yourself," Ira answered. "I'll wait."

McClelland whirled around and walked into the store. A crowd began gathering at a discreet distance away. This was the long-anticipated meeting between a man still regarded as a Ranger and one known as a rascal. The store door swung open. Out stepped the lawyer, flourishing two forty-fives he had just bought.

The politician raised his guns and fired. The bullets went wide of their target. Andrew McClelland's haste to kill had spoiled his aim. As he attempted a second round, Ira fired. He heard the thud of bullet biting into flesh and the quick cry that followed.

The adventurer fell to the plank sidewalk. Blood spurted from his left arm, dyeing a sleeve of the broadcloth from black to scarlet. His face convulsed with agony, Andrew McClelland propped himself on his good elbow and shot again. A sigh wheezed from his lips when he saw his enemy standing there still untouched.

Ira had helped beat this man in the election, then bested him in a gun duel. These were triumphs enough to satisfy any reasonable man's honor. Anything else, Ira realized, would be "sending a game foe to hell ahead of his time."

"Get on your feet, Andrew," he called. "We're even now."

The remaining pistol slid from the lawyer's right hand. McClelland opened his mouth and spat contempt on it as it dropped. His cronies rushed forward to pick him up. Ira was shoving his gun back in his holster when a gunshot sounded and a bullet sang past him.

Ira swung around, pistol cocked, to see Hugh McClelland dodging behind a boxlike shanty at the end of the block. A gun was in the hand of the land agent.

Ira pulled trigger. His shot went through the corner of the shanty, tearing through pine board to hit Hugh McClelland. Ira heard a howl, then he ducked as a pistol barrel was poked from around the shanty wall. After another shot the gun disappeared.

Men yelled to Ira, urging him to take cover. But Ira was not retreating. Once more he lifted his revolver. Once more his shell splintered through the flimsy shack. Once more, so a sobbing moan told him, his shot had punctured flesh as well as wood.

After a brief silence Ira heard feet moving rapidly away from the shanty. Finally their sound was lost under the hoof tread of mule teams drawing farm wagons into town.

Ira turned. A man with a badge was pushing his way through the awed spectators. It was the cowhand sheriff, who had been too absorbed in a checker game at the town barber shop to notice the shooting until it was over.

The sheriff saw Andrew McClelland stretched on a bench outside the store and Ira Aten soberly contemplating the gun he still hadn't put away. The sheriff's eyes bulged.

"Golly!" he croaked. "Whatinell happened?"

"I've just shot the McClelland brothers," Ira answered him tightly. "So I reckon I'm your first arrest and your first prisoner."

He handed the gun, butt forward, to the sheriff. "Send somebody to get the doctor for Andrew. And find Hugh. He swallowed a double dose of lead."

"I know that breaking my pledge will break your heart. But I feel it is my duty to help these people."

RUSTLER ROUNDUP

Ira's fight with the McClellands was a fateful disturbance of the life pattern he had been trying to find under the moderating influence of Imogen Boyce. Ballots, rather than bullets, were becoming the main solvents of the conflicts developing from an emerging new West. This change, a virtual revolution, was a welcome one to a man basically preferring the franchise to the forty-five.

Originally, Ira had wanted only to whip a pair of fortune hunters at the polls. Then he would go back to a quiet life centering around that waiting girl in Austin.

Years of modest, prudent living had been his goal. Years in which he'd add another stable, industrious family to those already transforming the Panhandle from a belt of prairie-dog towns to a prosperous center of human settlement. Mindful of its peculiar soil, he had planned to grow crops of grass-derived plants such as wheat and maize in this domain of grass. His essential frugality was irked whenever he saw East Texas emigrants despoiling its wide acres with the parasitic fluff called cotton.

He had thought that in some manner he might act as a mediator between the XIT and the nesters venting their resentments against bigness through the militant Populist party. Naturally there would be friction between land-hungry little men and that formidable beef-raising corporation managed by Imogen's cousin. Yet did not both the small and the great have a common interest in improving a section that held such a potential for everybody? Did not both face the common necessity of rustling, fence cutting, and other surviving remnants of outlawry? Could not some understanding be worked out within the West's traditional framework of neighborliness?

All these plans for the future had been so many projections of aims firmly fixed when he had relinquished the badge in Fort Bend County. All were dependent on commitments made to the woman he meant to marry.

The men he shot recovered quickly. Andrew McClelland's arm wound had been a flesh one with bone left intact. Ira's first bullet had grazed Brother Hugh's neck, the second his spine. A quarter of an inch deviation of either, and the speculator would have ended in the Dimmitt graveyard.

Ira knew that the legal consequences of his act might be serious. But he was less disturbed by a possible verdict of guilt than by worry over Imogen's opinion of the shooting scrape. A jury he could face on the merits understood between men. Facing a woman, with her baffling standards, was a more grueling prospect than cross-examination by the best prosecuting attorney in Texas.

Naturally, he had to face the woman before tackling the jury and prosecutor. Imogen sent him a brief, emphatic letter demanding an explanation after she had read a newspaper account of the fight. Meantime Judge Gough, helping Ira as much as possible, had also entered charges against the McClelland brothers and placed them under the same amount of bail. These two then closed their land business and hurriedly returned to Tennessee, though legally obligated to remain in Texas for the trial.

What went on with Imogen in Austin Ira never fully recorded. He declared in his memoirs that "she believed all I said." But her eyes must have flashed fire, she must have made some angry comments, as Ira explained why "honor" had required him to compound a sweeping political triumph with a subjectively personal one. Texas women seldom had patience for the irrelevant heroisms of men.

Imogen listened to the evidence and gave her verdict in advance of the one to be rendered by a jury:

"Ira, I won't let you go back to Castro County unless you marry me and take me with you."

It struck the former Ranger as being a light sentence.

On February 3, 1892, at Central Christian Church in Austin, Imogen Boyce became Imogen Aten. The bride was twenty-four years old, the groom, twenty-nine. With the fine adaptability of a pioneer woman, the young wife went with her husband to the Panhandle and turned a bachelor dugout into as pleasant a home as a hole in the ground could be.

She sat through every day of the trial held a little later at the district court in another county seat named Tulia. The McClellands did not appear either as defendants to be judged or as witnesses to complain. Ira didn't know a man on the jury. But after the judge had been handed a verdict of acquittal, every juror filed by him to shake hands and offer "a kind word of encouragement."

Two old farmers on the panel particularly impressed Ira. "We thought you were a little hasty in shooting two men just because one of them called you a liar," the first granger said, "but we weren't willing to send you to prison for it."

"I wish you'd killed the sons of bitches," remarked the second.

All his life Ira retained a list of the jurors and it was one of his most prized keepsakes. After the trial he and his bride returned to their ranch. While she cooked meals considerably better than bachelor's beans, he began building a substantial frame house to replace the dugout.

As each man remembers some idyll intimately personal, Ira never forgot that half year of quiet contentment. Trouble he recalled only as so much spent fury. Kitchen smoke trailing from his chimney meant more to him than all the gunsmoke spouted from Ranger carbines. And "one hug from my good woman," he wrote wistfully, "more than all the citations ever handed me by Ranger captains."

Yet life, as such, inhibits a gifted man from sustaining a posture palpably less than himself. Ira Aten could no more

be the ordinary domesticated male than a veteran soldier
can be a pacifist. He had intended to keep faithfully all the
promises made to Imogen before their marriage. Then another crisis of conscience was forced upon him by a challenge to the law.

In the fall of 1892 a horde of range thieves descended on
Castro County from lawless areas of New Mexico Territory.
Thousands of cattle were stolen from the ranches; farmers
lost even their plow horses to the plundering gangs. A vicious local mob led by the thieving Cordele brothers—Oscar
and Fred—scraped up the leavings.

The whole flimsy structure of law began collapsing in this
newly-organized county. Citizens appealed to their elected
sheriff for leadership and protection. But that jovial soul
preferred jumping kings at the barbershop checkerboard to
apprehending rustlers on a range.

His indifference to duty encouraged other types of criminals to make Castro County their hunting ground. Card
sharps and bushwhackers from all over the West gathered
in Dimmitt to turn it into another Panhandle hell-hole like
tough Tascosa. Decent women hesitated to walk on the main
street. The fading jezebels from the tamed towns came
flocking in.

Once more harassed settlers begged Ira Aten to help them.
But Ira stood firm on the promises he had made to his wife
that he'd forget the badge and the chase. There was an added reason now for keeping those pledges: Imogen was preg-
nant. So he kept referring them, though it scorched his gall,
to the barbershop loafer who wore the star.

During March of 1893 Imogen took their first-born to visit
his two sets of grandparents in Austin and Round Rock. The
baby son was christened Marion Hughes Aten, the middle
name honoring John Hughes, now a Ranger sergeant. Si-
multaneously the Cordele gang began harassing Dimmitt by
stealing calves in broad daylight from back-yard pens.

This was the last straw for a law-abiding people. The sore-
ly beset citizens had had enough. The sheriff's guarantors

went to the county clerk and erased their signatures from his bond. Nobody else would sign for him so that he was automatically out of office.

Judge Gough called an urgent meeting of the county commissioners to name a successor. Only one man was proposed, he being the only one who had the background to cope with this fresh onslaught of outlawry. Ira was making the best of temporary batching when Gough rode to his house and informed him that he'd been drafted as sheriff of Castro County.

It was then that the former Ranger broke the most solemn pledge of his lifetime. His neighbors were facing the stark issue of life or death. Honest men or bad men, one or the other, were going to have to move out of the county.

"I don't know how my wife will take it, Judge," he said soberly, "but I've got to accept."

Gough, the dugout intellectual, swore him in on the spot. Ira went to the courthouse and told the deposed sheriff to vacate. Then he sat down and wrote his first letter on Castro County's official stationery. It was a letter to his wife.

I've just been made sheriff of Castro County, he wrote. I know that breaking my pledge will break your heart. But I feel it is my duty to help these people.

A few days later there came a one-line reply from Imogen: *I will never return home until you resign.*

Eventually, it took an interfamily council of Boyces and Atens to reverse that ultimatum from a furious wife. But when Imogen did come home, she showed the mettle of a pioneer woman.

A daughter of a cultured family buckled two six-shooters around her waist to begin serving as county jailer. Some of the deadliest cutthroats in the West were her wards during her husband's tenure as sheriff. Not one of them ever escaped.

Few men have ever served as sheriff of two counties, in Texas or anywhere else. In both counties where Ira had worn the badge he had been appointed to accomplish a specific purpose.

In Fort Bend County his paramount job was to quell an organized vendetta. There all the offenders had been people of respectable origins. But in Castro County, as Ira put it, "I realized that I had been appointed sheriff for the duty of cleaning up the county of horse and cattle thieves. So started in on what proved to be a real job."

The job had to be done, this time, on the dregs and scourings from all over Texas, New Mexico, and Oklahoma.

Ira began his campaign by declaring war on the Cordeles. Before many weeks he was riding after them with writs and warrants. Those brothers of the long rope got the jump on a determined sheriff by slipping out, between suns, with scores of cattle belonging to different settlers.

Nobody seemed to know where they had gone. Any who actually did were afraid to tell. Some whispered that they'd shoved west to New Mexico, some that they'd headed south toward the Cap Rock, others that their destination was the Cimarron section in No-Man's Land, north of the Canadian River.

Finally Ira learned from a frightened informant that the brothers, with several other cattle thieves, had fled east to Oklahoma. With two cowboy deputies, Ira started trailing them across six Panhandle counties. All along the way friends and sympathizers of the outlaws tried to throw the small posse off the track. But the pursuers trailed the wideloopers to the Oklahoma line. There, Texas officers would ordinarily have turned back; but boundaries weren't halting those three as they splashed their horses across the Canadian.

Forty miles over the line they entered the deep bottoms of the Ouachita River. Near sundown they discovered a large bunch of the stolen cattle. Other bunches kept appearing as the trio of lawmen rode deeper into the bottoms. Steers, bearing brands of different ranchers along the pursuit route, were mixed with those whose marks identified them as belonging to Castro County citizens. It was obvious to Ira that the gang had appropriated every stray beef in sight during a long and leisurely raid on Panhandle ranges.

"Looks like they're loose-herding the cattle, Sheriff," a deputy observed. "Holding them by a watering place during the day, then rounding them up to march under cover of night."

Ira agreed, remarking that the rustlers must be nearby. Talk was stopped by a clatter of hoofs heard down a dim trail. Hastily the three lawmen pulled their mounts into a dense thicket. From that cover they trained their Winchesters on three men who were drawing near. Their voices came clearly over the first evening calls of wild birds.

"Time to git these critters moving," said a big fellow who seemed to be bossing operations. "I promised to git 'em to the Cordele boys by Saturday at sunup."

"Reckon so," answered a scrawny youth. "But I'm leavin' out soon as they pay me off. First time I ever worked a runnin' iron for any outfit."

"Eatin' three squares a day, ain't you?" the big man growled.

"Damned sight better'n you were doin' when the Cordeles gave you a feed and a job."

The third man nervously jingled his spurs. "I done many a chore for the Cordeles," he said. "But derned if I like the way we handled this one."

"What's wrong?" the big man demanded belligerently.

"Been movin' too slow," the perturbed thief answered. "And stoppin' to pick up too many cattle with a posse right on our tails. Ruck and Jack tipped us that danged Ranger sheriff and his deputies was after us."

The boss shrugged his heavy shoulders. "Hell, Aten and his posse had to stop at the line. They ain't got no authority this side of "

Ira raised his Winchester and gave his pony a swift jab with the spurs. The horse plunged forward through the thicket as the outlaws came abreast of the waiting officers. The mounts carrying the two deputies were right behind Ira's.

Three startled rustlers looked into the business ends of three loaded rifles. Three pairs of hands rose high.

"Here's our authority," Ira said tersely. "Our guns. You fellows want to make it easier on yourselves by waiving extradition back to Texas?"

The skinny youth started blubbering. "I'll go back like you say, Mr. Sheriff. Please make it light on me, I ain't never been in no trouble before."

The man who had been complaining spoke in words flat and resigned. "You called the draw, Aten, and I been expectin' you, anyhow. I'll go."

Ira turned to the big man. "You agree with your partners?"

"Hell, no!" the boss rustler snarled. "You ain't takin' me one hoofstep across that line without papers."

"I'll get the papers," Ira promised. "Strip them of their guns," he said to the deputies.

Ira decided to leave the cattle untended in the bottoms till the three prisoners were delivered to the nearest Oklahoma jail, which was at Cheyenne, in Roger Mills County. He knew that the slow-moving steers would not drift far from this lush grass and plentiful water. Besides, the posse should not be gone for much longer than twenty-four hours.

The three prisoners were taken to Cheyenne and lodged in a jail that looked insubstantial as a cheesebox while Ira hunted up a judge. Before that official the two who were cooperating signed confessions of cattle stealing in Texas and formal waivers of extradition. The third laughed in the court's face.

"I'm placing all three prisoners in your custody, Sheriff Aten," the judge said. "You'd better keep the big one locked up here until you get an extradition order from the territorial governor in Guthrie."

Ira thanked the court, but didn't trust Cheyenne's flimsy jail to contain the holdout desperado. He sent his deputies back to the Washita, instructing them to start toward Texas with the recovered cattle and the two prisoners. "Make these rustlers help drive the herd on the way back," he said. "I'll overtake you later."

Ira took the boss thief, handcuffed, on a stagecoach to Guthrie and had him locked up in the strong jail at Oklahoma's territorial capital. He sought out the governor, who proved cooperative.

"I'm at your service, Sheriff," he said. "But it would be best if I could have a formal extradition request from the governor of Texas so I could honor it and, thereby, make everything strictly legal."

"Could you give me thirty days to get those papers from Governor Hogg in Austin?" Ira asked. "And hold this man as a fugitive meantime?"

Oklahoma's chief executive agreed, reminding Ira that thirty days was the legal limit on a fugitive proceeding.

"I know," Ira said. "I promise that you won't have to turn him loose at the end of that time."

Ira left Guthrie and the next day he overtook his deputies, who reported that the prisoners were behaving in properly chastened fashion, helping to drive back the cattle they had stolen. The steers were herded across a shallow ford of the Canadian into Texas; then, mile after mile, they were driven back toward their home ranges.

Ira put the two prisoners on sorry horses to "ride drag" in the rear of the drive. He kept the best mounts for himself and his deputies so that the disarmed pair could be overtaken easily if they attempted flight. At night the rustlers were handcuffed together in their blankets. But they might have been a couple of ordinary herders, drawing thirty dollars a month and keep, for all the trouble they gave.

As days went by the drive turned into a continuous parade of triumph for law. Dozens of ranchers and cowboys lined the roads to look over the herd and pick out cattle bearing their brands. Hundreds of citizens rode up to shake hands with the first officers who had ever recovered steers from the plundering Cordeles. Hundreds laughed when they saw the sorry-looking prisoners "on drag," swallowing the choking hoof dust of the very cattle they'd helped steal.

But something worth more than the value of the steers—important as that was—stirred the minds of honest citizens enthusiastically congratulating the lawmen. Ira and his cowboy deputies had shown them that they didn't have to suffer the depredations of outlaws.

Law had won one of its first major victories in the outlaw infested area of the Panhandle. Those settlers saw a new day; it looked as if the days of the long riders were numbered.

Ira made a personal stop at Clarendon, in Donley County, long enough to get a grand-jury indictment against the man held at Guthrie. This was a prerequisite for the Texas extradition papers wanted by the Oklahoma governor. When Ira reached Castro County after a month's absence, he arrested a local henchman of the gang who gave bond. The older of the two prisoners caught on the Washita was lodged in the Dimmitt jail under the vigilant eye of Jailer Imogen Aten. Ira wanted to be lenient with the younger one, so he asked a justice of the peace to parole the boy in his custody pending trial.

Ira put the youngster to work tending cattle on his own ranch. Then he went to Austin and obtained the signature of Governor James Stephen Hogg on extradition papers for the desperado being held in Oklahoma. When Ira got to Guthrie he found that the big fellow had made an unsuccessful attempt to free himself on a writ of habeas corpus. He was brought in shackles to Dimmitt and kept under close surveillance pending trial.

As a matter of strategy, Ira then had additional indictments brought against all the rustlers in Armstrong County, on the eastern edge of the Panhandle. This county was less intimidated by cattle thieves than Donley because its first settler and the area's first rancher, Charles Goodnight, had done such a thorough job of outlaw extermination.

Three months later the three men faced a court at Claude, Armstrong County's seat. A Texas judge gave them the long sentences that a Texas sheriff requested. The young rustler was freed, as Ira had promised, after giving evidence for the prosecution. Two more state witnesses turned up, surprisingly, to clear themselves and then to clear out.

They were the Cordele brothers. Sniveling, hands quivering, they swore that their cowhands had stolen cattle without their knowledge or consent. By such subterfuge they managed to dodge conviction. Lawyers' fees cost them so much, however, that they afterward got on their horses and left the state.

The expert officer learns from his foes as well as his allies. Castro County's sheriff had learned a new way of fighting outlaws. Ira called in his deputies after the trial at Claude.

"Where we can't convict 'em, we'll break 'em," he announced. "I'm having the Castro County *News* print me up a bale of legal papers."

The three lawmen then began hounding different offenders on every charge that reasonably could be adduced. They booked chronic wrongdoers for vagrancy when their wallets were stuffed with the profits of brand burning or cold decking. They swore out complaints of attempted assault if some saddle thug even looked hard at a respectable citizen. Touts and tinhorns were hauled in for violating state law by carrying pistols, though no decent man was ever touched for packing a Colt to defend himself.

With writs and warrants, the three lawmen kept scourging lawbreakers. The Dimmitt jail bulged with prisoners awaiting trial. Sometimes they went off to the penitentiary. Sometimes they went free because a witness was too intimidated to testify or a jury too scared to convict a swaggering blackguard. "No matter," Ira told stiffening townspeople. "Lawyers and court costs don't come cut rate." No sooner did a bad man win acquittal on one charge than the law enforcers were pouncing on him with an other. All over the Panhandle lawyers were joking that "If it wasn't for Aten and his deputies we'd all be starving to death."

Throughout the Southwest a message buzzed along the out law grapevine: *Stay out of Castro County. The lawmen ruin your play and the lawyers get your roll.*

The county's outlaw element began to dwindle as sorry characters started toeing their stirrups, as soon as court proceedings ended, to ride out while they still had nickels in their Levis. The Oklahoma and New Mexico gangs started by-passing Castro County because everybody knew how Ira Aten and his men had sailed across a state line after the rustler band. Scores of desperadoes bagged in the Aten net had previously been giving posses the laugh for years.

Another rumor spread to alarm the demoralized circles of freebooters. It was reported that Ira Aten was returning to the Texas Rangers as captain of a special prairie detail to hang every outlaw from the Canadian River to the Brazos. Soon the Panhandle began seeing a grand exodus of criminals along with a healthier immigration of settlers.

Some of the departing ones ran squarely into New Mexico and Oklahoma sheriffs notified by Ira to look for them. Others, heading south toward Old Mexico, were halted on the Rio Grande by fast-riding Ranger patrols.

None, so far as is known, ever came back to court hemp in the Panhandle. The wheel prints of the covered-wagon caravans kept erasing the hoofmarks of the outlaw bands. Windmills were supplanting water holes; the saloon had started giving way to the schoolhouse. The solid folkways of hearth and home were prevailing over those ephemeral mores of the pistol and the pack saddle. After Ira's time, a certain group of Castro County homesteaders were to plat a town on the site of an abandoned outlaw roost; they would name their settlement Nazareth.

Ira was too busy with his office and his ranch to sift and analyze these changes. Yet the Old West was giving way to the new, and Ira Aten was playing a part in that process.

*"Don't ever leave this
camp at night, unless I
tell you to."*

ARSON ON THE RANGE

By the winter of 1894 not one running iron glowed on the eight hundred and seventy-six square miles that comprised Castro County. But another sort of spark was paralyzing operations on the ten-county spread that Albert Boyce operated for absentee owners in Britain.

The spark of arson kindled furtively on the choice pastures of the XIT. Flames often started by nesters resenting the scientifically run big enterprise as furiously as the English Chartists had despised the rising factories during the earlier decades of that same hectic nineteenth century.

"The XIT was the Goliath of the Cow Country," the Texas historian, Lewis Nordyke, has commented. "And the little Davids were swarming in with their slingshots."

During December of 1894 a nester slipped into the heavily fenced property of the big outfit. Thoughtlessly or on purpose, he tossed a match into a pack-rat hole. The result was the disastrous holocaust described in XIT records as "the Big Burn."

The blaze raged along an irregular course, seventy to a hundred miles in width. One of the big outfit's seven divisions was completely wrecked till new grass could grow the following spring. Two others were partially ruined. Four thousand prized breeding cattle were burned to ashy gristle that the coyotes nosed over. In effect, the whole southern half of the world's largest ranch had been reduced to a monstrous swath of ash.

After the fire Ira made an intensive investigation, since a substantial number of the XIT's three million acres lay in Castro County.

He worked closely with his cousin-in-law, Colonel Boyce
and XIT foremen in a careful effort to find possible accom-
plices of the firebug. Finally he told Boyce:

"There will be more fires like this unless you protect yourselves better. Nesters, who are otherwise honest citizens,
will think nothing of burning ranges that they think should
be open to their cattle. Or cutting your fences to make off
with a calf or two. You need your own police force and need
to work out some safety rules that every man on your ranch
will have to mind."

Colonel Boyce sighed, remembering the stinging rebukes
he had received from the XIT's main office in Chicago. "My
bosses have told me to do just that, Ira. Will you head that
force, and set up a fire department, too?"

With XIT support Ira had been elected sheriff for a full
term just two months before. But his family had grown
with the birth of a second son, Albert Boyce Aten, now
seven months old. Times were tight everywhere following
the great money panic of 1893. Ira's combined earnings
from both his office and his little ranch were small and
uncertain.

So in January of 1895 he resigned to become superintendent of the ranch's Escabarda division, which had been a
frequent target of arsonists. With his usual forethought, he
doubled his life insurance before taking the job. Six hundred
thousand acres of Texas's finest pastures were under his su-
pervision. Forty thousand of the XIT's best cattle grazed on
those ranges. Ira meant to guard them against both range
burners and brand burners.

His first step was to organize the twenty cowboys working
under him into the counterpart of a Ranger company. Two
of his old comrades of the Frontier Battalion came from El
Paso to act as company lieutenants. One, Big Ed Connell,
was placed in charge of a squad of heavily armed riders at
a line camp called Tombstone on the Oklahoma boundary.
The second, Wood Saunders, was stationed with a corps at
Trujillo Camp on the border of New Mexico.

Men with Winchesters patrolled fence lines to keep invaders out. Sentries were posted on windmill towers to lookout for prowlers who might have sneaked in with branding iron or matchbox. At each of the outfit's four camps a logbook was kept. On its pages was written the name of every visitor, the description of his horse, the time of his coming, and the place of his destination. This guest register was enough to cut down the number of predatory floaters because their kind didn't like their names on records.

Ira also introduced other techniques of range policing that are reportedly used by major western ranches to this day. He set up "mail boxes" on the range as drops for intradivision messages. Only he, Connell, and Saunders had keys to the boxes which were opened by all three at least once daily. Thus the XIT's protectors could notify each other quickly of troublesome characters and join forces to expel them.

Imogen and the children lived in an XIT house whose dark blinds were always drawn to protect the head of the house against assassination attempts. On his rounds by night Ira never sat within the circle of campfire light because any number of lurking prowlers by the fences would have relished the distinction of shooting the XIT's general in chief. When he journeyed to some place on the ranch, he always returned by a different route. XIT cowboys found it best to give strict attention to duty since Superintendent Aten might appear at any hour or minute to give the range a scrutiny with eye or lantern.

One of Ira's punchers, Joe Killough, had been a leader of the nester political opposition in the Panhandle. No doubt Killough had hired out to the enemy only to eat, after the money panic came with its harsh impact on small holders. Ira made him a windmill sentinel: a singularly confining job for a man used to the motion of the plow and the stirrup. So on a moonlight night, one summer, the disgusted cowhand decided to leave and let God protect the grass of the XIT.

Killough saddled his pony, slipped away from the lonely camp, bound eastward for eighty miles away. He had ridden only a short distance, however, when he saw coming toward him a man on a better horse. Moonbeams were dancing on the extended barrel of a forty-five in the rider's hand.

"Where in hell are you going?" came the challenging demand.

The cowboy, recognizing Boss Aten by his voice, made a hurried self-identification and then said: "I'm leaving the XIT and your goddam windmills."

Ira put away his gun. "Get back to your job, Joe," he advised Killough in a kindly tone. "I'll put you to riding herd tomorrow. But don't ever leave this camp at night again unless I tell you to."

In another Panhandle election, Ira was chosen county commissioner of Deaf Smith County, half of which lay in the XIT's Escabarda pastures. The electorate of this commissioner's district consisted of Ira's twenty cowboys. Only one of them ever scratched his name from the ballot during the eight years that he served. That voter was probably Joe Killough, making a defiant individual gesture against an agrarian monopoly, although the man came to like Ira personally.

Ira's vigilant security measures made the XIT one of the toughest of all ranches for cattle rustlers and horse thieves to crack. But there was no lasting protection against the match. As Ira realized, you could see a gun in a man's hand but not the deadly little stick of phosphorus in his pocket.

Fires—medium and small—kept popping up on Ira's thousand square miles of range in spite of all his careful patrolling. And one blaze burned itself on his memory above all the ones that his riders quelled.

The time was nightfall. Ira was riding back from New Mexico after a fruitless search for a man and a boy believed to have set a fire that had been extinguished on the XIT's ranges the day before. He was keeping his pony to a slow, disappointed trot. Gradually he became conscious of a gathering bright light creeping across the sky.

Ira pulled his horse to a dead stop. The light spread till the heavens were a solid red of reflected flame. It came from the direction of the winter pasture where Ira grazed bulls being fattened for spring shipment to eastern markets. He spurred his horse mercilessly forward. In less than an hour he pulled it up exhausted by the bull pasture.

Cursing, sweating cowboys were already fighting the blaze when Ira jumped down and began shouting orders. Some punchers were slaughtering beeves for fire drags. Others, mounted on horseback, were pulling the bleeding carcasses by lassos across flaming patches of grass.

Frightened, bellowing bulls were retreating before the advancing flames. They threw themselves in a mad rout against fence wire, then plunged back, hemmed in by fence and flame, as the fierce heat seared long-festering scars across the fresh barb cuts on their hides.

Ten more yearlings were slain by Ira's order, enough to stop any ordinary fire, what with the smothering weight of the beef and the blood gushing forth like water. But the carcasses became charred offerings to arson the minute they hit the flames.

The columns of flame leaped the wide furrows or "fire guards" that had previously been made by plows on the Escabarda. Patch after patch of rich high grass was swept by the blaze. Whirling hot billows of smoke caused men and horses to begin retreating.

"Come on, boys!" Ira yelled. "We've got to put this hell out."

With quirt and spur the punchers forced the resisting horses back toward the inferno. Sparks shot forward, singeing the eyebrows of the men and frizzling the hair on their hands. Riders and wagons, with barrels of water, began arriving from other XIT divisions. A little while later cowmen from New Mexico and Oklahoma charged in to help fight this danger threatening to jump state lines and ruin their ranges.

All night long, hour after hour, mile upon mile, coughing, weary men bucked the cyclone of flame. Water from barrels, placed on steer hides, pulled by horses and attached to chain drags finally began checking its raging fury.

By dawn the punchers and the XIT's neighbors had brought disaster under control. That December morning the sun rose chill and sullen over the great blackened swath that had once been the finest winter pasture in the Panhandle. Little slivers of roasted flesh and bits of bone, crumbling into ashes, were all that was left of valuable blooded steers. Dozens of fine cow ponies limped around on burned hoofs; they would be out of commission for a year till nature gave them new ones.

Ira gazed over the scorched earth of his range. Ashes of cremated steers were blending with the ashes of crumbled grass under the boots of the men. The damage he could not even begin to estimate in dollars.

Outlaws would hear and rejoice about the blow struck by a pair of tramps at this biggest of all outfits. The wide loops would swing throughout the Panhandle. The running irons would burn hotter than ever.

Not far from where Ira sat on his saddle, two XIT cowboys were flogging some last smoldering fire patches with their saddle blankets. Some Oklahoma cowpunchers were stamping out smoking cow chips. A New Mexico rancher was mounting, to ride out and look for other chips that might have been missed and still be burning.

There had never been any love lost between the XIT and its smaller neighbors. Till well into the twentieth century the big foreign-owned enterprise would be a recurrent political issue in Texas. Yet a common danger had caused many of the little people to rally with it in a common battle still to be fought.

The grass is gone, Ira thought, *but it will grow again—enough of it for everybody. Honest ranchers can make a new start from calamity. Together we put out this fire. Together we'll stamp out the grass burners and the wideloopers.*

From that time on XIT hands and smaller neighbors kept Ira informed about any suspicious drifters or hard-looking bands seen in the area. Cowboys from adjoining outfits rode with those from the XIT to run down gangs and bring back cattle. By a wise decision of its Chicago executive, John V. Farwell, the combine instituted a good-neighbor policy toward the nesters; it was one that Ira welcomed. Colonel Boyce, too, accepted the new order of things, if with some qualification.

Let the nesters turn in on us, he directed Ira in a written memorandum. *Don't let the thieves in.*

He meant that the XIT would no longer be the colossal roadblock that it had been for travel across the Panhandle or the states farther north. The ranch began giving square dances on its premises and inviting the homesteaders to come. John Farwell, lay preacher as well as astute business-man, came out from Chicago to try converting his cowboys, with nesters being cordially received at services.

Farwell—perhaps prematurely—dissolved the XIT police force. Ira managed to maintain some precautions against rustlers but his successor, John Armstrong, was killed by a band of cattle thieves. Ed Connell and Wood Saunders left the outfit after being demoted to ordinary cowhands. But they stayed with their friend until, by Ira's commemoration, "all was quiet and safe enough for me to lie down and take a quiet sleep."

The years marched on, at a pace somewhat faster than the tread of Texas cattle. The United States fought the Spanish American War and, thereby, established itself as a world power. The Populists declined after their thunder had been stolen by a western politician, half-mountebank and half-statesman, named William Jennings Bryan. More ter-ritories of the West were being admitted into the Union or readying themselves for statehood. Carrie Nation, whom Ira remembered so vividly, had dried up the state of Kansas. Dallas was taking on a conservative primness. Tascosa was barely alive after having been missed by a railroad stretch-ing across the Panhandle.

A few major outlaws, like Henry Starr, were still running loose. But an aging man named Frank James had settled down to the peaceful life of an Oklahoma farmer.

The Six-Shooter Age sank into further eclipse with the coming of the twentieth century. Ira was thirty-seven years old and the father of four children when he put up a calendar to mark its first year, 1900. And now as he rode the improved roads of the Panhandle he saw the first chugging gas buggies scaring horses whose sires had never flinched at gun shots.

More and more of the big ranches were being broken up into homesteads and family-sized stock farms, operational expenses having become so costly. By 1904 even the XIT was selling big chunks of its holdings to the settlers who kept streaming into the Panhandle. The big outfit, as such, had come too late on the scene of the grass empires, but it had swapped a magnificent new state capitol building in Austin in return for its broad acres.

That year Ira heard of a new frontier being developed in California—the Imperial Valley. He was told of its promise by a family whom he met on a train. It was a hard decision for a Texan to make, but he resigned his job with the ranch and began preparing for a move to a state where he had neither roots nor friends.

Ira had spent almost a decade on that vast cattle barony, which earned more controversy than it ever did money. It was a longer, if less significant, period than the one he had put in as a Texas Ranger. At its end the Texas where he had fought and ridden was largely history, like the men who had shaped it out of mesquite jungles and cactus patches.

On a day both solemn and exciting, Ira and his family went to Amarillo for the first lap of their journey. Just fifteen years before, migrants from Texas to California still had been going by covered wagon. For the Atens, it was a train whistle that blew, not an ox whip that cracked.

"A lawman til I die..."

RANGER FOREVER

Ira Aten was forty-two years old when he settled in California. On a second frontier, he was making his second effort at homesteading. A second time, also, he was trying to live by routine work, in pleasant obscurity.

Fifteen hundred miles he had journeyed from Texas, where his contemporaries lamented his departure and called him one of the greatest law enforcers in the state's turbulent history. Sometimes fame charitably forgets middle-aged men who cease to court it. Ira hoped that it would drape no more mantles on him.

He and Imogen were now interested only in accumulating a reserve of money and property to underwrite the futures of their four children. After they had relocated in the Imperial Valley, he renewed his promise, unkept in the Lone Star state, that he would hunt no more bad men and hold no more public offices. Again, as he had in the Texas Panhandle, he decided "to lay aside the old saddle, Winchester, and six-shooter, and start life again in a new country."

Significantly, his first homestead was in an area bordering Mexico. It was a few hundred acres of raw, semi-desert land located in Imperial County, a short distance from the boundary dividing California proper from the Mexican province of Lower California. Those years as an officer on the Texas–Mexico border had given Ira lasting feelings of sympathy and good will toward the dark-skinned people. Few Anglos ever became as good a friend to them as did Ira Aten. His word to them became his bond in California, as it had been in Texas.

Those first years in the new country were difficult ones for the transplanted family. This wasteland made the Texas border seem an Eden by contrast. The Imperial Valley was an ocean of sand flooding the oven-hot air with torrential storms of grit and dust. The grass for cattle to crop was sparse, except on occasional moist little "islands" centering around water holes. Other foliage was more stunted and thorny than Ira had ever seen on the grim savannahs of the Rio Grande.

Nearby was a sluggish, semi-dry river that was called the Colorado, like that other stream he had known in Texas. But water, as such, was scarce in the Valley and had to be hoarded like gold.

Yet the Atens adjusted themselves to struggle and hardship after all those years of relative comfort on the XIT. Imogen learned how to scrimp along with what they had, after the fashion of her pioneer ancestors in the Republic of Texas. Their three sons—Marion, who was twelve; Boyce, ten; and Ira, Junior, seven—began attending one of the new public schools that Imperial County was building for the recent influx of children. Imogen, the "baby," was only five, yet already she was learning how to cook, sew, and sweep. Four years after their arrival in California the Atens had their last child and second daughter, Eloise.

Ira kept wooing obscurity. He might have been successful if half the Valley's settlers hadn't been émigré Texans. Many of them had already heard or read of him, though he had known none of them back in the home state. They began seeking him out to listen to his Ranger experiences told first hand, and he was a man never sparing either of friendly talk or generous hospitality.

So the Aten legend became naturally re-created in California. Texans had brought it with them, as they had the epics of other Lone Star heroes like Sam Houston, Jim Bowie, and Governor Jim Hogg, who had put the rapacious railroad interests under public control. Because he had been a Ranger and a prominent citizen of the state, Ira Aten automatically became the leader of the Texas colony in the Valley.

The year was 1906 when shabby characters began drifting into the area and hiring themselves out as ranch hands to pick up anything portable they could lay hands on. Ira was doing some work at his home one day when a worried neighbor, Clarence Conant, came over with an urgent problem.

"Mr. Aten," Conant said, "I'd like to get rid of two men I hired to work on my place. After I'd brought them with me from town, they threw their hats in a corner, sprawled out in chairs, and demanded food at once. Since then they've done mighty little work and my wife is having to treat them like star boarders."

Ira frowned. "Why don't you just tell 'em to start moving, Clarence?"

Clarence Conant looked frightened. "I—I don't want my family hurt and—well, I'd be no match for them."

Ira put aside his task. "Let me take a look at 'em, Clarence."

He accompanied the young settler to the Conant ranch. There he found two hard-bitten drifters, lounging in the shade when there was work to be done. The face of one was familiar—very familiar—to the former Ranger. Ira had seen it on many a reward poster.

Ira gave the rancher an eye signal and the pair of neighbors walked away from the house to confer. "Clarence," Ira said quietly, "the worst-looking of those tramps is an escapee from the Texas penitentiary. I'm seeing that he goes back to Texas."

Ira went home, saddled a horse, rode into the little desert town of Imperial, and sent an urgent wire to Texas officials. They, in turn, sent a telegram to the sheriff of Imperial County, asking that the fugitive be apprehended and held pending extradition proceedings. County officers came to the Conant ranch and arrested the bullying convict. The sheriff ordered his partner to leave the place or face charges of intimidating his employer.

Next day the remaining tough strode into the Stevenson Brothers general store in Imperial. He picked up an ax from a rack of cutting blades and, swinging it at the Stevensons, began demanding the name of the man responsible for having his friend recaptured.

"When I find out who the goddamned so-and-so is," he snarled, "I'll go to his place and chop his head off with this here ax."

Flourishing the implement, the drifter strode up and down the aisle threatening the petrified storekeepers with violence unless they told him the name. Happening to walk into the store, the gentleman in question stood quietly behind the man while he listened to his ravings.

Finally he tapped the hoodlum's shoulder. "I sent your friend back to jail," he said. "My name is Ira Aten."

The hoodlum wheeled around, and for a moment looked into those blazing blue eyes. "Ira Aten, the Texas Ranger?" he asked, deflating like a pierced balloon.

Ira looked at him contemptuously. "Yes, you cheap tinhorn—Aten, the Ranger."

The ruffian dropped the ax. "All right, Mr. Aten," he answered meekly, ran from the store, and took the next train out.

Whenever Clarence Conant told the story in later years, which he did many times, he always finished by saying, "To this day I don't know whether Mr. Aten had a gun."

In due time Texas officers who knew and respected the name of Ira Aten came to fetch the escaped convict. Ira went with them to the Imperial County jail at El Centro and, under oath, made identification of the glowering wretch. After this affair Ira's desert neighbors, as had those in the Panhandle, began begging him to pin on a badge.

They wanted him to run for sheriff. When he declined, they urged him to accept the less-exacting job of precinct constable. To all their soliciting Ira returned courteous refusals. "My days as a lawman are over," he kept telling them. "I left all that behind in Texas."

But it was Ira Aten, the unforgotten Ranger, whom citizens kept asking for help against assorted roughnecks from both sides of the California-Mexico border. It was he whom local officers consulted when they were faced with a difficult crime and scarce or conflicting evidence. Then an Imperial County sheriff named Mobley Meadows determined to wreck the bases of several law breaking combines by cleaning out El Centro's saloons.

Resignedly, Imogen saw Ira ride away in a posse led by Meadows. Refusing to accept a deputy's commission, her husband moved against the grog dens as rapidly and efficiently as those he had cleaned out in Dimmitt. As a public-spirited citizen, he helped round up thieves and killers, then appeared in different courts to give clinching testimony against them.

On one occasion Ira was present in El Centro police court, waiting to testify against an offender involved in a liquor case. He kept looking at the fellow and sensed intuitively that he was in imminent personal danger. Ira arose from a seat and shouted to Sheriff Meadows: "Take him out!"

The defendant was dragged outside and searched. Two pistols were found in the man's jacket pockets. After the commotion had subsided, Ira told the spectators calmly, "I'm glad it ended that way. If that roughneck had started to draw those pistols, I'd have had to shoot him."

Ira kept on riding with the official organization known as the Sheriff's Mounted Posse to round up smugglers and other outlaws operating along the boundary. These offenders, while not of the stature of those he had pursued on the Texas–Mexican border, were dangerous and lawless pests impeding the development of civilization on this lingering last frontier of a great American state. Ira, as a champion and builder of civilization, helped sweep them away like so much accumulated trash.

For Ira Aten was the type of pioneer who seeks frontiers not to escape society but to expand it. There were misanthropic wanderers in Kentucky before Daniel Boone and in Texas before Stephen F. Austin: the anti-social ones reverting, by some curious atavism, to a primitive, untamed kind of existence. With these, the element personified by Ira Aten had nothing in common. His kind brought with them an inherent stability typified, perhaps, by the Conestoga wagon in one era and the R. F. D. mailbox in another.

Ira himself found more scope to build in his second environment of California than in his earlier one of Texas. California had a characteristic business cast, dating from the 1849 gold rush, far preceding the aggressive economic push that contemporary America has come to associate with the Lone Star State. The legislature at Sacramento regularly appropriated generous funds for internal improvements and the development of natural resources. In contrast, the legislature at Austin had been grudging and parsimonious, too often dominated by the demagogic conservatism of the South. Texas kept clinging to the umbilical cord of Dixie, even while asserting its own boisterous identity. California never had any such clinging tie to break, nor any troublesome aftermath of the Civil War to contend with.

California's pioneers of the early twentieth century saw how the Mormon pioneers of adjoining Utah had converted arid wastelands into blooming fields and gardens through scientific irrigation. A water-conservation program was enacted at Sacramento to transform California's desert areas, including the Imperial Valley where Ira had grown one of the first commercial citrus crops. These sections were divided into irrigation districts governed by elected five-member boards of directors.

However, the California legislature failed to provide for public ownership of power resources. Consequently, its desert settlers found themselves at the mercy of powerful monopolies that gained control of the state's chain of rivers, charging exorbitant rates for water and electricity in communities they condescended to serve, ignoring the lesser-populated localities which offered no margin of profit.

Ira worried along with the situation, as other agricultural producers did, till the end of World War I. Then urban and rural citizens throughout southern California organized a movement for cheap public power to insure full development of the region's economic and social potential. Advocates of public ownership concentrated on electing members of the irrigation boards as a preliminary step toward securing appropriate legislation in Congress.

For twenty years straight, Ira had kept his pledge to Imogen about never again seeking public office. But in 1923, with her enthusiastic consent, he accepted nomination for the board of the Imperial Valley district. His election was an impressive moral victory for the public power group because the directors had been divided three to two in favor of ending the monopoly. Now the line-up was four to one, with but a lone supporter of the power companies being left on the board.

Other candidates sharing Ira's views won in other districts. A California congressman had introduced a bill in Washington for the colossal Boulder Canyon Project, which would include the construction of the Hoover Dam to conserve river waters, as well as the All-American Canal, which farmers and ranchers would be able to tap for their irrigation needs.

Ira was now sixty. He and Imogen were happy, respected, and moderately well off. Their lives were correspondingly full and placid. Then a gentle old warrior found a last series of battles forced upon him. A campaign fought this time for different objectives and with weapons different from those he had used on hills and plains. The main weapon, flourished by his opponents, was money.

Ira himself made the comparison between his former conflicts with evil and this present one. "The great electrical power trust is not unlike the cattle rustler who took the unbranded mavericks and calves," he noted thoughtfully in his memoirs. He felt that the power magnates, like the rustlers, took "an unjust toll" from western ranchers and farmers. But, he commented: "Going out and catching a few criminals or settling feuds and riots in the many different counties of Texas is a small job compared to this one."

How much harder the new job was Ira learned as he fought a ring far more formidable than run-of-the-mill bandits—a group whose leaders were rich and influential figures in the nation's life. Against their weapons of big money and big propaganda, the consumers had only the counter-instruments of their ballots and their convictions.

Someday historians may equate the battle for public power in the West with such definitive earlier struggles as the ones for law and for equitable division of the grazing lands. Eventually the consumers won in California because history was marching on their side. But the power trust spent twenty million dollars to stay that march before the Boulder Canyon project and its dependent undertakings came into being during 1932. An elderly former Ranger had done much to score one of the greatest popular victories in the whole tumultuous epic of the West's far-flung domain.

"Ira Aten was our wheel horse," Munson H. Dowd, his friend and ally in the Power War, has written. "He worked and traveled all over California to secure support and help for that vital legislation in Washington. Never once did he waver as a board member or as a citizen."

The lights went on in the Imperial Valley. Rural electrification lines were extended into the tiniest, most remote communities. Farmers and ranchers stowed discarded kerosene lamps with other relics in their attics. Business expanded as Valley merchants found new buyers of toasters and radios and washing machines.

More years passed in California, cut like Texas from the titan mold. The former Texan's hair grew grayer as the prodigious acres of California grew greener. Ira served on the board of the irrigation district for sixteen years, finally retiring because of age. Other positions of honor and responsibility had come to him during his long residence in the Valley. He had helped organize the first Chamber of Commerce in El Centro, and served as its vice president when the straggling border village was swiftly evolving into a trim Western city. Later he had been elected a director of the town's first bank and president of the Imperial Valley Pioneers Association.

The five Aten children grew up to follow in the footsteps of the distinguished pioneer who was their father, and the sedate, matronly woman who was their mother. The two eldest sons, Marion and Boyce, enlisted in the Allied forces during World War I. Marion won wings as a captain of the British Royal Flying Corps. Boyce was killed in the Battle of the Argonne Forest. The Boyce Aten Post of the American Legion in El Centro is named for him.

Ira, Jr., settled on a second ranch owned by the Atens at Calipatria in the Valley, but later moved to Albuquerque, New Mexico, where he became a prosperous cattleman. Imogen, the elder daughter, joined the staff of Stanford University. Eloise, the younger, married R. W. Radder, of Burlingame, California, and gave Ira one of his favorite grandchildren, Gary Boyce Radder.

Few of the West's old lawmen were alive now. Fewer still were the survivors among the West's old outlaws, whose fatality rate had been higher during the decades of cut and shoot. The few former long riders still living felt that the less history, written or spoken, the better. But the remaining veterans of the badge learned that a subdued America still insisted on remembering its last living links with the past.

Texas remembered the gallant lawman who had lingered on to see a future that his brain and his Winchester had helped shape.

In 1936 Walter Prescott Webb published his great book, *The Texas Rangers*. Ira Aten was one of the Rangers who received most attention in the book, with a score or so of pages devoted to his crushing of the Navarro County fence cutters. Earlier, another Texas writer, J. Evetts Haley, had visited Ira in California to obtain firsthand material for a notable account of the XIT. This history paid tribute to the former range boss for his security techniques and his bristling offensive against the rustlers.

During 1942 another Texan named Jack Martin published a biography of Ranger Captain John R. Hughes, which contained many admiring references to Ira Aten. Ira, Martin declared, "was a top-notch frontier officer."

Ira, meantime, had been working on his own memoirs, which were issued, though not in chronological sequence, by the Texas magazine, *Frontier Times*, in 1945. This material was incomplete, being a series of random recollections put down spontaneously when their author was past seventy. But it provided, if scrappily, authentic information on one of the West's history-makers.

Modestly but gratefully, Ira accepted this new surge of publicity. Visitors came from far and near to talk with the hale and hearty octogenarian who had fought outlaws and subdued feudists.

One result was that he began making more frequent visits to Texas which had already enshrined him during his lifetime. His old cow-country friends of the XIT Association elected him as their "trail boss" or president. Ira enjoyed the annual reunions held at Dalhart, in the Panhandle, though each year fewer of the gray-haired men with the saddle-bowed legs answered the roll call.

On May 12, 1938, Ira was present in El Paso to attend the unveiling of a monument to his old friend and commander, Captain Frank Jones, slain in the bloody battle of Pirate Island on June 30, 1893. Pirate Island had been a rustler-populated enclave of Mexico on the north bank of the Rio Grande but dumped into Texas by one of the constant shifts in the river's channel. A Ranger named Aten had been in that fight—Ira's younger brother, Edwin, who had quit cowboying in the Panhandle to join the force. Still a third brother, Calvin Aten, had worn the badge of the Frontier Battalion. No Aten ever compromised or dishonored the emblem.

John Hughes, who had succeeded Jones as captain of Company D, also attended the ceremonies, as did Ed Aten and an other venerable former Ranger Ed Bryant, whose mother had been a Texas Mexican woman. Following the unveiling, Hughes spoke reminiscently:

"You know, after that ruckus on Pirate Island, nineteen rustlers committed suicide by getting tangled in Ranger ropes."

John Hughes was a regular visitor at Ira's California home till Hughes's death at ninety-two, in 1947. Other guests—friends and strangers—flocked to the Aten ranch as one of the last out posts of the boundless hospitality that Old West tradition nourished. Religious and service organizations, Boy Scouts and Girl Scouts held encampments and picnics in a big grove of eucalyptus trees on Ira's property. He never accepted a penny of rent, never turned away any group. "Glad to have you," he would say when adults and youngsters began unloading baskets. "Make yourselves at home, and just ask me if you need anything."

His main interest now, in a benign and prosperous old age, was people. So concerned was he for the feelings of Texans who were descended from outlaws that he was very reluctant to tell, in word or print, the name of any man he had ever trailed or arrested. Judd Roberts, the worst outlaw he had ever pursued, had respectable kinsmen living. So did many other desperadoes.

In 1944 Ira celebrated his eighty-second birthday. Forty-nine years had elapsed since he had unpinned that last badge when resigning as sheriff of Castro County. Now, though the gesture was one of sentiment, with Imogen not objecting, Imperial County decided to give him another star.

The presentation was made at a meeting of the Boyce Aten Post of the American Legion, called to honor the father of the fallen soldier who had given the post its name. After Ira had made a speech, from trembling lips, Sheriff Robert W. Ware pinned a gold deputy's badge on him. The old officer, recovering his composure, then said jokingly, "Thank you, Bob. This is the first time I've been higher than a deputy constable."

Then Ira turned to the audience, and his eyes were twinkling. "You know, folks, I guess I'll always be a lawman. A lawman till I die."

But death kept withholding its summons. When Ira reached eighty-five, in 1947, his step was hale and his handshake hearty. At ninety, in 1952, he still could swing into a stirrup like a young man; still, with a little more time for aiming, shoot as straight as he had in the Texas Rangers, generations before.

By that time he had probably outlived every other man who ever served with him on a force since become an adjunct of a more complex state police organization in a modern Texas of smoking factories and spewing oil wells. But with the calm resignation shown by the very aged, the last illustrious Ranger knew that he must pass on like that older Texas of the trail drive and the long ride.

During the summer of 1953 Ira had a tombstone, inscribed with his name, placed in the Aten family plot at Evergreen Cemetery in El Centro. A few months later he decided to visit Imogen, now an invalid, who was being cared for by their daughter, Eloise Radder, in Burlingame. There, the man who was wont to say proudly that he had never been sick a day in his life came down with pneumonia.

Germs did the job that bullets never could, on August 5, 1953. That very month *Zane Grey's Western Magazine*, one of the few literate publications of its kind, published one of a series of three articles, "I Rode with the Texas Rangers," done by Ira in collaboration with a Texas writer who was fortunate enough to become his literary executor. Ira would have been ninety-one had he lived just one month longer. Imogen survived him by four years, passing on in 1957.

Texas, which Ira Aten helped so decisively to shape, has not yet erected the formal monument to his memory that he deserves. But two years before his death the commissioners of his California county named the thoroughfare spanning his ranch Ira Aten Road.

When the soil was heaped on him, a spur must have clicked in some rawhide Valhalla. The roster of the immortal Rangers was now complete.